Deep Learning on Windows

Building Deep Learning Computer Vision Systems on Microsoft Windows

Thimira Amaratunga

Apress®

Deep Learning on Windows: Building Deep Learning Computer Vision Systems on Microsoft Windows

Thimira Amaratunga
Nugegoda, Sri Lanka

ISBN-13 (pbk): 978-1-4842-6430-0
https://doi.org/10.1007/978-1-4842-6431-7

ISBN-13 (electronic): 978-1-4842-6431-7

Copyright © 2021 by Thimira Amaratunga

Managing Director, Apress Media LLC: Welmoed Spahr
Acquisitions Editor: Smriti Srivastava
Development Editor: Matthew Moodie
Coordinating Editor: Shrikant Vishwakarma

Cover designed by eStudioCalamar

Cover image designed by Pexels

Distributed to the book trade worldwide by Springer Science+Business Media LLC, 1 New York Plaza, Suite 4600, New York, NY 10004. Phone 1-800-SPRINGER, fax (201) 348-4505, e-mail orders-ny@springer-sbm. com, or visit www.springeronline.com. Apress Media, LLC is a California LLC and the sole member (owner) is Springer Science + Business Media Finance Inc (SSBM Finance Inc). SSBM Finance Inc is a **Delaware** corporation.

For information on translations, please e-mail booktranslations@springernature.com; for reprint, paperback, or audio rights, please e-mail bookpermissions@springernature.com.

Apress titles may be purchased in bulk for academic, corporate, or promotional use. eBook versions and licenses are also available for most titles. For more information, reference our Print and eBook Bulk Sales web page at http://www.apress.com/bulk-sales.

Any source code or other supplementary material referenced by the author in this book is available to readers on GitHub via the book's product page, located at www.apress.com/978-1-4842-6430-0. For more detailed information, please visit http://www.apress.com/source-code.

Printed on acid-free paper

To my loving wife, for all your support

Table of Contents

About the Author

Thimira Amaratunga is an inventor, a Senior Software Architect at Pearson PLC Sri Lanka with over 12 years of industry experience, and a researcher in AI, machine learning, and deep learning in education and computer vision domains.

Thimira holds a Master of Science in Computer Science with a Bachelor's degree in Information Technology from the University of Colombo, Sri Lanka.

He has filed three patents to date, in the fields of dynamic neural networks and semantics for online learning platforms. Thimira has also published two books on deep learning: *Build Deeper: The Deep Learning Beginners' Guide* and *Build Deeper: The Path to Deep Learning*.

In addition, Thimira is the author of Codes of Interest (`www.codesofinterest.com`), a portal for deep learning and computer vision knowledge, covering everything from concepts to step-by-step tutorials.

LinkedIn: `www.linkedin.com/in/thimira-amaratunga`.

About the Author

About the Technical Reviewer

 **Sarani Mendis** is currently working as a Software Engineer at Pearson Lanka, with six years of industry experience. She is an enthusiast and a researcher in UI/UX, AI and machine learning in natural language processing, and computer vision domains. Sarani is also an active volunteer at Lanka Software Foundation and has worked on many of their projects under Code for Sri Lanka-Elections.

She holds a Master of Science in Computer Science and a Bachelor of Information Technology from University of Colombo School of Computing–Sri Lanka.

Acknowledgments

Like many others, this book also started as a single thought. Even with experience in publishing two earlier books, it was a challenging journey. From the beginning and along the way, I have received support and encouragement from many, and I would like to express my sincere gratitude here.

First, I would like to thank the team at Apress, especially Smriti Srivastava, the acquisitions editor; Shrikant Vishwakarma, the coordinating editor; Matthew Moodie, the developmental editor; and everyone else involved in the publishing of this book.

I would also like to thank Sarani Mendis, the technical reviewer, for the excellent feedback and suggestions that added immense value to this book.

To my loving wife, Pramitha: Thank you for the encouragement and the motivation you provided from the inception of the idea to the completion. Without your support throughout the long hours and days spent writing and perfecting this book, completing it might not have been possible.

To my managers at Pearson PLC, who have guided me throughout the years, I would like to express my gratitude for the guidance and encouragement. And to my team and colleagues, thank you for all your support that allowed me to achieve this.

And last but not least, to my parents and sister, thank you for the endless support throughout the years.

Introduction

Do you wish to learn to build practical deep learning and computer vision Systems, but are reluctant to switch to Linux for the development? Do you feel like you are more familiar with Windows, and wish that you could build everything on Windows? Well, you do not need to worry anymore. The latest deep learning and computer vision libraries have matured to the point that almost everything now can be made to work seamlessly on Windows as well. This book will show you how.

Windows OS accounts for over 70% of desktop PC usage. Windows provides many conveniences, with a wide variety of available productivity tools, causing it to gather a large user base. Furthermore, due to the better hardware compatibility and driver support, most decently to high-powered personal PCs tend to run Windows. This means that there is a large percentage of AI enthusiasts and developers out there who would like to jump into learning the remarkable capabilities of deep learning / AI. But they are reluctant or afraid to take the first steps because of the fear of the complexity of the tools and a widely held belief that AI systems can only be built on developer-friendly operating systems such as Linux. This book aims to help them move past those mental blocks and start building practical deep learning systems.

Deep learning on Windows will help you learn to build deep learning and computer vision systems using Python, TensorFlow, Keras, OpenCV, and more, right within the familiar elements of Microsoft Windows. The goal of this book is to get as many of you interested in the field of deep learning and have the OS you build upon a nonbarrier to begin learning.

Along the way, we will learn what deep learning is and how it came to be. We will clarify some misconceptions and confusion surrounding deep learning and look at some of the major milestones it has achieved throughout the years. We will dive into coding, while learning how to apply the concepts as you build. You will learn how to set up all the tools and technologies you will need to start coding deep learning systems on a Windows system.

In this book, you will:

- Learn the concepts, history, and milestones behind deep learning and how it relates to machine learning and AI while resolving some misconceptions surrounding those AI concepts.

- Learn the tools you would require (TensorFlow, Keras, OpenCV, CUDA, etc.) to successfully learn building deep learning systems, and learn how to set up, configure, and troubleshoot them step by step. Learn to get the tools working on Microsoft Windows and learn why the OS or the hardware you are developing in does not hold you back in building state-of-the-art AI systems. This should allow you to break any mental barriers and apply what you have learned in any OS or other system.

- Learn to build your first deep learning model and understand how the concepts of each step of it work through code examples. Learn how to visualize the internal workings and the structure of a model to gain a deeper understanding of how they work, and apply that experience to develop more complex models in the future.

- Learn to build real-world, practical deep learning computer vision systems with limited amounts of data with the concepts of transfer learning and fine-tuning. Learn how to configure training of larger models with large datasets, and ways you can deploy your application once trained.

- Once you have mastered the basics, learn more exciting and advanced concepts such as generative adversarial networks, and reinforcement learning (for basics in game programming).

The book is meant for you if you are an enthusiast of machine learning and AI—from the beginner to intermediate level—and would like to get a taste of what deep learning can do. It is meant for you if you prefer to jump in and learn through a hands-on, practical way by trying out coding and are not afraid to get your hands dirty with code. And finally, this book is meant for you if you desire to build practical, real-world AI systems.

## CHAPTER 1

What Is Deep Learning?

We live in the era of artificial intelligence (AI).

We may be born a little too late to explore earth, and born too early to explore the universe. Yet we may be here just in time to witness the rise of AI.

And we can help build that future.

Innovation in the field of AI is happening daily, from smart consumer devices to AI personal assistants to self-driving cars. The technology giants—Google, Facebook, Amazon, Microsoft, Apple, IBM, and AI-specialized organizations like DeepMind and OpenAI—strive to build AI technologies in a variety of fields that solve problems and improve the quality of life.

Deep learning is the latest iteration of AI. Although the concept itself has been around for many years, deep learning has become popular during the past few years due to the remarkable breakthroughs it continues to achieve. What was science fiction a decade ago is now becoming a reality.

Thanks to deep learning, AI technologies are increasingly becoming a part of our household. Today, most of our consumer devices and services have some sort of AI built into them. Maybe it is time you joined the revolution. You too can start contributing to this AI drive.

But first, we need to make sure that we understand what deep learning is.

Defining Deep Learning

Whether you are coming from a traditional AI background or just starting in the AI field, you might be wondering what the terms "artificial intelligence," "machine learning," and "deep learning" mean, as well as the other terminology surrounding it (Figure 1-1).

© Thimira Amaratunga 2021
T. Amaratunga, *Deep Learning on Windows*, https://doi.org/10.1007/978-1-4842-6431-7_1

Figure 1-1. *The deep learning confusion*

With the term "deep learning" becoming a buzzword, and becoming a part of some consumer technologies as well, it may be hard to figure out what each of these terms mean and how they relate to each other. You might be trying to figure out whether these three terms can be used interchangeably, and where each of them came from.

These are common questions that come to all of us when we are beginning the deep learning journey. Let us see how we can answer them.

Deep learning is a subset of machine learning that deals with hierarchical feature learning.

Machine learning is an approach to artificial intelligence that aims at providing machines with the ability to learn without explicitly programming them.

As for artificial intelligence, we should probably start from the beginning. It all started with the idea of *intelligent machines*.

Intelligent Machines

The concept of intelligent machines is the idea that machines can be built with parallel (or greater) intelligence of a human being, giving them the capacity to perform tasks that require human intelligence.

Human beings have been obsessed with this idea since ancient times, and written records of it can be traced back to the 1300s (from the works of Ramon Llull, 1232–1315). By the seventeenth century, Gottfried Leibniz expanded on this idea with his *calculus ratiocinator*—a theoretical universal logical calculation framework. By the nineteenth century, the concept of *formal reasoning* had begun, with the introduction of concepts such as *propositional logic* by George Boole and *predicate calculus* by Gottlob Frege.

However, there was no formal research concept for AI until the Dartmouth Conference in 1956.

Artificial Intelligence

In June 1956, many experts in the field—scientists and mathematicians—came together at Dartmouth College in New Hampshire. This conference, titled "The Dartmouth Summer Research Project on Artificial Intelligence," was the starting point of the formal research field of artificial intelligence. The Logic Theorist, developed by Allen Newell, Herbert A. Simon, and Cliff Shaw, now considered to be the first artificial intelligence program, was also presented in the Dartmouth conference. The Logic Theorist was meant to mimic the logical problem solving of a human and was able to prove 38 out of the first 52 theorems in *Principia Mathematica* (a book on principles of mathematics written by Alfred North Whitehead and Bertrand Russell).

By the 1960s, AI research was in full swing. It had funding from the US Department of Defense, more and more AI research labs were being established, and researchers were optimistic. Herbert A. Simon had predicted in 1965 that "machines will be capable, within twenty years, of doing any work a man can do."[1]

But AI did not progress quite that fast.

Around the late 1990s and early 2000s, researchers identified a problem in their approach to AI: to artificially create a machine with intelligence, *one needed to first understand how intelligence worked.*

Even today, we do not have a complete definition of what we call "intelligence."

To tackle the problem, researchers decided to work from the ground up: rather than trying to build intelligence, they investigated building a system that could grow an intelligence on its own.

This idea created the new subfield of AI called *machine learning*.

---

[1]Herbert A. Simon, *The Shape of Automation for Men and Management* (New York: Harper & Row, 1965), p. 96.

Machine Learning

Machine learning is a subset of artificial intelligence and aims at providing machines the ability to learn without explicit programming. The idea is that such machines (or computer programs), once built, will be able to evolve and adapt when they are exposed to new data.

The main idea behind machine learning is the ability of a learner to generalize from experience. The learner (or the program), once given a set of training samples, must be able to build a generalized model upon them, which would allow it to decide upon new cases with sufficient accuracy.

Based on this approach, there are three learning methods for machine learning systems:

- **Supervised learning:** The system is given a set of labeled cases (a training set), based on which it is asked to create a generalized model that can act on unseen cases.

- **Unsupervised learning:** The system is given a set of unlabeled cases and asked to find a pattern in them. This is ideal for discovering hidden patterns.

- **Reinforcement learning:** The system is asked to take any action and is given a reward, or a penalty based on how appropriate that action is to the given situation. The system must learn which actions yield the most rewards in given situations over time.

With these techniques, the field of machine learning flourished. They were particularly successful in the areas of computer vision and text analysis. Over the years, many models have been introduced as means of implementing machine learning techniques, such as artificial neural networks (models inspired by how neurons of the brain works), decision trees (models that use tree-like structures to model decisions and outcomes), regression models (models that use statistical methods to map input and output variables), and so on.

Around 2010, a few things happened that influenced machine learning research:

- Computing power became more available, and evaluating more complex models became easier.

- Data processing and storage became cheaper. More data became available for consumption.

- Our understanding of how the natural brain works increased, allowing us to model new machine learning algorithms around them.

These breakthroughs propelled us into a new area of machine learning called *deep learning*.

Deep Learning

Deep learning is a subset of machine learning that focuses on an area of algorithms inspired by our understanding of how the brain works to obtain knowledge.

It is also referred to as *deep structured learning* or *hierarchical learning*.

Deep learning builds upon the idea of artificial neural networks and scales it up, to be able to consume large amounts of data by deepening the networks in a specific way. Through a deeper network, a deep learning model has the capability of extracting features from raw data and "learn" about those features little by little in each layer, building up to a higher-level knowledge of the data. This technique is called *hierarchical feature learning*, and it allows such systems to automatically learn complex features through multiple levels of abstraction with minimal human intervention.

Following are some definitions of deep learning from some pioneering work in the field:

A sub-field within machine learning that is based on algorithms for learning multiple levels of representation to model complex relationships among data. Higher-level features and concepts are thus defined in terms of lower-level ones, and such a hierarchy of features is called a deep architecture.

—*Deep Learning: Methods and Applications*[2]

The hierarchy of concepts allows the computer to learn complicated concepts by building them out of simpler ones. If we draw a graph showing how these concepts are

---

[2]Li Deng and Dong Yu, *Deep Learning: Methods and Applications* (Redmond, WA: Microsoft Research, 2014), p. 200.

built on top of each other, the graph is deep, with many layers. For this reason, we call this approach to AI, deep learning.

—*Deep Learning*[3]

One of the most distinct characteristics of deep learning—and one that made it quite popular and practical—is that it scales well; that is, the more data given to it, the better it performs. Unlike many older machine learning algorithms that have an upper bound to the amount of data they can ingest—often called a *plateau in performance* (Figure 1-2)—deep learning models have no such limitations (theoretically), and they may be able to go beyond what humans can comprehend. This is evident with modern deep-learning-based image processing systems that are able to outperform humans.

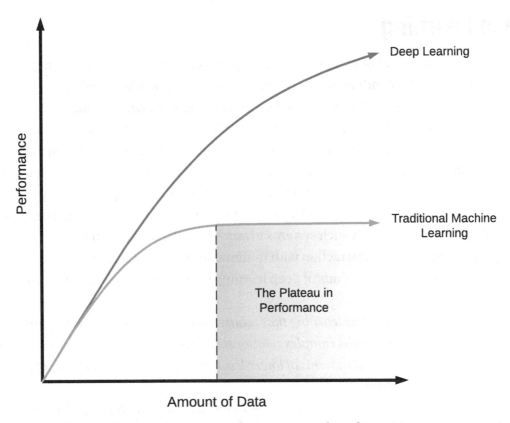

Figure 1-2. *The lack of plateau in performance in deep learning*

---

[3]Ian Goodfellow, Yoshua Bengio, and Aaron Courville, *Deep Learning* (Cambridge, MA: MIT Press, 2016), p. Back Cover Text.

Convolutional Neural Networks

Convolutional neural networks (CNNs) are a prime example of deep learning. They were inspired by how the neurons are arranged in the visual cortex (the area of the brain which processes visual input). Here, not all neurons are connected to all the inputs from the visual field. Instead, the visual field is "tiled" with groups of neurons (called receptive fields) that partially overlap each other.

CNNs work in a similar way. They process their input in overlapping blocks of the input using mathematical convolution operators, which approximates how a receptive field works (Figure 1-3).

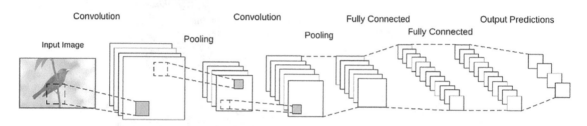

Figure 1-3. *A convolutional neural network*

The first convolution layer uses a set of convolution filters to identify a set of low-level features from the input image. These identified low-level features are then pooled (from the pooling layers) and provided as input to the next convolution layer, which uses another set of convolution filter to identify a set of higher-level features from the lower-level features identified earlier. This continues for several layers, where each convolution layer uses the inputs from the previous layer to identify higher-level features than the previous layer. Finally, the output of the last convolution layer is passed on to a set of fully connected layers for the final classification.

How Deep?

Once you grasp the capabilities of deep learning, there is one question that usually surfaces: If we say that deeper and more complex models give deep learning models the capabilities to surpass even human capabilities, then *how deep a machine learning model should be to be considered a deep learning model?*

It turns out that there is no clear response to this question. What we need to do instead is to look at deep learning from a different angle to understand it better. Let us take a step back and see how a deep learning model works—for example, with CNNs.

As mentioned earlier, the convolution filters of a CNN attempts to identify lower-level features first and use those identified features to identify higher-level features gradually through multiple steps.

This is the hierarchical feature learning we talked about earlier, and it is the key to understanding deep learning and what differentiates it from traditional machine learning algorithms (Figure 1-4).

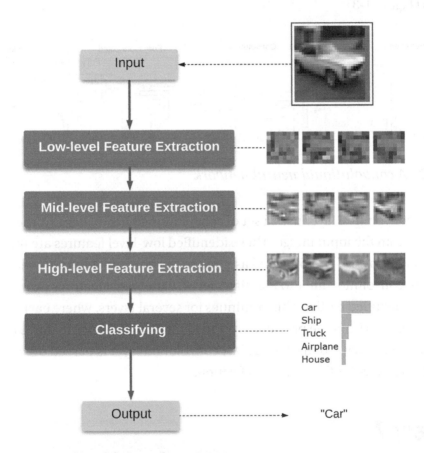

Figure 1-4. *Hierarchical feature learning*

A deep learning model (such as a CNN) does not try to understand the entire problem at once; that is, it does not try to grasp all the features of the input at once, as traditional algorithms tried to do. What it does look at is the input, piece by piece, so that it can derive from its lower-level patterns/features. It then uses these lower-level features to gradually identify higher-level features, through many layers, hierarchically. This allows deep learning models to learn complicated patterns, by gradually building them up from simpler ones. This also allows deep learning models to comprehend the world better, and they not only see the features but also see the hierarchy of how those features are built upon each layer.

Of course, having to learn features hierarchically means that the model must have many layers in it. This means that such a model will be "deep."

That brings us back to our original question: it is not that deep models are deep learning, but rather that to achieve hierarchical learning, the models need to be deep. The deepness is a by-product of implementing hierarchical feature learning.

So how do we identify whether a model is a deep learning model or not?

Simply put, if the model uses hierarchical feature learning—identifying lower level features first, and then building upon them to identify higher-level features (e.g., by using convolution filters)—then it is a deep learning model. If not, then no matter how many layers your model has, it is not considered a deep learning model. This means that a neural network with 100 fully connected layers (and only fully connected layers) would not be a deep learning model, but a network with a handful of convolutional layers would be.

Is Deep Learning Just CNNs?

When we talk about deep learning, we talk about CNNs a lot. You might be wondering whether deep learning is only CNNs.

The answer is no.

The following models, among others, are considered deep learning:

- Convolutional Neural Networks

- Deep Boltzmann Machine

- Deep Belief Networks

- Stacked Autoencoders

- Generative Adversarial Networks (GANs)

- Transformers

We take CNNs as examples for deep learning more often because they are easier to understand. As they were based on how biological vision works, it is easier to visualize and apply how they are based on the cognitive workflow of vision.

But we should keep in mind that CNNs are not the whole picture of deep learning.

Why Computer Vision?

Looking at the history of deep learning and some recent achievements of it,[4] you will notice that most of the projects it has been applied to deal with computer vision. Even the ImageNet competitions focus on visual recognition.

Why is that? Does deep learning only work on computer vision?

Not really.

Vision—understanding and giving meaning to visual inputs—is something humans are exceptionally good at. The ability to understand one's surroundings is considered a sign of intelligence. So when it comes to building intelligent machines, vision is one of the core capabilities that we wish an intelligent machine to possess. It is also easy to validate, as we can easily compare it with the ability of a human.

Therefore, exploring vision capabilities has become a core area in deep learning research.

The achievements deep learning gathers in the vision field may shape how we approach other fields as well. Thanks to the capability of transfer learning (which we will discuss in a later chapter), deep learning can apply knowledge gained from one domain to another domain. While typically this capability is used to apply knowledge from one vision model to another, it is speculated (and there is much ongoing research) how the knowledge from a model trained on visual input may apply in a nonvisual context.

How Does It All Come Together?

Returning to our original questions: *How do the areas of artificial intelligence, machine learning, and deep learning relate to each other?*

---

[4]A more detailed look at the milestones of deep learning throughout the years is available in Appendix 1.

Simply put, machine learning is a subset (an approach) of artificial intelligence, and deep learning is a subset of machine learning, all working toward the common goal of creating an intelligent machine (Figure 1-5).

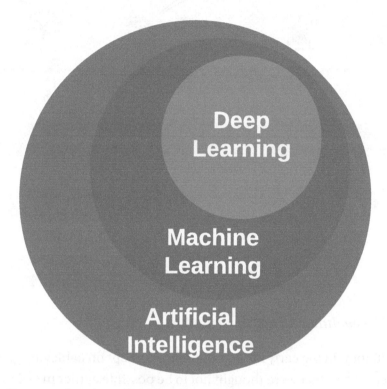

Figure 1-5. *How artificial intelligence, machine learning, and deep learning relate to one other*

See Figure 1-6 for a quick look back at how deep learning, machine learning, and artificial intelligence evolved through the years.

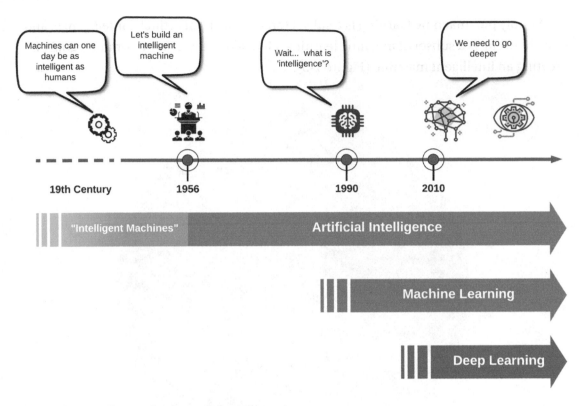

Figure 1-6. *The evolution of deep learning*

With its initiation in the early 2010s, deep learning kept on achieving groundbreaking results, with accuracies that were thought not to be possible earlier in tasks that were previously thought to be only possible to perform by humans, such as image recognition, language processing, and speech recognition. Shown in Figure 1-7 are a few of the noteworthy deep learning milestones in image recognition over the past decade.

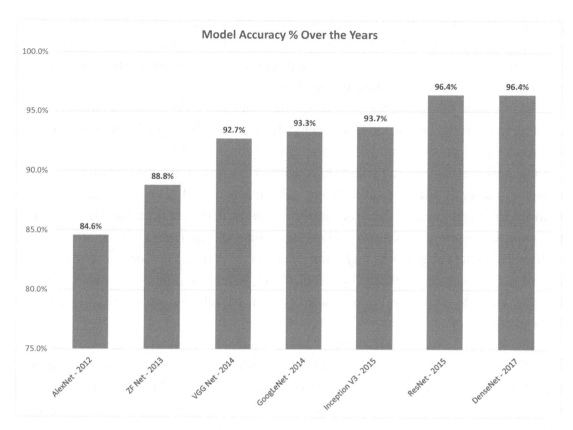

Figure 1-7. *Deep learning model accuracy over the years*

You can learn more about these specific models and their importance to deep learning in Appendix 1.

With the capabilities demonstrated and the success achieved by deep learning, we may be a step closer to the ultimate goal of artificial intelligence: building a machine with human (or greater) level intelligence.

Is an Artificial Intelligence Possible?

Despite everything AI has already achieved, there still exists some skepticism out there as to whether true AI (also referred to as artificial general intelligence) is possible.

One of the reasons for these skepticisms is due to a misunderstanding of the term "artificial intelligence." This has caused doubts in the approach AI is taking toward its goals.

The term "artificial intelligence" is an unfortunate mis-term, which has led to many misinterpretations. When the Dartmouth conference of 1956 named the new research field as artificial intelligence, they had good intentions for that name. But, as always, intentions are not preserved nor are they obvious.

The common misconception—by taking the name literally—is that AI aims to build "intelligence" artificially. However, in reality, the term "artificial intelligence" was and was always meant to be "artificial" + "Intelligence," meaning that it was meant to *bridge* artificial and intelligence. The goal of AI is to observe and understand "intelligent" behavior inherently found in natural constructs (human or otherwise) and attempt to build the intelligent behavior into artificial constructs. These artificial constructs could be computer programs, machines/robots, algorithms, or theoretical frameworks.

This concept is what has brought us models such as neural networks and genetic algorithms, among many others. If you look closely at these models, it becomes apparent that they are all applying modified versions of natural intelligence concepts on top of artificial constructs.

The ultimate goal of AI was—and is—to build a machine with a human or greater level of intelligence. (Note that a "machine" is a subjective term here, which can mean any artificial construct.) We do not want to reinvent "intelligence" for it. We just need to adapt the character and concept of natural intelligence to the artificial constructs we build.

We do not build intelligence artificially. We build machines inspired by nature.

## CHAPTER 2

Where to Start Your Deep Learning

Welcome to the exciting world of deep learning, AI, and computer vision.

With a high-level understanding of what deep learning is and its capabilities from the last chapter, you might be eager to learn building practical deep learning and computer vision systems.

But are you reluctant to switch to Linux for the development? Do you feel like you are more familiar with Windows, and wish that you could build everything on Windows?

Well, you do not need to worry anymore. The latest deep learning and computer vision libraries have matured to the point that almost everything now can be made to work seamlessly on Windows as well.

We will look at building deep learning systems on Windows step by step.

But first, let us answer a concern you might be having.

Can We Build Deep Learning Models on Windows?

If you have been a developer for long, you might have noticed that Windows did not used to work well with cutting-edge development, especially open-source projects.

While deep learning and computer vision frameworks weren't necessarily limited to a particular OS, the ease of development on Linux or Unix-based systems and the pace of which the development happened meant that the latest features and options were either delayed or not available on Windows. And thus for a time, if you wanted to make any serious machine learning, AI, or computer vision models, it seemed like you would have to stick with Linux or a Unix-based system.

But fortunately, things have improved for Windows greatly in recent years.

Cutting-edge deep learning frameworks like TensorFlow and Keras, as well as computer vision libraries like OpenCV and Dlib, now have their newer versions working natively on Windows. Driver support and GPU acceleration also work seamlessly on Windows now.

© Thimira Amaratunga 2021
T. Amaratunga, *Deep Learning on Windows*, https://doi.org/10.1007/978-1-4842-6431-7_2

In fact, in some cases, it is easier to get GPU acceleration such as NVIDIA CUDA support working with Windows than on Linux. Windows driver support for consumer graphics cards has been ahead for many years.

Advantages of Using Windows

Windows is the most popular operating system in the world, with over 70% of desktop PCs using some version of it (see Figure 2-1).[1]

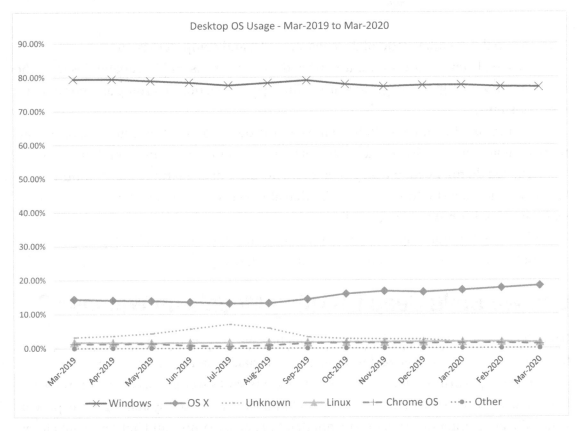

Figure 2-1. *Windows usage on desktop PCs[1]*

---

[1]Statistics from GS Statcounter, "Desktop Operating System Market Share Worldwide, Sept. 2019–Sept. 2020," https://gs.statcounter.com/os-market-share/desktop/worldwide, accessed [19 Apr 2020] and Wikipedia, "Desktop/Laptop Operating System Browsing Statistics," https://en.wikipedia.org/wiki/Usage_share_of_operating_systems#Desktop_and_laptop_computers, accessed [17 Apr 2020].

In most cases, unless you are a dedicated DL/ML researcher, if you already have a decently powerful general-purpose PC—or are thinking of getting or building one—you tend to use Windows on it. Probably you are more familiar with using Windows as the OS of your home PC and are using other software on your PC that is only available on Windows.

So, if you are thinking of learning to build deep learning models, it is easier when you do not need to switch your OS to do so.

If you are planning to use GPU accelerations on your models—which we cover later in this chapter—then getting them working on Windows is much easier than other operating systems due to better driver support (although Linux GPU driver support is now improving).

And if you do have a good GPU in your PC, chances are that you want to use that for other things like gaming or productivity instead of dedicating it to deep learning. By sticking to Windows, you get the best of both worlds.

Limitations of Using Windows

In addition to the advantages we discussed, there are some limitations in using Windows that you should be aware of.

While most of the frameworks and libraries for deep learning and computer vision are now available on Windows, you may find that the latest versions of them are typically delayed more than their Linux counterparts.

If you try to customize or build the libraries from source, you may find that the requirements to build them on Windows are a little bit strict. It is the main reason that the native packages tend to be delayed for Windows.

Because support for Windows was recent, you may also find that the community support for issues on Windows is also less than that for Linux. This will hopefully improve in the future, with more people starting deep learning development on Windows.

The bottom line is that you do not have to switch from Windows to an OS like Linux in order to learn deep learning if you don't want to. In this book, we will see how to get everything needed to build deep learning systems that work on Windows.

Linux is a great OS for developers. If you feel like it, you should definitely check out developing on Linux. Serious researchers on deep learning and computer vision do tend to use Linux systems for their development due to the flexibilities it provides. But it is not a must for you to start learning.

You can start building practical deep learning systems right on Windows. And once you learn how, you can later switch to any OS for your development if you prefer.

So what do you need to start?

You need to select a programming language to write your code and select a couple of deep learning frameworks for that language, throw in a selection of utility libraries and tools to help you, and then just start coding.

Does that sound too overwhelming?

Let us look at these requirements one at a time.

Programming Language: Python

You might wonder, why Python? Is it the only language for deep learning? Definitely not.

When you understand the concepts, you can use pretty much any language to implement deep learning. But some languages have already established tools, libraries, and frameworks for supporting machine learning and deep learning tasks. To avoid reinventing already existing elements, we chose a language that has a lot of such pre-existing support.

Is Python the best language for deep learning? That is a tricky question.

When we look for the most popular languages for machine learning, a couple of languages stand out: Python, R, C++, C, and MATLAB. Each of them has its advantages and disadvantages.

We chose Python for several reasons that are especially important when you are just starting to learn deep learning.

For a beginner in deep learning—especially for someone with a programming background—writing code in Python would be more natural. You can use most of the familiar object-oriented and functional programming concepts. While performance may not be as good as C or C++, Python is still quite fast. Having the capability to run the code on multiple CPUs and GPUs helps a lot too. Another plus point is that most C and C++ libraries tend to have Python interfaces as well (e.g., OpenCV, Dlib, Caffe). Compared to R and MATLAB, the availability of deep learning and machine learning libraries are similar in Python. But considering the maturity of the libraries, Python libraries seem to be more bleeding edge. Most of the latest deep learning frameworks are currently being developed primarily targeting Python (e.g., TensorFlow).

One of the biggest advantages of using Python is its deployability. Say you build an awesome deep learning program, and you want to deploy it as a web service. With Python, it is fairly straightforward. With R, MATLAB, or C/C++, it will take quite a bit of effort.

Considering all these benefits, we are going to use Python for our deep learning experiments.

Package and Environment Management: Anaconda

Anaconda is an open source platform of Python and R languages meant for machine learning, data science, large-scale data processing, and scientific computing. Anaconda contains optimized versions of Python for many platforms and architectures.

It is not only a Python distribution, but also a package, dependency, and environment manager for Python. Through its conda package manager, Anaconda allows easy creation of virtual isolated environments—with its Python binaries and packages—to experiment with. You can create multiple independent Python environments of multiple Python versions, and their own independent installed packages, based on your needs.

Anaconda also contains hundreds of prebuilt and tested packages for machine learning, scientific computing, and data processing that you can directly install through the conda package manager. It removes the hassle of finding, building, installing, and dependency managing of packages and libraries.

Python Utility Libraries for Deep Learning and Computer Vision

When working with Python and the deep learning frameworks (which we will be looking at in a bit), having the following set of utility libraries will make a lot of tasks easier:

- **NumPy:** adds support to handle large multidimensional arrays in Python, along with a collection of high-level mathematical functions that can be applied across arrays.

- **SciPy:** the scientific cousin of NumPy. SciPy adds support for mathematical optimization, linear algebra, integral and differential equations, interpolation, special functions, Fourier transforms, and signal processing to Python.

- **Pillow:** pillow is a fork of PIL (Python Image Library), which adds image processing capabilities to Python. It adds extensive file format support for images, with efficient internal representation mechanisms.

- **Scikit-Image:** adds a set of higher-level image processing capabilities to Python, such as edge detection, equalization, feature detection, and segmentation.

- **h5py:** adds the support of the HDF5 binary data format to Python. The HDF5 format is used in many of the machine learning frameworks, as it allows easy storage and handling of large, terabyte-level data as if they were internal data arrays.

- **Matplotlib:** Matplotlib is a sophisticated 2D and 3D plotting and data visualization library for Python, allowing you to create publication-quality plots and figures on a variety of platforms.

Note   These are just a few of the utility libraries that we would need to get our code working. We will be needing more as we go along. But having these will help make things easier from the start.

With Anaconda, we also do not need to install them one by one. Anaconda has utility functions to quickly install these—and more—which we will investigate in the next chapter.

Deep Learning Frameworks

TensorFlow

TensorFlow is currently one of the most actively developed machine learning libraries in the world. At its core it is a symbolic math library, which specializes in applications such as neural networks.

TensorFlow is the second-generation machine learning library by the Google Brain Team, and has gained huge popularity in recent times due to its deep learning capabilities. First released in November 2015, as the successor to DistBelief (Google Brains first-generation machine learning library), TensorFlow initially only supported Python and C on Linux. Since then it has added support to C++, Java, Go, JavaScript, and experimental support for Swift. Third-party support is also available for C#, Haskell, Julia, MATLAB, R, Scala, Rust, OCaml, and Crystal. TensorFlow now works on Windows and Mac OS natively.

TensorFlow is capable of running on either CPU or GPU (with NVIDIA CUDA). It also runs on Google's proprietary Tensor Processing Units (TPUs)—application-specific integrated circuit (ASIC) units built specifically for machine learning and tailored for TensorFlow. TensorFlow can also run on lower-end devices like mobile phones—on Android and iOS—and Raspberry Pi devices when running inference.

TensorFlow uses stateful data flow graphs for its numerical calculations, where the nodes of the graph represent mathematical operations, while the edges of the graph represent the data that flows through the nodes. The data is represented as multidimensional arrays (tensors), hence the name "TensorFlow."

In February 2017, TensorFlow released version 1.0.

TensorFlow.js 1.0 was released in March 2018.

TensorFlow 2.0 was released in January 2019, version 2.1 in January 2020, and version 2.2 in May 2020.

The 2.x versions come with many new features and improvements, such as eager execution, multi-GPU support, tighter Keras integration, and new deployment options such as TensorFlow Serving (Figure 2-2).

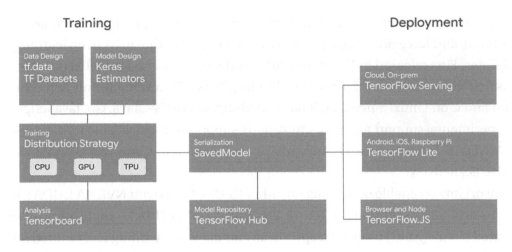

Figure 2-2. *The TensorFlow 2.0 Ecosystem[2]*

Keras

Keras is a higher-level neural networks library for Python, which can run on top of TensorFlow, CNTK (Microsoft Cognitive Toolkit), or Theano, and has limited support for MXNet and Deeplearning4j. The focus on Keras is to allow fast experimentation and prototyping of code by being user-friendly, minimal, modular, and extensible. Keras gives you a more clean and structured code than when using the backend libraries directly.

Keras supports convolutional networks and recurrent networks, as well as combinations of the two, and can run on both CPU and GPU, based on the capabilities of the backend being used.

With the release of TensorFlow v1.0 in February 2017, the TensorFlow team added dedicated support to Keras in the TensorFlow library.

With TensorFlow 2.0, released in January 2019, the Keras library is fully integrated into the TensorFlow library and is available through the tf.keras interface. The multibackend Keras implementation is also maintained as a separate branch, but the main development now happens on tf.keras.

---

[2]Image is from [https://blog.tensorflow.org/2019/09/tensorflow-20-is-now-available.html], "TensorFlow 2.0 is now available!," [30 Sept 2019].

Other Frameworks
Scikit-Learn

Scikit-Learn (formerly scikits.learn) is a library for machine learning, data mining, and data analytics. It gives capabilities such as classification, regression, clustering, dimensionality reduction, model selection, and preprocessing (feature extraction and normalization). Scikit-Learn has one of the best collections of machine learning and utility algorithms for data processing.

Theano

Theano is a machine learning and numerical computation library developed by the researchers at the University of Montreal. The idea behind Theano is to allow developers to write symbolic expressions, which it would then dynamically compile to run on various architectures. The dynamic C code generation feature of Theano allows programs to efficiently run and take advantage of different CPU or GPU architectures. Theano has tight integration with NumPy, which it uses to represent its multidimensional data structures.

Theano has been in active development since 2007 and is considered as a good alternative to TensorFlow, as both support similar features.

Computer Vision Libraries

Why do we need computer vision libraries?

As we discussed in the previous chapter, when working with deep learning, you will run into many tasks requiring computer vision and image processing.

Having these libraries will make things easier.

OpenCV

OpenCV (open source computer vision) is the de facto standard library when it comes to computer vision. Aimed at real-time computer vision applications, OpenCV is loaded with vision and image processing algorithms. It also has some machine learning capabilities built in to aid with building computer vision applications.

Originally developed by Intel and initially released in June 2000, OpenCV has since been made open-source and is now released under the BSD license. The current versions of OpenCV is primarily written in C++, but still contains some legacy C components as well as C interfaces. OpenCV has interfaces for C, C++, Python, MATLAB, and Java. It can run on Windows, Linux, Mac OS, iOS, and Android.

As well as the computer vision aspect of it, OpenCV provides excellent image processing and manipulation options such as cropping, resizing, transforming, color channel manipulating, and many more options on a variety of image types. This makes it essential to many applications in which images are used, such as building deep learning computer vision models with frameworks such as TensorFlow. OpenCV is also able to process video streams from cameras as well as video files (Figure 2-3).

Figure 2-3. *OpenCV processing a video file*

Currently there are two major branches of OpenCV: v3.x and v4.x. The 4.x branch contains the latest development and is more optimized. However, the 3.x versions may be more cross-compatible with other libraries we are using.

Dlib

Dlib is a toolkit for C++ and Python containing machine learning algorithms and tools for creating complex software to solve real-world problems. Dlib provides algorithms for machine learning and deep learning, multiclass classification and clustering models, support vector machines, regression models, a large set of numerical algorithms for areas such as matrix manipulations and linear algebra, graphical model inference algorithms, and utility algorithms for computer vision and image processing. And due to C++ implementations backing most of these implementations, they are optimized to the point that can be used in some real-time applications as well.

If you're interested in facial recognition models or facial emotion processing, then Dlib is a library you should try out, as Dlib has some of the most optimized out-of-the-box face detection and face landmark detection models available (Figure 2-4).

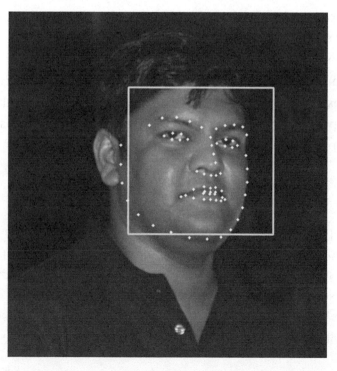

Figure 2-4. *Dlib Face Landmark Detection in action*

Dlib also has easy to use functions to train your own object detectors, shape predictors, and deep learning–based semantic segmentation of images.

Optimizers and Accelerators

Building and training deep learning models are computationally complex tasks, usually taking a lot of processing power and time of a system. Optimizers and accelerators are libraries and tools which help to perform those steps faster. Most optimizers and accelerator tools work by giving your deep learning code direct access to the capabilities of the hardware of the system, allowing them to harness the full potentials of the hardware.

NVIDIA CUDA and cuDNN

CUDA is a parallel computing platform and programming model invented by NVIDIA. It enables dramatic increases in computing performance by harnessing the power of the GPU. cuDNN—CUDA Deep Neural Network library—is a GPU-accelerated library of primitives for deep neural networks. cuDNN provides highly tuned implementations for standard routines such as forward and backward convolution, pooling, normalization, and activation layers.

Using CUDA and cuDNN along with either Theano or TensorFlow can speed up your neural networks extensively (networks that took hours to train might take just minutes, but this would depend entirely on your model). The only requirement is that you need to have a CUDA supported NVIDIA GPU in your system.

OpenBLAS

OpenBLAS is an open-source implementation of the BLAS (basic linear algebra subprograms), containing optimizations for many specific processor types. Machine learning libraries such as Theano can speed up certain routines by utilizing BLAS libraries. You will see a noticeable speed difference when running your models with OpenBLAS on CPU. However, some libraries, such as TensorFlow, have their internal optimizers, and will not see any improvements with OpenBLAS.

What About Hardware?

The next question that might strike you is: What kind of hardware do I need to do deep learning experiments?

It is a tricky question, as we need to think about the two phases of a deep learning system: *training* and *inference*.

To build a deep learning system—or any machine learning system—we first gather some data to train the system on. We then build a deep learning model and run it through the training dataset. This is where our model "learns" the characteristics of the data. Once the system runs through the training dataset, we typically do some validation steps to make sure it has been trained properly. These steps are called the *training phase* of the system.

Once the system completes the training phase, it is ready to be put to real use. This is where the system is presented with new, real-world data and utilizes what it has learned. The system will use what it has learned, to infer things about the new data it is being presented. This is called the *inference phase* of the system.

So how does this relate to our question about hardware?

The training phase is the most resource-intensive of the two. It requires high computation power (either CPU or GPU) to run the training through a deep learning model, and large amounts of memory to hold the data needed for the training. So for training deep learning models, you will need a machine with sufficient computing power and memory. The more power you have, the faster and the more complex the models you can train. Having GPU-computing capable graphics card (such as a one with an NVIDIA CUDA enabled GPU) would be a plus here.

But remember, even a moderate PC is capable of training sufficiently large deep learning models. There are techniques you can use to handle large data sets with limited memory. So do not let your PCs specs discourage you from experimenting. All the code we discuss in this book can run on a standard PC or laptop.

If you feel that your local computing power is not sufficient for your experiments, you can easily use cloud computing services to train your deep learning models. Amazon Web Services provides their P3 GPU Compute instances, which are backed by NVIDIA Tesla GPUs (see AWS P3 Instances[3]), which should be able to handle massive deep learning models, or Google Colab Notebooks (see Google Colaboratory[4]).

What about the inference phase?

---

[3]AWS P3 Instances are from [https://aws.amazon.com/ec2/instance-types/p3/]," "Amazon EC2 P3 Instances," [20 Apr 2020.]

[4]Google Colaboratory, "Welcome To Colaboratory," https://colab.research.google.com/, [20 Apr 2020.]

A properly optimized deep learning model would be able to run inference on a limited resource device such as a Raspberry Pi device or a smartphone. This typically depends on the size of the final trained model. There are deep learning architectures— such as MobileNet and SqueezeNet, which are specifically designed to be fast and smaller in size, so they can fit into mobile devices.

Recommended PC Hardware Configurations

If you are thinking of building (or upgrading) or buying a PC that you plan to use for deep learning, machine learning, or computer vision tasks, here are some recommendations for the hardware.

Note   Please note that these are only recommendations. The libraries and frameworks mentioned in this book can be set up and will work on a variety of hardware configurations.

As mentioned earlier, the main requirements for a machine aimed at deep learning and computer vision are processing power and memory. Processing power dictates how fast the required calculations can be performed and is determined by how fast your CPU and GPU are. The number of processor cores your CPU has will also have an impact on the speed as it dictates how parallel the operations can be. Memory dictates how complex your models can be (as they need to be loaded into the memory) as well as how much of the training data can be loaded into the memory at a time, indirectly affecting the training speed. The complexity of the models you will be able to train will be determined by both the amount of RAM the machine has and the amount of VRAM the GPU has.

Therefore, the ideal deep learning PC would consist of a faster, powerful CPU with a high core count, with large amounts of RAM, and a faster GPU with higher VRAM.

But unless you have an unlimited amount of money to spend on the absolute highest-end PC, you would have to balance out these requirements. So let us see what we should practically look in to.

For the CPU, balance out the power and affordability. Something like an Intel Core-i5 or an AMD Ryzen 5 would be sufficient as a minimum. A Core-i7 or higher (eighth-generation or higher) for Intel,[5] or Ryzen 7 or higher (second-generation or higher) for AMD,[6] would be a better choice if you can go for it. Consider the core count as well as the single-core performance when selecting. An overclockable processor (i.e., multiplier unlocked processor, such as the Intel K series) is only recommended if you are experienced with overclocking, as we prefer stability over raw speed for deep learning workloads. You can usually save several hundred dollars by going for a non-overclockable processor.

Pair up the processor with a decent motherboard. You will not need a fancy gaming-featured motherboard. But look for a one with good power distribution, with a higher number of VRMs (voltage regulator modules). In deep learning workflows, both the CPU and GPU would be running at their max, so better power delivery will keep them stable. Also, look for the expandability of the motherboard as well. Having more RAM slots would allow you to add more RAM later, while more PCIe 16x slots will allow you to go for a multi-GPU option later. However, these are optional features if you are just starting.

Go for the highest amount of RAM you can afford. It is recommended to have 16GB of RAM at a minimum. Also, be aware of the recommended speed of the RAM that your processor and motherboard support. Higher speed RAM with XMP profiles may introduce instabilities if you are unfamiliar with how they work.

As mentioned with the motherboard, stable power is essential to the stability of the system. Some deep learning training tasks can take hours, if not days. Therefore, a stable power supply is a must. When selecting a power supply look for a one with an energy efficiency rating of "80+ Gold" or better. Based on the processor and the graphics card you select, typically a 500W power supply may suffice. But you may go for a higher one if, for example, you plan to go for multiple GPUs later.

Selecting a GPU can be a bit tricky, as they are usually the most expensive component of a PC build. Since most deep learning and machine learning frameworks and libraries use NVIDIA CUDA for GPU processing, we would need to select an NVIDIA graphics card.

---

[5]List of Intel microprocessors from [https://en.wikipedia.org/wiki/List_of_Intel_microprocessors], "List of Intel processors," [21 Nov 2020].

[6]AMD Ryzen from [https://en.wikipedia.org/wiki/Ryzen], "Ryzen," [20 Nov 2020].

Note   While AMD has some excellent graphics card models, their compatibility and support with ML tasks are still experimental. So we will need to stick to NVIDIA here.

When considering a graphics card for deep learning, machine learning, or computer vision tasks, few things needs to be considered:

- **CUDA core count:** The higher the core count, the better it can parallelize the processing.

- **Memory:** Higher memory allows you to fit more training data at a time for processing. (If your dataset is bigger than the available GPU memory, you will have to chunk it and perform incremental learning.)

- **Clock speed:** The higher the clock speed, usually the better (if you're just starting, don't think too much about numbers such as "base clock" and "boost clock," as several other factors are affecting the speed of the card).

- **Other features:** Having additional features such as Tensor Cores found in GPUs with NVIDIA Turing microarchitecture (GeForce RTX 20 series or newer), might help increase the training speed of your models. But you may need to tune your models to utilize these features.

Based on these factors, the following graphics cards families can be recommended:

- **GeForce 10 series:** An older generation, but still fairly good performance. You may also be able to find these very cheaply in the used market if you are comfortable getting a used GPU. Recommended cards: GTX 1070Ti or better (1070Ti, 1080, 1080Ti).

- **GeForce 16 series:** The same Turing architecture as the 20 series, but without the Tensor Cores and RT Cores (Ray-Tracing). Recommended cards: GTX 1660 or better (1660, 1660Ti).

- **GeForce 20 series:** The latest generation of NVIDIA GeForce (at the time of this writing). Turing architecture with Tensor Cores and RT Cores. Recommended cards: RTX 2060 Super or better (2060 Super, 2070 Super, 2080 Super, 2080Ti, Titan RTX).

- **GeForce 30 series:** It is still too early to say anything about the deep learning performance of the next generation of NVIDIA GeForce. But with the new Ampere microarchitecture, it is expected to outperform the previous generations.

NVIDIA graphics cards are sold either directly through NVIDIA—the "Founders Edition" cards—or through NVIDIA partners such as ASUS, MSI, EVGA, Gigabyte, and many more. When selecting a graphics card, it is better to select one from a well-known brand, as those tend to have better build quality, better and stable power delivery, and better cooling. Deep learning tasks will stress your GPU and sustain the stress more than any game or application.

In addition to this, faster storage such as an SSD would also help to speed up your system.

What we discussed here are only recommendations; it is possible to build deep learning models with much older or slower hardware than this. Therefore, do not be discouraged if your current machine does not meet these recommendations. As mentioned in the previous section, optimizing your models plays a larger role than the speed of the hardware you train on. So start learning, and start building.

## CHAPTER 3

Setting Up Your Tools

Now that we know what we need to get started, let us begin setting up our tools.

Since we will be using packages from several different sources—from Anaconda package channels, pip packages, and so on—the order in which we install them is somewhat important in order to get a smoother installation experience without any conflicts. We recommend the following order of operations:

1. Install Visual Studio with C++ Support

2. Install CMake

3. Install Anaconda Python

4. Set up the Conda Environment and the Python Libraries

5. Install TensorFlow

6. (Optional) Install Keras multibackend version

7. Install OpenCV

8. Install Dlib

9. Verify Installations

Let us look at how to set up each of them.

Step 1: Installing Visual Studio with C++ Support

The first step we need to do is to install a compiler for C++.

Why do we need C++? Aren't we going to code in Python?

Yes, we are going to use Python. And no, you do not need to learn C++ to learn deep learning (although C++ is a wonderful language).

© Thimira Amaratunga 2021
T. Amaratunga, *Deep Learning on Windows*, https://doi.org/10.1007/978-1-4842-6431-7_3

But some of the more advanced Python libraries have parts that were written with C++ to improve their performance. So to install some of the libraries, we need to have a C++ compiler installed in our system.

On Windows, we use Visual Studio as the compiler.

Due to various compatibility issues of different Visual Studio versions with various packages, it is recommended that we stick with an older version of Visual Studio rather than the latest version. This older version can be downloaded from the Visual Studio Older Versions page.[1] Visual Studio 2015 is a good choice (Figure 3-1). The free community edition will be enough for our tasks.

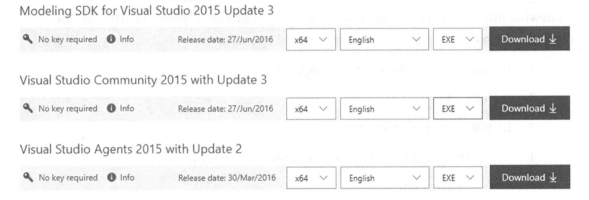

Figure 3-1. *Select to download "visual studio community 2015 with update 3" from the Visual Studio older versions page*

When installing VS 2015, make sure to select the "custom" install option (Figure 3-2).

---

[1]Visual Studio (older versions page), https://visualstudio.microsoft.com/vs/older-downloads/, [22 Nov 2020]; you will need to register (free) for a Microsoft Online account in order to download older versions of Visual Studio.

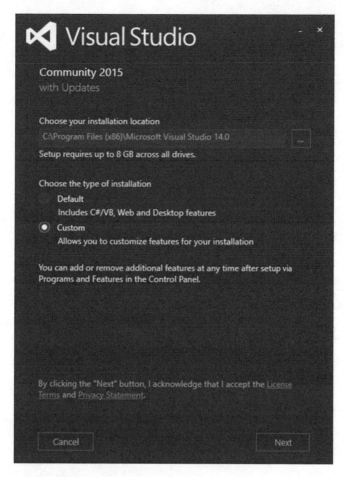

Figure 3-2. *Visual Studio custom install*

Select to install the Visual C++ option in the next screen (Figure 3-3).

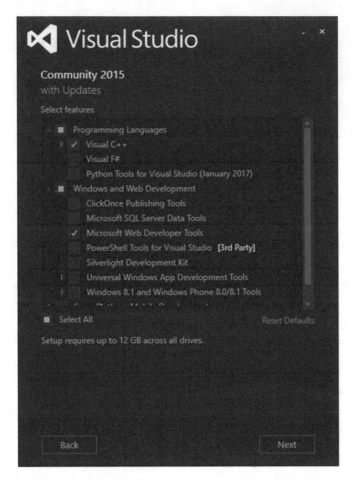

Figure 3-3. *Select to install Visual C++*

After the installation is completed, you can verify that C++ is available by launching Visual Studio and checking whether the 'Visual C++' option comes up (Figure 3-4).

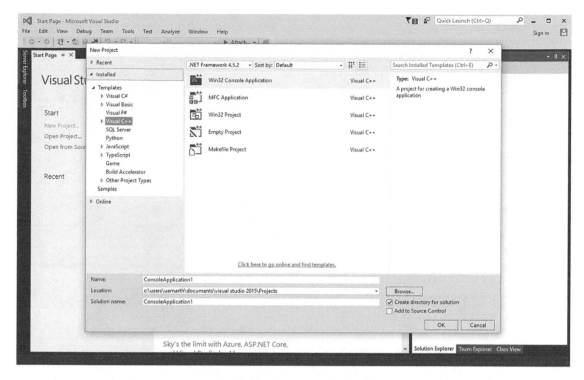

Figure 3-4. *Visual Studio 2015 with Visual C++*

Step 2: Installing CMake

CMake is a cross-platform build tool used to compile, test, and package software projects. CMake is used as a build tool in many open-source projects with C++ libraries, such as Dlib. CMake requires to have a C++ compiler installed on the system, which is why we installed Visual Studio with C++ tools before installing CMake.

In order to install CMake, head over to the CMake Downloads page[2] and download the latest Windows win64-x64 installer package (Figure 3-5) and run the installation.

---

[2]CMake (downloads page), `https://cmake.org/download/`, [9 Apr 2020].

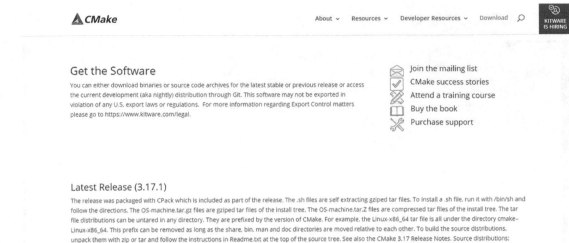

Figure 3-5. *Download the latest CMake package*

When installing, make sure to add CMake to the system path (Figure 3-6).

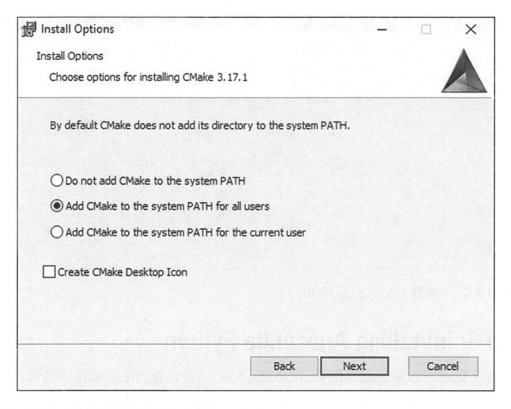

Figure 3-6. *Add CMake to the system path*

Once the installation is completed, you can verify the installation by running the following on the Windows command prompt (Figure 3-7).

```
cmake --version
```

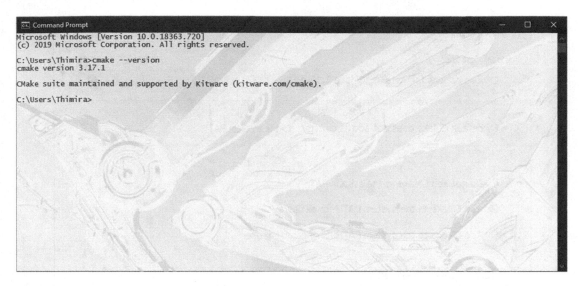

Figure 3-7. *Verify CMake version*

Step 3: Installing Anaconda Python

Installing Anaconda is straightforward: simply head over to the Anaconda individual edition downloads page[3] and download the latest Python 3.x 64-Bit package for Windows (Figure 3-8). The full installer is about 470MB in size, and contains the conda package manger, Python 3.8, and a set of prebundled commonly used packages. While the base installer comes with Python 3.8, we will be able to use other Python versions when creating the conda virtual environments.

---

[3]Anaconda (individual edition downloads page), `https://www.anaconda.com/products/` `individual`, [19 Nov 2020].

[4]Anaconda (package lists), `https://docs.anaconda.com/anaconda/packages/pkg-docs/`, [19 Nov 2020].

Figure 3-8. *The Anaconda individual edition downloads page*

The list of packages bundled in the installer, as well as the full list of conda packages available to install, can be found at the Anaconda package lists.[4]

Tip   If you do not need the full installer with the prebundled packages, and only need the conda package manager and Python, you can get the **Miniconda** distribution,[5] which has a much smaller size (~60MB). The miniconda installer package is also available with Python 3.8, but allows us to set up virtual environments with other Python versions.

---

[5]Miniconda (distribution), `https://docs.conda.io/en/latest/miniconda.html`, [28 Jul 2020].

Installing is as simple as running the downloaded graphical installer.

Tip   In the graphical installer, the "add Anaconda to my PATH environment variable" option might be unchecked by default (Figure 3-9). It is better to check this option, as it allows us to run the conda commands from the Windows command prompt.

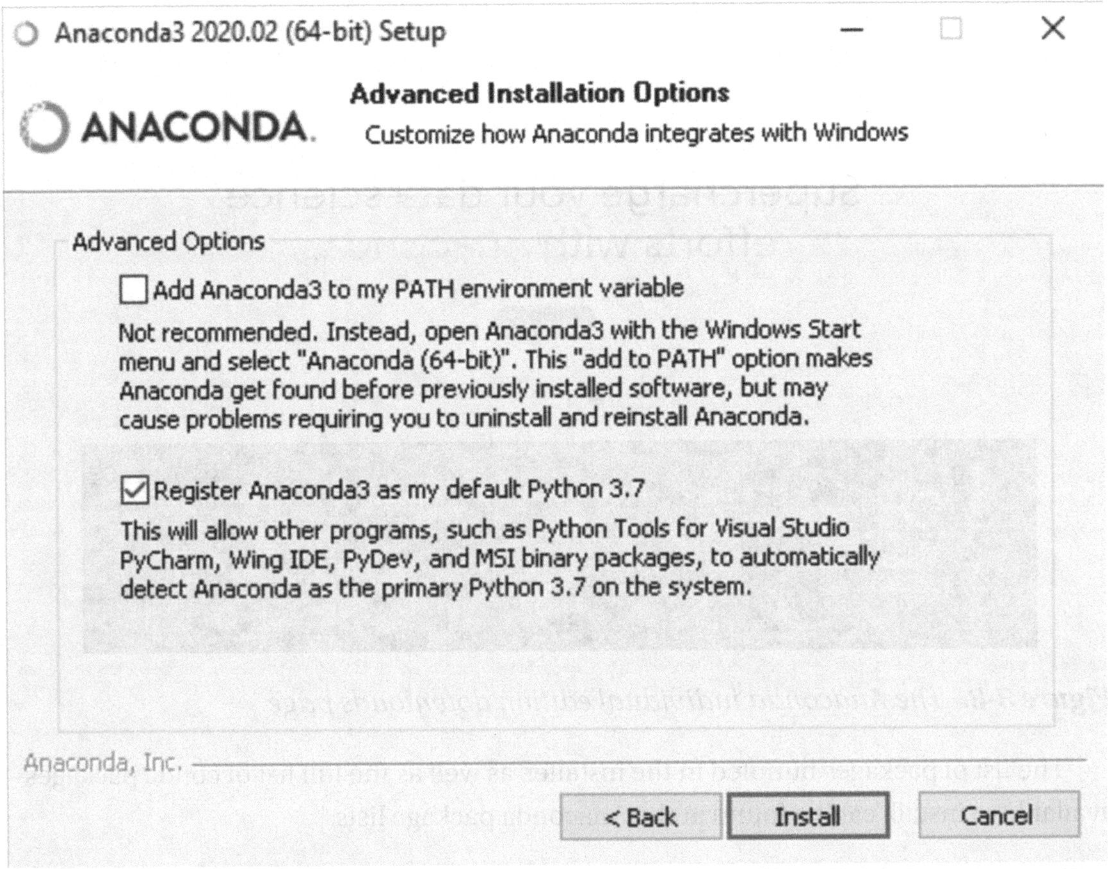

Figure 3-9. *The "add Anaconda to my PATH environment variable" option in the Anaconda installer*

If you forget to check this option, do not worry. You can add Anaconda to the PATH manually by adding the following to the system PATH variable (where \path\to\ anaconda3 is the Anaconda installation directory):

```
\path\to\anaconda\path\to\anaconda\Library\mingw-w64\bin\
path\to\anaconda\Library\usr\bin\path\to\anaconda\Library\
bin\path\to\anaconda\Scripts
```

For an example, if the user profile is at C:\Users\Thimira\, the paths should be:

```
C:\Users\Thimira\Anaconda3C:\Users\Thimira\Anaconda3\
Library\mingw-w64\binC:\Users\Thimira\Anaconda3\Library\usr\
binC:\Users\Thimira\Anaconda3\Library\binC:\Users\Thimira\
Anaconda3\Scripts
```

Once the installation is completed open a Windows command prompt and run the following command:

```
conda list
```

If you get a list of installed conda packages, then Anaconda is installed and working properly.

Note   If you get an error message, make sure you closed and reopened the terminal window after installing, or do it now. Then verify that you are logged into the same user account that you used to install Anaconda.

At this point, if you have not used Anaconda Python before, it is better to go through the "getting started with conda" guide.[6] This a tutorial that should take you less than 30 minutes, and helps you get familiarized with the commands and capabilities of Anaconda.

---

[6]Conda, "Getting Started with Conda," https://conda.io/projects/conda/en/latest/user-guide/getting-started.html, [31 Jan 2020].

Step 4: Setting up the Conda Environment and the Python Libraries

Once you get the hang of conda, it is time to create the conda environment and install the necessary packages.

Note   Make sure you performed the "`conda update conda`" command as mentioned in the getting started guide before proceeding.

When creating the conda environment we also need to install the utility libraries we discussed in the previous chapter. We can install them one by one. But with conda, we do not have to.

Conda has a *metapackage* named 'anaconda' that bundles many of the commonly used utility packages.

So we just need to run the following command to create the conda virtual environment and install all the utility packages we want in it (this is a single command; see Figure 3-10).

```
conda create --name deep-learning python=3.7 anaconda
```

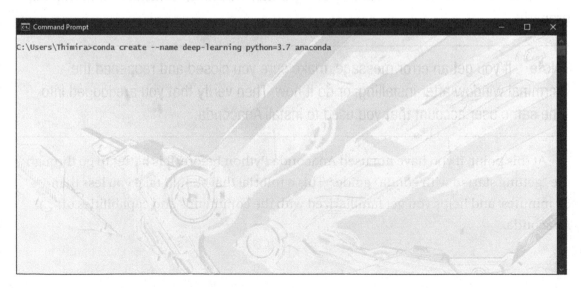

Figure 3-10. *Creating the Conda environment*

- **--name deep-learning:** We set the name of the environment to be "deep-learning." You can change that to anything you like.

- **python=3.7:** We tell conda to create the new environment with Python 3.7. You can specify another version of Python if you want to. But 3.7 is the one that is recommended now.

- **Anaconda:** We tell conda to install the anaconda metapackage into the created environment. This will install the bundle of commonly used utility packages, which includes the set of utility libraries we discussed earlier.

Note   Instead of using the metapackage—which installs a lot of packages that you might not need—you can also specify the list of packages to be installed when creating the environment:

```
conda create --name deep-learning python=3.7 numpy scipy
scikit-learn scikit-image pillow h5py matplotlib
```

Once the environment is created (which may take several minutes to download and install all the required packages; Figure 3-11), you can activate it by running:

```
conda activate deep-learning
```

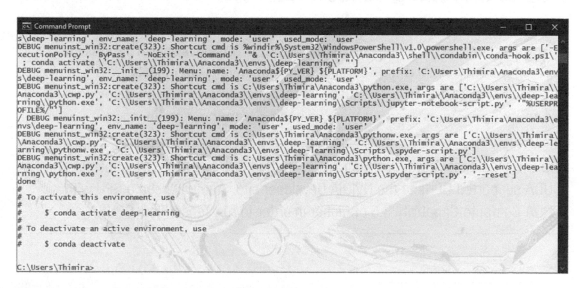

Figure 3-11. *Environment creation finished*

When an Anaconda environment is activated, the name of the environment will get prepended to the command prompt (Figure 3-12).

You can use this to verify that you are working on the correct environment. Always make sure that you have activated and working on the correct environment for all the following steps.

Figure 3-12. *Conda environment activated*

Step 5: Installing TensorFlow

TensorFlow has both a CPU version and a GPU version. If your system has a CUDA capable NVIDIA GPU installed, the TensorFlow GPU version is able to harness the processing power of that GPU to accelerate the training of your models.

If you have a CUDA capable NVIDIA GPU I highly recommend installing the GPU version, as it gives massive speed-ups to your deep learning experiments.

Tip   You can check whether your NVIDIA GPU is CUDA capable from the list of CUDA supported GPUs at the NVIDIA Developer site.[7] You will need a GPU with CUDA Compute Capability 3.5 or higher in order to run TensorFlow GPU.

---

[7][https://developer.nvidia.com/cuda-gpus], "CUDA supported GPUs," [22 Nov 2020].

As TensorFlow now has an Anaconda-native package, we will be using it to install TensorFlow, as it simplifies the installation of its dependencies such as the CUDA Toolkit and cuDNN libraries.

To install the GPU version of TensorFlow, run the following command (make sure you are in the activated conda environment we created earlier):

```
conda install tensorflow-gpu==2.1.0
```

Note   We are specifying the version number of the package also as tensorflow-gpu==**2.1.0** because anaconda tends to install an older version. Hopefully this will be fixed in the future, but until then it is better to specify the package version.

Tip   Always check for the latest available TensorFlow package version from the Anaconda package lists[8] and install that version. At the time of this writing the Anaconda package lists shows version 2.2.0 as the latest TensorFlow version available. However, if you attempt to install it, you may get a "PackagesNotFoundError" due to an issue with the conda package registry. Until that is fixed, we will stick with TensorFlow 2.1.0.

For the CPU version:

```
conda install tensorflow==2.1.0
```

Caution   Do not attempt to install both the GPU and CPU versions in the same conda environment. If you want to switch the versions, uninstall the other version first, or use a different conda environment.

---

[8]Anaconda (package lists), https://docs.anaconda.com/anaconda/packages/pkg-docs/, [19 Nov 2020].

Conda will take care of installing all the dependencies for you. If you opted to install the GPU version, this will also include the CUDA Toolkit and cuDNN libraries as well (Figure 3-13).

```
Select Command Prompt - conda install tensorflow-gpu - conda install tensorflow-gpu==2.1.0                              —   □   ×
  astor                 pkgs/main/win-64::astor-0.8.0-py37_0
  backports.os          pkgs/main/win-64::backports.os-0.1.1-py37_0
  blinker               pkgs/main/win-64::blinker-1.4-py37_0
  cachetools            pkgs/main/noarch::cachetools-3.1.1-py_0
  cudatoolkit           pkgs/main/win-64::cudatoolkit-10.1.243-h74a9793_0
  cudnn                 pkgs/main/win-64::cudnn-7.6.5-cuda10.1_0
  gast                  pkgs/main/win-64::gast-0.2.2-py37_0
  google-auth           pkgs/main/noarch::google-auth-1.13.1-py_0
  google-auth-oauth~    pkgs/main/noarch::google-auth-oauthlib-0.4.1-py_2
  google-pasta          pkgs/main/noarch::google-pasta-0.2.0-py_0
  grpcio                pkgs/main/win-64::grpcio-1.27.2-py37h351948d_0
  keras-applications    pkgs/main/noarch::keras-applications-1.0.8-py_0
  keras-preprocessi~    pkgs/main/noarch::keras-preprocessing-1.1.0-py_1
  libprotobuf           pkgs/main/win-64::libprotobuf-3.11.4-h7bd577a_0
  markdown              pkgs/main/win-64::markdown-3.1.1-py37_0
  oauthlib              pkgs/main/noarch::oauthlib-3.1.0-py_0
  opt_einsum            pkgs/main/noarch::opt_einsum-3.1.0-py_0
  protobuf              pkgs/main/win-64::protobuf-3.11.4-py37h33f27b4_0
  pyasn1                pkgs/main/noarch::pyasn1-0.4.8-py_0
  pyasn1-modules        pkgs/main/noarch::pyasn1-modules-0.2.7-py_0
  pyjwt                 pkgs/main/win-64::pyjwt-1.7.1-py37_0
  requests-oauthlib     pkgs/main/noarch::requests-oauthlib-1.3.0-py_0
  rsa                   pkgs/main/noarch::rsa-4.0-py_0
  tensorboard           pkgs/main/noarch::tensorboard-2.1.0-py3_0
  tensorflow            pkgs/main/win-64::tensorflow-2.1.0-gpu_py37h7db9008_0
  tensorflow-base       pkgs/main/win-64::tensorflow-base-2.1.0-gpu_py37h55f5790_0
  tensorflow-estima~    pkgs/main/noarch::tensorflow-estimator-2.1.0-pyhd54b08b_0
  tensorflow-gpu        pkgs/main/win-64::tensorflow-gpu-2.1.0-h0d30ee6_0
  termcolor             pkgs/main/win-64::termcolor-1.1.0-py37_1
```

Figure 3-13. *The CUDA-toolkit and cuDNN libraries being installed*

Step 6: (Optional) Installing Keras Multibackend version

This is an optional step.

With TensorFlow versions 2.0 and up, Keras is integrated into the TensorFlow library and is available through its tf.keras Python interface.

But if you need to install the multibackend version of Keras for experimentation with other backends such as Theano, you can install it using pip:

```
pip install keras
```

Switching the backend of Keras is done in the keras.json file, which is located at *%USERPROFILE%\.keras\keras.json* on Windows. The default keras.json file looks like this:

```
{
    "floatx": "float32",
    "epsilon": 1e-07,
```

```
    "backend": "tensorflow",
    "image_data_format": "channels_last"
}
```

When switching the backend, you need to be aware of the image_data_format parameter of Keras also. You can read more about it in Appendix 2.

If you are sticking with TensorFlow, the default settings of Keras will work fine.

Step 7: Installing OpenCV

OpenCV has prebuilt binaries for Windows that can be downloaded from their official site. But you may run into issues with getting the Python bindings working with 64-Bit Python 3.7.

The easiest way to get OpenCV working on Windows with 64-Bit Python 3.7 is to use the Anaconda package (Figure 3-14). As with TensorFlow, conda will handle all the dependency management.

```
conda install opencv
```

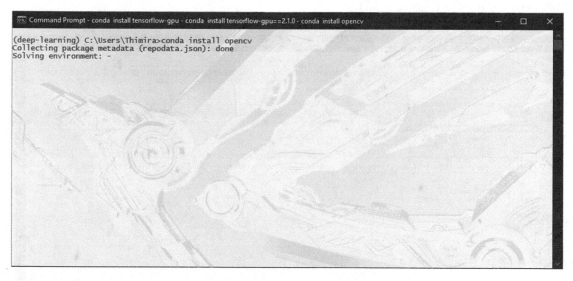

Figure 3-14. *OpenCV being installed*

Step 8: Installing Dlib

With all the great features in Dlib, installing it has always been a little bit troublesome because of some specific dependency requirements it needs that have a habit of almost always conflicting with your other libraries. With the latest versions, however, installing Dlib has become somewhat simple.

If you want the latest official package of Dlib installed, then using the pip package is the way to go.

Note   You need to have Visual Studio and CMake installed before attempting to install Dlib. Make sure CMake is available in the system path by running `cmake --version.`

You can install the Dlib pip package with:

```
pip install dlib
```

It will collect the package, build the wheel using CMake, and then install it in your conda environment (Figure 3-15).

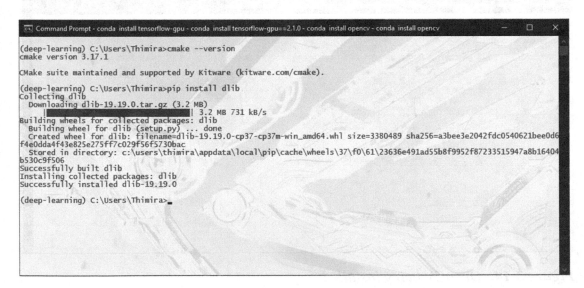

Figure 3-15. *Dlib PIP installation successful*

Step 9: Verifying the Installations

After you install all the required packages and libraries, it is best to do some preliminary checks to ensure that everything is installed correctly. Otherwise, you will run into issues later when running your code and wouldn't know whether there's a bug in the code, or an issue with the installation.

We will not be able to test everything without attempting to run a few deep learning models. But these steps will help you make sure everything is ready.

First, make sure you have activated the conda environment we created earlier:

```
conda activate deep-learning
```

You can verify that the environment activated correctly by looking at the command prompt (Figure 3-16).

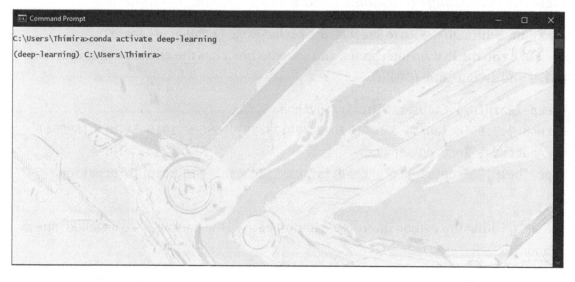

Figure 3-16. *Conda environment activated*

Run the following to see a list of all the installed packages:

```
conda list
```

You will get a long list like the following (Figure 3-17):

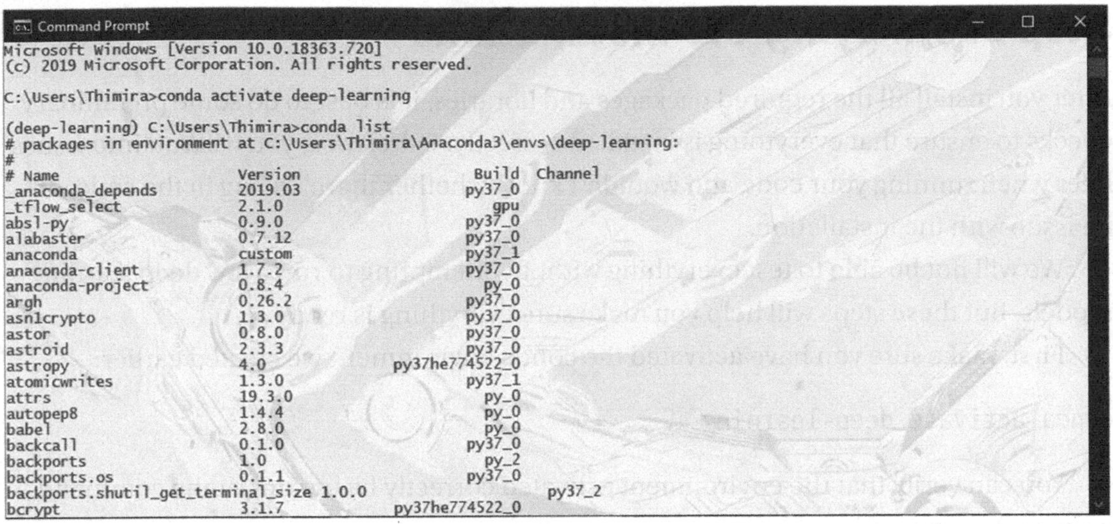

Figure 3-17. *Listing the installed packages in our Conda environment*

Glance through the list to see if all the packages we installed are there.

Then run the Python interpreter, and see whether it has the correct Python version (3.7.*) and architecture (64-Bit).

```
(deep-learning) C:\Users\Thimira>python
Python 3.7.6 (default, Jan  8 2020, 20:23:39) [MSC v.1916 64 bit (AMD64)]
:: Anaconda, Inc. on win32
Type "help," "copyright," "credits" or "license" for more information.
>>>
```

Next, within the Python interpreter, import each of the packages we installed, one at a time:

- TensorFlow

  `import tensorflow as tf`

- OpenCV

  `import cv2`

- Dlib

  `import dlib`

- Multibackend Keras (if you installed it)

  `import keras`

If everything is set up properly, all these imports should complete without any errors. Some packages, such as TensorFlow and Keras, may display some info messages while importing (Figure 3-18).

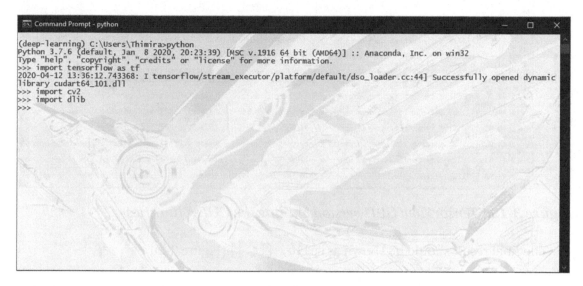

Figure 3-18. *Test importing the installed packages*

Finally, let us check TensorFlow functionality. Run each of the following commands, one after the other, in the Python interpreter:

```
import tensorflow as tf
x = [[2.]]
print('tensorflow version', tf.__version__)
print('hello, {}'.format(tf.matmul(x, x)))
```

If you have the TensorFlow GPU version installed, you may see some info messages of CUDA libraries being loaded (Figure 3-19).

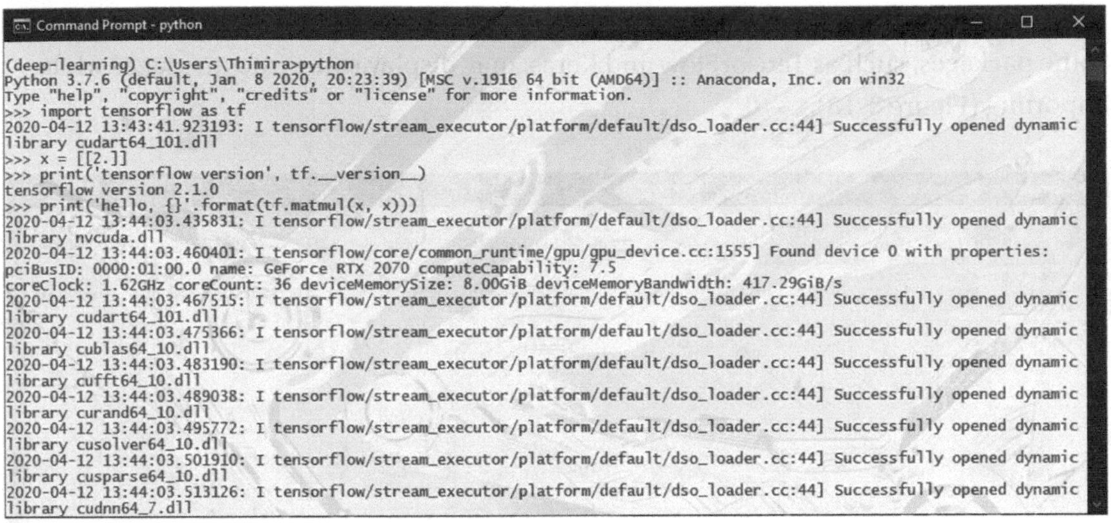

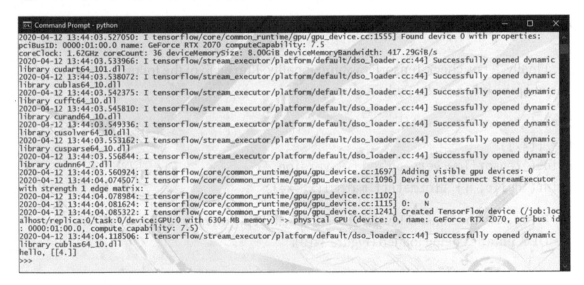

Figure 3-19.   *TensorFlow GPU version loading the CUDA libraries*

The final result should be shown as `hello, [[4.]]` (Figure 3-20):

Figure 3-20.   *TensorFlow test successful*

If all commands ran without errors, then we are good to go.

You can run `quit()` to exit the Python interpreter.

Step 10: (Optional) Manually Installing CUDA Toolkit and cuDNN

When we installed the TensorFlow GPU version via the conda package, you will notice that the CUDA Toolkit and the cuDNN library got also installed as conda dependencies. While this works with the TensorFlow conda package (and few other conda packages), for other libraries that might require CUDA functionality, you may need to install the CUDA toolkit globally.

You can download the CUDA Toolkit from the NVIDIA CUDA downloads page,[9] which lists the latest CUDA Toolkit binaries. Older versions of CUDA can be downloaded from the CUDA toolkit archive page.[10] Select the toolkit version you require, and then select the appropriate package for your version of Windows (Figure 3-21).

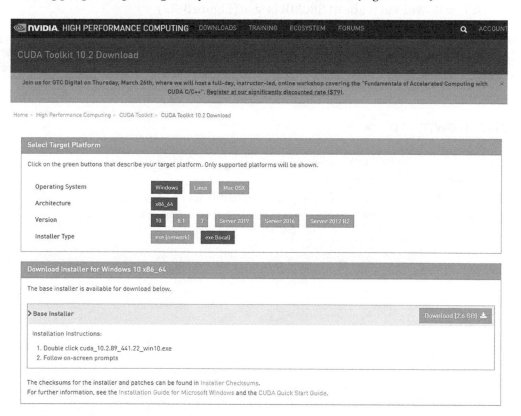

Figure 3-21. *NVIDIA CUDA toolkit downloads page*

---

[9]NVIDIA (CUDA downloads page), `https://developer.nvidia.com/cuda-downloads`, [9 Apr 2020].

[10]NVIDIA (CUDA toolkit archive page), `https://developer.nvidia.com/cuda-toolkit-archive`, [20 Nov 2019].

Note   Selecting the exe (local) installer will greatly reduce the installation time and is the better option if your Internet connection is slow or unreliable. Also, you can reuse the same installation package to start the installation over if anything goes wrong. Note that the download size is around 2.6GB in the latest version.

Next, you need to download cuDNN by heading over to NVIDIA cuDNN Page.[11] The downloads page for cuDNN will list multiple versions of cuDNN. You must make sure to download the latest version of cuDNN that is compatible with the CUDA Toolkit version you are using. For example, if we selected CUDA Toolkit v10.2 then we need to select Download cuDNN v7.6.5 (November 18, 2019), for CUDA 10.2 or whatever the latest version is. The download is about 280MB is size (Figure 3-22).

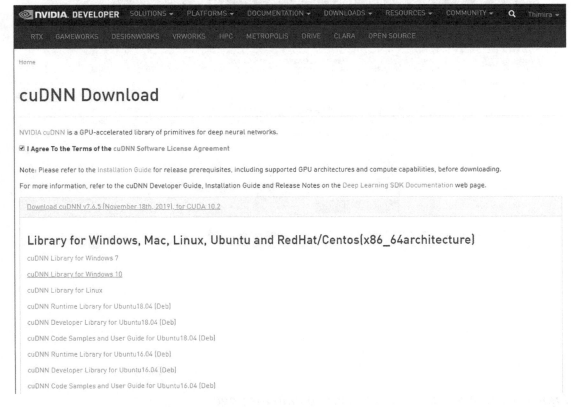

Figure 3-22.   *The cuDNN downloads page*

---

[11]NVIDIA (cuDNN page), `https://developer.nvidia.com/cudnn`, [12 Apr 2020]; you will need to register (free) for a NVIDIA developer account in order to download cuDNN.

Once both packages are downloaded, start by running the installer for the CUDA Toolkit. In the install options select the **Custom Install** option (Figure 3-23). In the Custom Install Options page, **deselect** the options for GeForce Experience, Display Driver (Figure 3-24), and Visual Studio Integration (Figure 3-25).

Figure 3-23. *Select the custom install option in the CUDA toolkit installer*

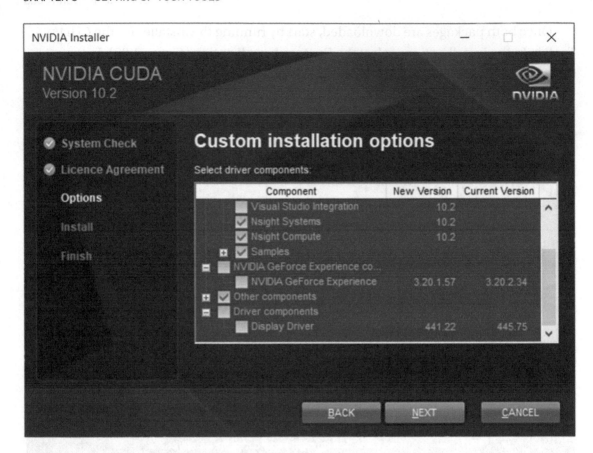

Figure 3-24. *Deselect GeForce experience and driver components*

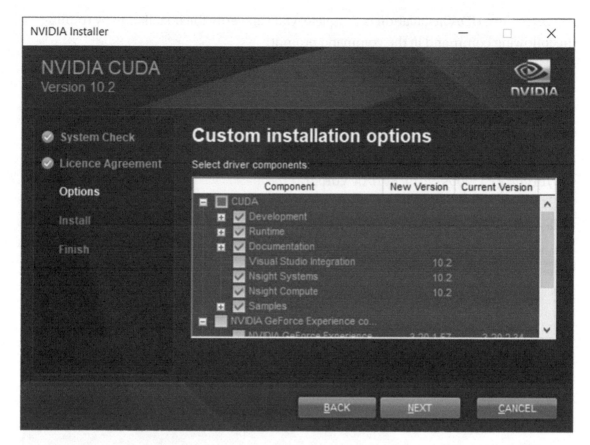

Figure 3-25. *Deselect the Visual Studio integration option under CUDA*

Caution   If you go with the *Express Installation* option, and you already have the latest display driver for your GPU installed, the installer may attempt to overwrite the already installed display driver with an older version driver. Therefore, if you already have the latest driver (and GeForce Experience installed), it is better to go in the *Custom Installation* path.

The *Visual Studio Integration* option is known to cause issues with some versions of Visual Studio. Therefore, it is better to deselect it if you do not plan to build Visual C++ CUDA applications.

You can keep the defaults for everything else in the CUDA installer.

Once the CUDA installation is complete, you can verify the installation by running the following command in the command prompt:

nvcc -V

(Note the uppercase "V.")

This will give an output of something like (Figure 3-26):

nvcc: NVIDIA (R) Cuda compiler driver
Copyright (c) 2005-2019 NVIDIA Corporation
Built on Wed_Oct_23_19:32:27_Pacific_Daylight_Time_2019
Cuda compilation tools, release 10.2, V10.2.89

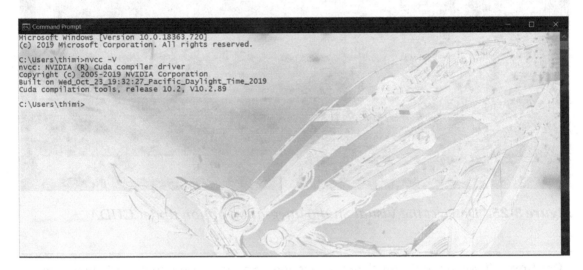

Figure 3-26. *CUDA toolkit installation verification*

Once the CUDA Toolkit is installed, you can install cuDNN.

cuDNN is not an installer. It is a zip file. You *install* it by extracting it and copying its content to the CUDA installation directory. When you extract cuDNN, you get a cuda directory, with 3 subdirectories: bin, include, and lib (Figure 3-27).

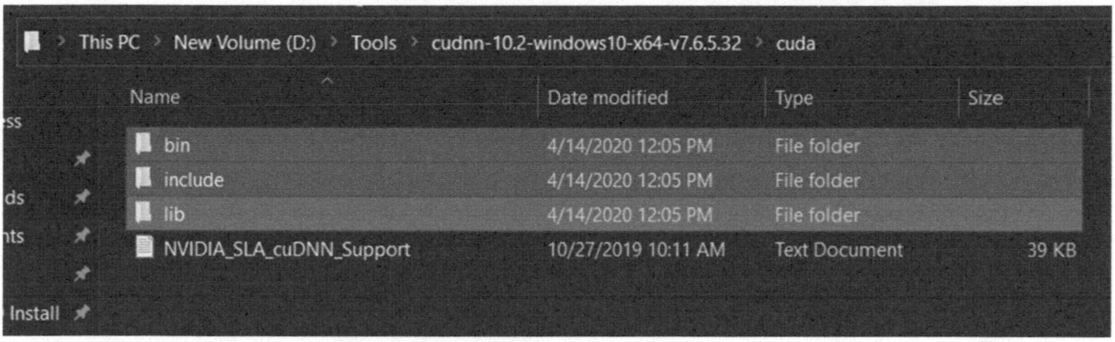

Figure 3-27. *cuDNN zip file extracted*

If you go to your CUDA installation directory (by default it is `C:\Program Files\ NVIDIA GPU Computing Toolkit\CUDA\vx.x`, where x.x. is the version you installed), you will see that it also contains directories named bin, include, and lib, with several other directories.

You need to copy the contents of each directory in the cuDNN to the respective directory in the CUDA installation directory (Figure 3-28). In other words, copy the contents of bin from cuDNN to bin of CUDA; lib of cuDNN to lib of CUDA; and include of cuDNN to include of CUDA.

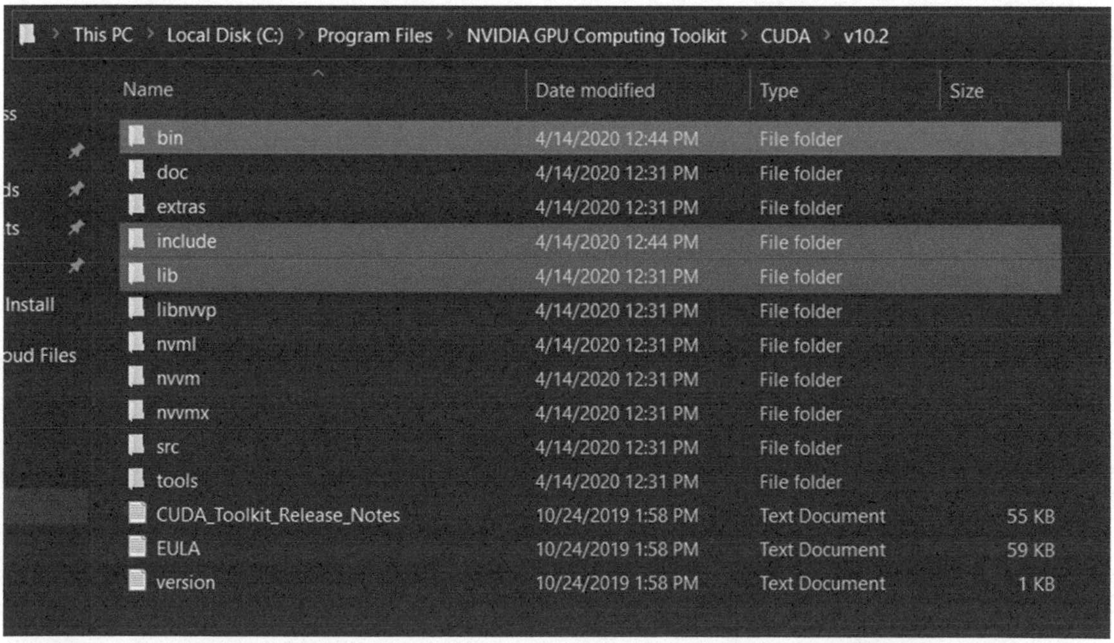

Figure 3-28. *cuDNN files extracted to the CUDA toolkit installation directory*

Once everything is copied, the CUDA Toolkit and cuDNN will be ready for your CUDA experiments.

Troubleshooting

To avoid most of the installation errors, make sure you perform the conda upgrade step before installing any packages (Figure 3-29).

```
conda update conda
```

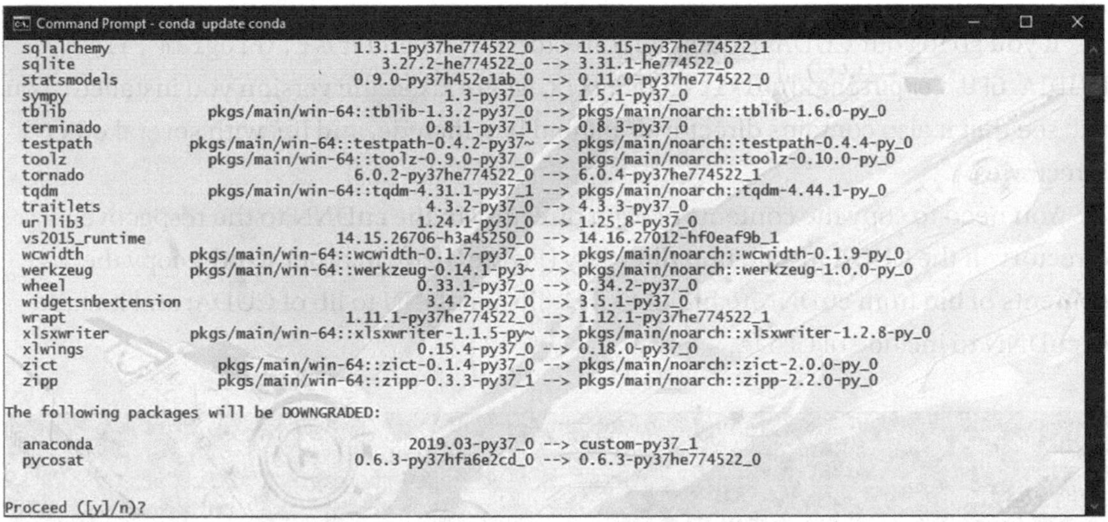

Figure 3-29.   *Conda upgrade step running*

Following are a set of issues that you might encounter, and how to fix them.

Matplotlib Pyplot Error

At the time of writing, there is an issue with a one specific build of the Matplotlib library available on conda. You can check it by running the following commands in the Python interpreter.

First, try importing the Matplotlib package. It should not generate any errors:

```
import matplotlib
```

Next, try importing the matplotlib.pyplot package:

```
import matplotlib.pyplot as plt
```

If the issue exists, it will crash your python interpreter.

If you have this issue, in order to solve this, you need to uninstall the Matplotlib library from conda and reinstall it using pip:

```
conda remove matplotlib
pip install matplotlib
```

You only need to do this if you have that error; it is possible that the faulty build will be fixed by the time you read this.

Not Getting the Latest Versions

While you are installing packages in conda, you might notice that you are not getting the latest available versions of the packages. This may be due to one of several reasons.

Conda package manager considers the inter compatibility between all the packages in an environment when installing, and may decide to go with an older version of a package for compatibility reasons.

Conda also caches the packages it downloads and installs. Therefore, it might sometimes use an older cached version of a package rather than fetching the latest one. You clean the cache using the following command:

```
conda clean –all
```

Cleaning the cache might allow conda to fetch the new versions.

If not, you can force conda to install the specific version of a package by specifying it in the install command (you can find the available package versions from the Anaconda package lists):[12]

```
conda install tensorflow-gpu==2.1.0
```

Conda will analyze the package version specified and will let you know whether it is compatible with the packages already installed in the conda environment, and whether

---

[12]Anaconda (package lists), https://docs.anaconda.com/anaconda/packages/pkg-docs/, [19 Nov 2020].

any package upgrades or downgrades are required. It will wait for you to confirm whether to proceed with the installation or not, so that you can safely check whether the specific version you want will work or not.

Not Using the Latest Version of OpenCV

If you recall, when we were installing OpenCV, we did not use the latest version, instead we let conda install an older version (version 3.4.1 in this case). Why didn't we force conda to install the latest version as we discussed in the previous section?

Well, if you try to install OpenCV v4 using the following command:

```
conda install opencv==4.0.1
```

you will get an error such as the one shown in Figure 3-30.

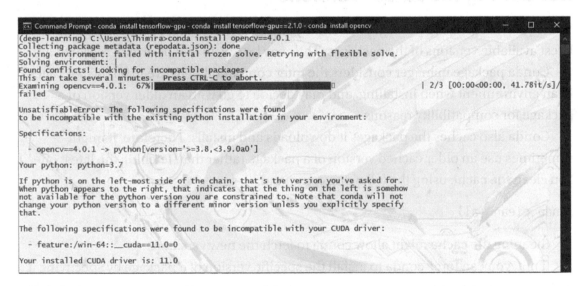

Figure 3-30. *OpenCV v4 Conda install error*

Basically, the OpenCV v4 conda package requires Python 3.8 or higher and CUDA version 11.0, which does not work with the other libraries—such as TensorFlow—that we are using.

So we will stick with the 3.4.x version for now, which has all the functionality we will be exploring in this book.

Dlib Build Errors

While installing Dlib pip package, you might run into an error such as this (Figure 3-31):

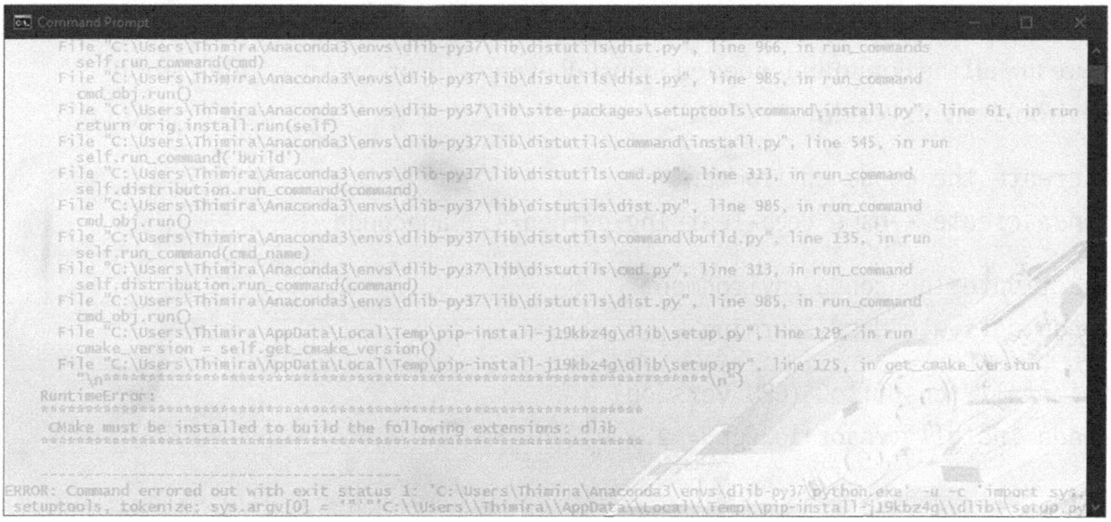

Figure 3-31. *Dlib build error*

This happens when CMake is either not installed properly, not added to the system path properly, or when the Windows command prompt window was not closed and reopened after CMake was installed.

If you encounter this, make sure CMake was properly installed and added to the path, and make sure you closed and reopened the command prompt window after it was installed.

You can verify CMake is properly installed by running:

```
cmake --version
```

Summary

In this chapter, we learned how to set up all the tools needed to start building deep learning models.

You need to install Visual Studio, CMake, and Anaconda Python as prerequisites. Here are all the commands needed to install everything on an Anaconda Python environment on Windows:

```
# create the conda environment
conda create --name deep-learning python=3.7 anaconda

# activate the conda environment
conda activate deep-learning

# install tensorflow (GPU version)
conda install tensorflow-gpu==2.1.0

# install opencv
conda install opencv

# install dlib
pip install dlib
```

These are only the core set of tools needed for learning to build deep learning models. You will install many more tools as you start building.

## CHAPTER 4

Building Your First Deep Learning Model

We are now ready to start building our first deep learning model.

But where do we begin?

To see deep learning in action, let us start with something that deep learning systems are extremely good at: a convolutional neural network built for image classification. For this, we will build what's commonly considered the "hello world" program of deep learning—that is, to write a program to classify images of handwritten digits. Think of it as a simple OCR system.

But don't we need a lot of data to train the system?

Well, luckily for us, since handwritten digits classification is a very popular problem to solve (even before deep learning), there is a publicly available dataset called the *MNIST dataset*.

What is the MNIST Dataset?

Back in 1995, the National Institute of Standards and Technology (NIST) in the United States created a dataset of handwritten characters to be used in machine learning and image processing systems. While this dataset worked for the most part, since the training and validation sets did not come from the same source, and due to some preprocessing applied on the images, there were some concerns about the validity of the dataset in a machine learning context.

In 1998, the data from the NIST dataset were cleaned up, normalized, and reorganized to resolve its issues, and this created the MNIST dataset (Modified National Institute of Standards and Technology dataset). The MNIST contains 70,000 images—60,000 training images and 10,000 testing/validation images—of 28x28 pixels.

© Thimira Amaratunga 2021
T. Amaratunga, *Deep Learning on Windows*, https://doi.org/10.1007/978-1-4842-6431-7_4

The MNIST dataset is publicly available from its official website.[1] However, due to its popularity, many machine learning and deep learning frameworks either have it built in, or provide utility methods to fetch and read the dataset. Keras, Scikit-Learn, and TensorFlow all provide such built-in methods, which spare us from having to retrieve, read, and format the data ourselves. A few samples from the MNIST dataset are shown in Figure 4-1.

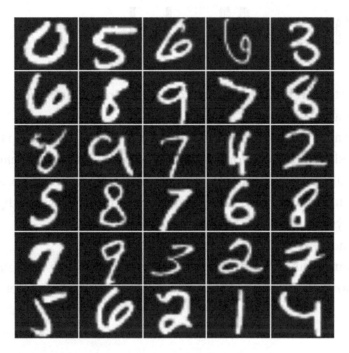

Figure 4-1. *A few samples from the MNIST dataset*

With a dataset at hand, we now need to decide on the architecture of the convolutional neural network we are going to build. In deep learning, since there can be so many variations of the way we can structure a model, it is typically better to start with a known and proven deep learning model and then make adjustments on it. So for our task, we will choose the **LeNet** architecture.

---

[1]MNIST website, http://yann.lecun.com/exdb/mnist/, [14 May 2013].

The LeNet Model

LeNet is a 7-layer Convolutional Neural Network (CNN) introduced by Y. LeCun, L. Bottou, Y. Bengio, and P. Haffner. In 1998 they introduced LeNet-5, their fifth successful iteration of the architecture.[2] It was designed specifically for handwritten and printed character recognition, so it fits perfectly with our requirements.

LeNet uses two sets of convolution operations (Figure 4-2). The first set uses 20 convolutional filters, and uses ReLU (Rectified Linear Units) as the nonlinearity function (the original LeNet architecture from the 1998 paper used Tanh as the nonlinearity function instead of ReLU), followed by a Max-Pooling layer. The second set uses 50 convolutional filters, again followed by ReLU and Max-Pooling. The output of these are then flattened, and sent through two fully connected (dense) layers to get the output predictions.

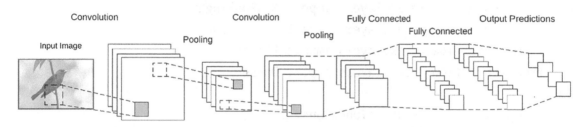

Figure 4-2. *The LeNet architecture*

The LeNet architecture is simple, but provides excellent accuracy for small image classification tasks. And since it is small, it can be easily trained on a CPU.

Let us Build Our First Model

We now have the data and have selected an architecture for our first deep learning model. So let's start building.

We will be using TensorFlow 2.1 and tf.keras (the TensorFlow version of Keras), in the Python 3.7 environment we created earlier.

Create a new Python file and name it `lenet_mnist_tf_keras.py`.

---

[2]Y. Lecun, L. Bottou, Y. Bengio and P. Haffner, *"Gradient-based learning applied to document recognition,"* in Proceedings of the IEEE, vol. 86, no. 11, pp. 2278-2324, Nov. 1998, doi: 10.1109/5.726791.

In this new file we will start by importing the necessary packages:

```
14:
15: # first, let's import tensorFlow
16: import tensorflow as tf
17: import numpy as np
18:
19: # import the mnist dataset
20: from tensorflow.keras.datasets import mnist
21:
22: # imports used to build the deep learning model
23: from tensorflow.keras.optimizers import SGD
24: from tensorflow.keras.models import Sequential
25: from tensorflow.keras.layers import Conv2D
26: from tensorflow.keras.layers import MaxPooling2D
27: from tensorflow.keras.layers import Activation
28: from tensorflow.keras.layers import Flatten
29: from tensorflow.keras.layers import Dense
30:
31: # import the keras util functions
32: import tensorflow.keras.utils as np_utils
33:
34: import argparse
35: import cv2
36: import matplotlib.pyplot as plt
37:
```

We start with importing TensorFlow, which is needed for us to use the tf.keras functions.

The `tensorflow.keras.datasets` package contains several commonly used built-in datasets of Keras. We import the MNIST dataset from it.

The `tensorflow.keras.optimizers`, `tensorflow.keras.models`, and `tensorflow.keras.layers` contains the core set of functions we would need to build our deep learning model.

The `tensorflow.keras.utils` package has several utility functions which would help us the build our model.

We import the argparse package to handle command line arguments, which allows us to train and evaluate the model.

OpenCV (imported as cv2) is used to display the results from evaluating the trained model.

The matplotlib package is used to visualize/graph the training performance of the model, as it is always better to see how well a model gets trained.

There will be two phases to our digit classification system: training and evaluating (for this application, we are not building an inference phase). The training phase takes time and is usually the most resource intensive phase. We certainly would not want to run the training every time we run our program. So we define a couple of command line arguments to trigger the two phases:

```
37:
38: # Setup the argument parser to parse out command line arguments
39: ap = argparse.ArgumentParser()
40: ap.add_argument("-t", "--train-model", type=int, default=-1,
41:                 help="(optional) Whether the model should be trained on
the MNIST dataset. Defaults to no")
42: ap.add_argument("-s", "--save-trained", type=int, default=-1,
43:                 help="(optional) Whether the trained models weights
should be saved." +
44:                 "Overwrites existing weights file with the same name.
Use with caution. Defaults to no")
45: ap.add_argument("-w", "--weights", type=str, default="data/lenet_
weights.hdf5",
46:                 help="(optional) Path to the weights file. Defaults to
'data/lenet_weights.hdf5'")
47: args = vars(ap.parse_args())
48:
```

We define three arguments:

- **--train-model:** indicates whether the model should be trained. Pass 1 to it to train the model.

- **--save-trained:** When the model is trained, we have the option to save the model weights to a file to be loaded back later. Pass 1 to this parameter, to indicate to save the weights.

- **--weights:** By default, we will be saving the models weights to data/
  lenet_weights.hdf5 (set by the default parameter of this argument). If you
  want to override that path, you can pass a custom path to this parameter.

Now, we load and preprocess our dataset:

```
49:
50: # Get the MNIST dataset from Keras datasets
51: # If this is the first time you are fetching the dataset, it will be
downloaded
52: # File size will be ~10MB, and will placed at ~/.keras/datasets/mnist.npz
53: print("[INFO] Loading the MNIST dataset...")
54: (trainData, trainLabels), (testData, testLabels) = mnist.load_data()
55: # The data is already in the form of numpy arrays,
56: # and already split to training and testing datasets
57:
58: # Reshape the data matrix from (samples, height, width) to (samples,
height, width, depth)
59: # Depth (i.e. channels) is 1 since MNIST only has grayscale images
60: trainData = trainData[:, :, :, np.newaxis]
61: testData = testData[:, :, :, np.newaxis]
62:
63: # Rescale the data from values between [0 - 255] to [0 - 1.0]
64: trainData = trainData / 255.0
65: testData = testData / 255.0
66:
67: # The labels come as a single digit, indicating the class.
68: # But we need a categorical vector as the label. So we transform it.
69: # So that,
70: # '0' will become [1, 0, 0, 0, 0, 0, 0, 0, 0, 0]
71: # '1' will become [0, 1, 0, 0, 0, 0, 0, 0, 0, 0]
72: # '2' will become [0, 0, 1, 0, 0, 0, 0, 0, 0, 0]
73: # and so on...
74: trainLabels = np_utils.to_categorical(trainLabels, 10)
75: testLabels = np_utils.to_categorical(testLabels, 10)
76:
```

Most of the cleaning up of the dataset has been already done for us by Keras. It is already in the format of numpy arrays, and already split to training and testing data.

If this is the first time you are using the MNIST dataset from Keras, it will be downloaded (around 10MB file size), and placed at `%USERPROFILE%/.keras/datasets/mnist.npz`.

The numpy arrays are in the format of [samples, height, width]. But Keras (and TensorFlow) expects one more dimension in the data arrays, which is the depth—or the channels—dimension. In a color image, there would be three channels—red, green, and blue. But since our digit images are grayscale images, there will only be one channel. So we reshape the arrays to add one more axis, so that the arrays become [samples, height, width, depth] shaped.

Since these are image data—each value being the gray value of a pixel—the values are in the range of 0–255. But for a neural network, it's better to always have the values in a range of 0–1. So we divide the entire array by 255 to get it in range.

The labels for the dataset come as single digits. But to train a neural network model, we need them as categorical vectors. We use the util function `to_categorical` to transform them so that:

'0' will become [1, 0, 0, 0, 0, 0, 0, 0, 0, 0]

'1' will become [0, 1, 0, 0, 0, 0, 0, 0, 0, 0]

'2' will become [0, 0, 1, 0, 0, 0, 0, 0, 0, 0]

And so on.

Now we come to the core part of the code, defining the structure of our model. We'll define a function named build_lenet() for this:

```
077:
078: # a function to build the LeNet model
079: def build_lenet(width, height, depth, classes, weightsPath=None):
080:     # Initialize the model
081:     model = Sequential()
082:
083:     # The first set of CONV => RELU => POOL layers
084:     model.add(Conv2D(20, (5, 5), padding="same",
085:                      input_shape=(height, width, depth)))
086:     model.add(Activation("relu"))
```

```
087:        model.add(MaxPooling2D(pool_size=(2, 2), strides=(2, 2)))
088:
089:        # The second set of CONV => RELU => POOL layers
090:        model.add(Conv2D(50, (5, 5), padding="same"))
091:        model.add(Activation("relu"))
092:        model.add(MaxPooling2D(pool_size=(2, 2), strides=(2, 2)))
093:
094:        # The set of FC => RELU layers
095:        model.add(Flatten())
096:        model.add(Dense(500))
097:        model.add(Activation("relu"))
098:
099:        # The softmax classifier
100:        model.add(Dense(classes))
101:        model.add(Activation("softmax"))
102:
103:        # If a weights path is supplied, then load the weights
104:        if weightsPath is not None:
105:            model.load_weights(weightsPath)
106:
107:        # Return the constructed network architecture
108:        return model
109:
```

Our function takes five parameters: the width, height, and depth of the input; the number of classes; and the path to the model weights file if given, and returns the model structure (with the model weights loaded if passed via the weightsPath parameter).

We use the Keras Sequential model to build our network. The Keras Sequential model makes building sequential network architectures (where all the layers are stacked up sequentially) much simpler. For more complex, nonsequential architectures (such as Inception modules) Keras provides the Functional API. But for simple sequential ones like LeNet, the Sequential model is the easiest.

We start with the first Convolutional, ReLU, and Pooling layer set. In the sequential model, the first layer needs to know the shape of the input to expect, so we pass it with the input_shape parameter. The subsequent layers can infer the shape on their own. We first define 20 convolutional filters of size 5x5, followed by a ReLU activation, and a

Max-Pooling layer of 2x2. The strides parameter defines how much the pooling window should slide on the feature map for each pooling operation. We will go through how each of these operations work in the next chapter.

The second set of Convolutional, ReLU, and Pooling layers are almost the same, with the number of convolutional filters increased to 50.

We then flatten the input, and add a Dense (fully connected) layer of 500 units.

The final layer is again a Dense layer, where the number of units is equal to the number of output classes of our data. We set a Softmax classifier as its activation.

If a path to a model weights file is passed, we load the weights to the constructed model. Otherwise, we return just the model.

Note   Don't worry if you do not yet understand what each of these layer types and parameters are and how they work. We will investigate them in more details later in the book.

Once we have the function to build the model, we can specify the optimizer for the model and then compile it:

```
142:
143: # Build and Compile the model
144: print("[INFO] Building and compiling the LeNet model...")
145: opt = SGD(lr=0.01)
146: model = build_lenet(width=28, height=28, depth=1, classes=10,
147:                     weightsPath=args["weights"] \
148:                     if args["train_model"] <= 0 else None)
149: model.compile(loss="categorical_crossentropy",
150:               optimizer=opt, metrics=["accuracy"])
151:
```

Here, we use the **SGD** Optimizer (Stochastic Gradient Descent), with a learning rate of 0.01 (set by the **lr** parameter).

We specify the width and height of the input as 28x28 as those are the dimensions of the images in the MNIST dataset. The depth parameter is set to 1, as we're dealing with grayscale images which has only one color channel.

Once the model is compiled, we train our model:

```
152: # Check the argument whether to train the model
153: if args["train_model"] > 0:
154:     print("[INFO] Training the model...")
155:
156:     history = model.fit(trainData, trainLabels,
157:                         batch_size=128,
158:                         epochs=20,
159:                         validation_data=(testData, testLabels),
160:                         verbose=1)
161:
162:     # Use the test data to evaluate the model
163:     print("[INFO] Evaluating the model...")
164:
165:     (loss, accuracy) = model.evaluate(
166:         testData, testLabels, batch_size=128, verbose=1)
167:
168:     print("[INFO] accuracy: {:.2f}%".format(accuracy * 100))
169:
```

We check the command line arguments (which were handled through argparse) to see whether we should run the training or not.

We pass our trainData and trainLabels (which we preprocessed/cleaned earlier) in to the model.fit() function.

We set the batch size to 128, which means the model will be trained with batches of 128 images at a time. Training in batches reduces the training time significantly. Batch size also controls the accuracy of the estimate of the error gradient when training using gradient descent. Because of that, deep learning models are almost always trained in batches. A batch size of 128 should work fine for our dataset here. You can change it later to see how it affects training.

An epoch is an iteration over the entire dataset. The epochs parameter tells how many times the model needs to be trained over the entire dataset. We set our epoch count to 20.

Along with our trainData and trainLabels, we pass the testData and testLabels also (using the validation_data parameter). This allows us to validate the model performance over the epochs.

Once the training is complete, we use the model.evaluate() function to evaluate the trained model with the full test dataset to get the final loss and accuracy of the model.

You may have noticed that the model.fit() function returns a value which we have captured in the history variable. This history value contains the accuracy and loss values of both training and validation for each epoch as the model trained. Using this value, we can draw a graph of how well the model was trained. Let's define a new function— graph_training_history()—to accept this history object and draw the graph:

```
109:
110: # a function to graph the training history of the model
111: def graph_training_history(history):
112:     plt.rcParams["figure.figsize"] = (12, 9)
113:
114:     plt.style.use('ggplot')
115:
116:     plt.figure(1)
117:
118:     # summarize history for accuracy
119:
120:     plt.subplot(211)
121:     plt.plot(history.history['accuracy'])
122:     plt.plot(history.history['val_accuracy'])
123:     plt.title('Model Accuracy')
124:     plt.ylabel('Accuracy')
125:     plt.xlabel('Epoch')
126:     plt.legend(['Training', 'Validation'], loc='lower right')
127:
128:     # summarize history for loss
129:
130:     plt.subplot(212)
131:     plt.plot(history.history['loss'])
132:     plt.plot(history.history['val_loss'])
133:     plt.title('Model Loss')
```

```
134:      plt.ylabel('Loss')
135:      plt.xlabel('Epoch')
136:      plt.legend(['Training', 'Validation'], loc='upper right')
137:
138:      plt.tight_layout()
139:
140:      plt.show()
141:
```

The history object contains four keys: [acc, loss, val_acc, val_loss].

We use matplotlib to draw the graph.

We start by specifying the graph size (12, 9) and style (ggplot).

We define two subplots to draw the accuracy matrices and the loss matrices for training and validation separately. Each subplot will show the matric for both training and validation.

We pass the history object to this function after the model training completes, right after the print statement for the morel accuracy at line 168:

```
169:
170:      # Visualize the training history
171:      graph_training_history(history)
172:
```

Once all the training and validation is complete, we save the model weights to a file:

```
172:
173: # Check the argument on whether to save the model weights to file
174: if args["save_trained"] > 0:
175:      print("[INFO] Saving the model weights to file...")
176:      model.save_weights(args["weights"], overwrite=True)
177:
178: # Training of the model is now complete
179:
```

We use the value of the **weights** command line argument as the path, which is by default set to data/lenet_weights.hdf5 if you did not override it. If a file with a same name is already there in the specified location the save_weights() function will not overwrite it by default. This is to avoid accidentally overwriting your trained models. Here we allow it to overwrite the file by setting overwrite=True.

Now our model is built, compiled, trained, and evaluated. We can use this trained model to test a few random digits:

```
179:
180: # Randomly select a few samples from the test dataset to evaluate
181: for i in np.random.choice(np.arange(0, len(testLabels)), size=(10,)):
182:     # Use the model to classify the digit
183:     probs = model.predict(testData[np.newaxis, i])
184:     prediction = probs.argmax(axis=1)
185:
186:     # Convert the digit data to a color image
187:     image = (testData[i] * 255).astype("uint8")
188:     image = cv2.cvtColor(image, cv2.COLOR_GRAY2RGB)
189:
190:     # The images are in 28x28 size. Much too small to see properly
191:     # So, we resize them to 280x280 for viewing
192:     image = cv2.resize(image, (280, 280), interpolation=cv2.INTER_
LINEAR)
193:
194:     # Add the predicted value on to the image
195:     cv2.putText(image, str(prediction[0]), (20, 40),
196:                 cv2.FONT_HERSHEY_DUPLEX, 1.5, (0, 255, 0), 1)
197:
198:     # Show the image and prediction
199:     print("[INFO] Predicted: {}, Actual: {}".format(
200:         prediction[0], np.argmax(testLabels[i])))
201:     cv2.imshow("Digit", image)
202:     cv2.waitKey(0)
203:
204: # close all OpenCV windows
205: cv2.destroyAllWindows()
```

We pick 10 random digits from the test dataset.

We then pass each of these images to the model.predict() function to get a prediction of what that digit is. The model.predict() function—much like the model.fit() function—expects the input as batches for predicting. Since we are only passing one sample at a time, we add a new axis to the data array—testData[np.newaxis, i]—to indicate that there's only one sample in this input.

The predictions come as a vector of probabilities for each class in the data. So we use the argmax function to get the array index of the class with the highest probability. Since our classes are the digits 0 to 9, the array index is the class label of the digit.

We now have the prediction. But rather than printing it out in the console alone, we want to display it along with the digit. We are going to use OpenCV for that. But we need to do some slight adjustments/postprocessing to the data before we can show them on OpenCV.

Remember that earlier we rescaled all the data to be in the range of [0.0–1.0]. Now we need to rescale it back to [0–255], so we multiply everything by 255.

OpenCV expects the image data to be unsigned 8-bit integers. This means that we convert the entire array to uint8 format with astype("uint8").

Now the image is in grayscale format. We convert it to a colour image by calling cv2.cvtColor(image, cv2.COLOR_GRAY2RGB). The image will still look grayscale. But now, we can draw text on it with color.

And finally, having the images at 28x28 pixels size is much too small. So we need to resize them to 280x280 size using the cv2.resize() function.

With the image data ready, we put the predicted digit value on the top left corner of the image and display it. By specifying cv2.waitKey(0) we keep the window open till any key is pressed. And since we are in a loop, we can switch through the 10 random digits we choose from the test dataset.

Along with displaying the digit, we also print the predicted digit with the actual value of the samples to the console.

Finally, as a good coding practice, we will also add some instructions on how to run the code as comments on the top of the file:

```
01: # How to use
02: #
03: # Train the model and save the model weights
04: # python lenet_mnist_tf_keras.py --train-model 1 --save-trained 1
05: #
06: # Train the model and save the model weights to a give directory
```

```
07: # python lenet_mnist_tf_keras.py --train-model 1 --save-trained
1 --weights data/lenet_weights.hdf5
08: #
09: # Evaluate the model from pre-trained model weights
10: # python lenet_mnist_tf_keras.py
11: #
12: # Evaluate the model from pre-trained model weights from a give
directory
13: # python lenet_mnist_tf_keras.py --weights data/lenet_weights.hdf5
14:
```

This completes the coding for our first deep learning model.

Running Our Model

We are now ready to run our first deep learning model. Let us do a few prechecks before we hit run to make sure it runs smoothly:

1. Make sure you have installed all the required libraries mentioned in the last chapter. TensorFlow, OpenCV, and Matplotlib are the main requirements for this example.

2. Make sure you have activated the conda environment which you installed all the libraries. You can double check by looking at the command prompt to see whether the activated environment's name is displayed.

3. In the directory where you have your lenet_mnist_tf_keras.py file, create a directory named data if you have not done so already. This is where the model weights will be saved by default. Make sure this data directory is writable.

If all prechecks are good, we can run our code.

Since this is the first run of our model, we need to train the model. So we set the command line arguments to train the model, and save the weights of the trained model:

```
python lenet_mnist_tf_keras.py --train-model 1 --save-trained 1
```

If you have not used the MNIST dataset before, Keras will automatically download the MNIST dataset. The download is about 10MB, so it should not take long.

Once the data is downloaded, our code will build the deep learning model, compile it, and will start the training (Figure 4-3).

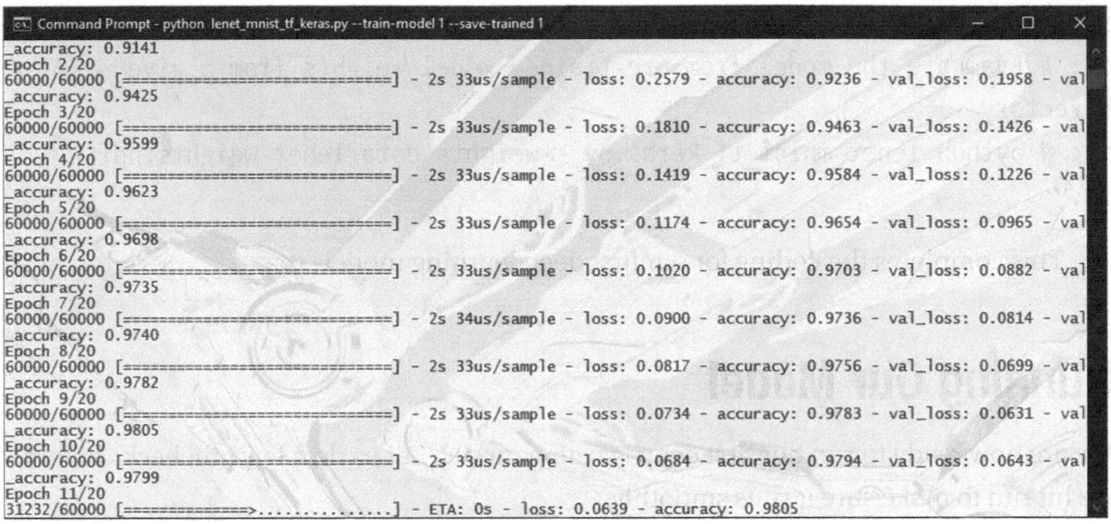

Figure 4-3. *Our model being trained*

The training will run for 20 epochs, as we specified.

If you are running this with the TensorFlow GPU version, the training will take less than two minutes. On a CPU however, it may take up to 30 minutes.

The console will show the progress of the training, accuracy and loss of training and validation.

Once the training is complete, it will evaluate the model on the test dataset and give the final accuracy value (Figure 4-4).

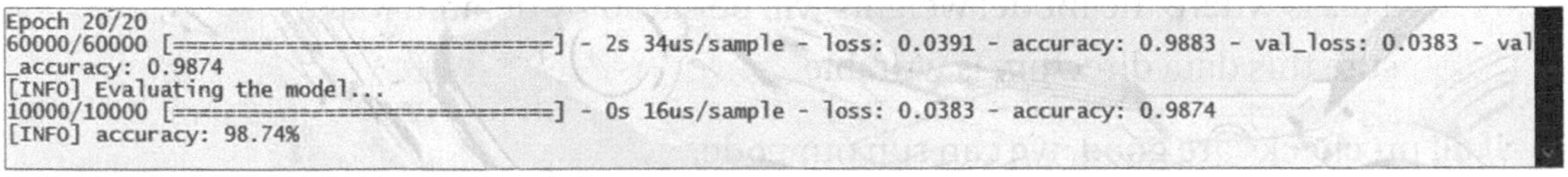

Figure 4-4. *Training completed and evaluation running*

Deep learning is exceptionally good at classification of simple images such as these. We should be getting around 98–99% accuracy with our simple model.

Once the evaluation step is done, the code will use Matplotlib to open a window to show the training history of the model (Figure 4-5).

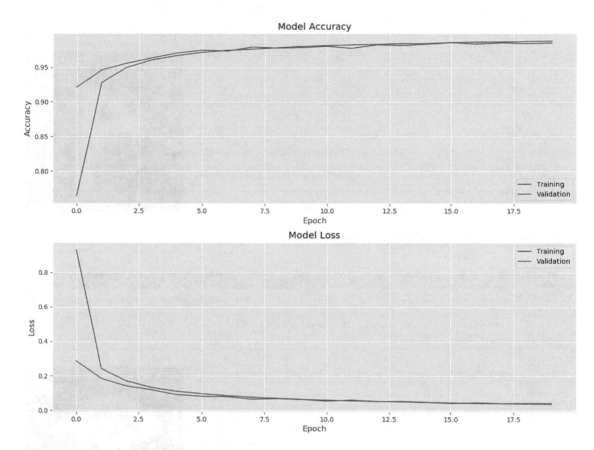

Figure 4-5. *The model training history*

The validation matrices follow the trend of the training, which is a good indication, as it does not look like the model is overfitting on the training data.

Note   The code execution will be on hold until you close the Matplotlib window. So remember to close it once you have reviewed the graph. You can also save the graph as an image from the Matplotlib window.

Now, the fun part. OpenCV will open the 10 random test digits one at a time, along with the predicted value of the digit (in green at the top-left of the image). Here are some examples (Figures 4-6, 4-7, and 4-8):

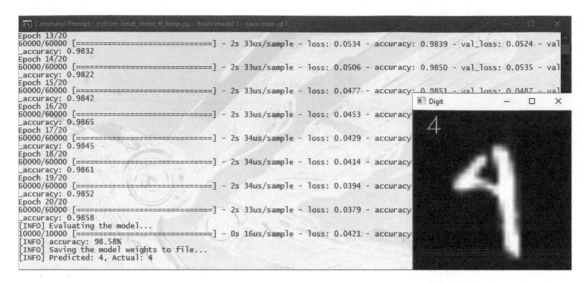

Figure 4-6. *Model prediction: digit 4*

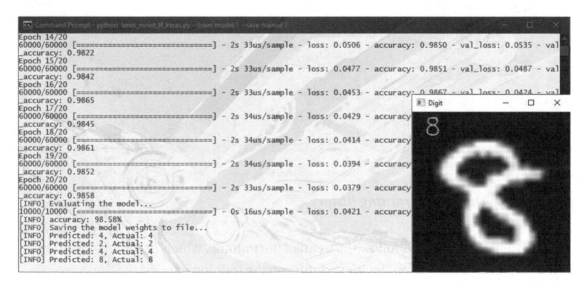

Figure 4-7. *Model prediction: digit 8*

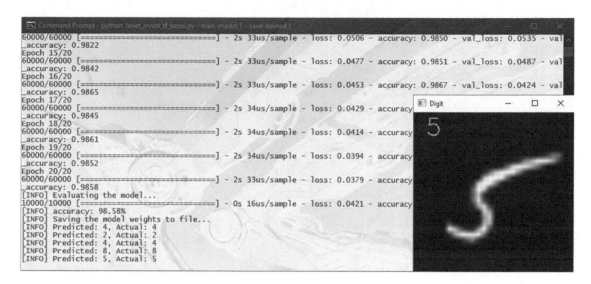

Figure 4-8. *Model prediction: digit 5*

You can switch through the digits by pressing any key.

Note   In some Windows builds of OpenCV, there's a bug in the code for opening an image window where if you try to manually close the window (by clicking the window close button), the code execution gets stuck. So it's better to let the code close the window properly by just switching between the results by pressing any key.

Along with showing the digit, we also print the predicted and actual values to the console (Figure 4-9).

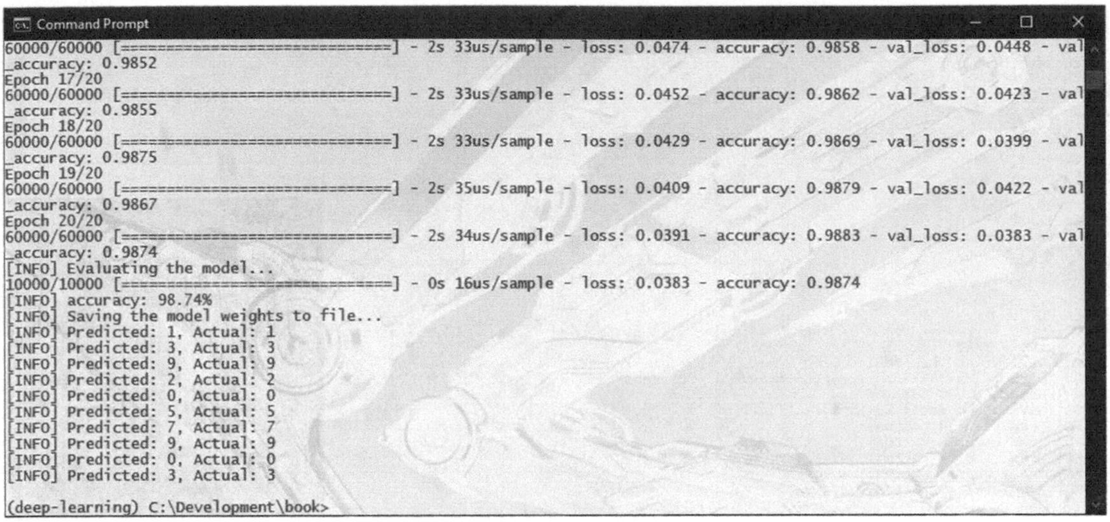

Figure 4-9. *The testing digit predictions and actual values printed on the console*

After training our model, the model weights will be saved to data/lenet_weights. hdf5. You can run the model again without training by running:

```
python lenet_mnist_tf_keras.py
```

Trying a Different Dataset

Once you are satisfied with the way the LeNet model classifies digits from the MNIST dataset, you might like to try out a different dataset that is a little bit more complex.

The Fashion-MNIST dataset would be the next best choice.

Fashion-MNIST consists of 10 classes of images of clothing. The images are in 28x28 pixel grayscale format, and has the following 10 classes labeled 0 to 9:

- 0: T-shirt/top

- 1: Trouser

- 2: Pullover

- 3: Dress

- 4: Coat

- 5: Sandal

- 6: Shirt

- 7: Sneaker

- 8: Bag

- 9: Ankle boot

Following are a few examples from the dataset (Figure 4-10):

Figure 4-10. *Samples from Fashion-MNIST dataset*

Like the MNIST dataset, Fashion-MNIST consists of 70,000 images—60,000 training and 10,000 test images. Because of the similarities between the two datasets, Fashion-MNIST can be a drop-in replacement to any model that uses the MNIST dataset.

You can download Fashion-MNIST from its official website.[3] But, as with MNIST, due to the popularity of the dataset, many machine learning and deep learning frameworks has it built-in.

Clothing Image Classification using Fashion-MNIST

Let us build a deep learning model to classify images of clothing from the Fashion-MNIST dataset.

As we talked about earlier, Fashion-MNIST is designed to be a drop-in replacement wherever MNIST can be used. So, we can start with the same LeNet model structure and the code we used earlier.

Let's create a new Python file for it and name it `lenet_fashion_mnist_tf_keras.py`.

We will start by importing the necessary packages:

```
01: # How to use
02: #
03: # Train the model and save the model weights
04: # python lenet_fashion_mnist_tf_keras.py --train-model 1 --save-trained 1
05: #
06: # Train the model and save the model weights to a give directory
07: # python lenet_fashion_mnist_tf_keras.py --train-model 1 --save-trained 1 --weights data/lenet_fashion_weights.hdf5
08: #
09: # Evaluate the model from pre-trained model weights
10: # python lenet_fashion_mnist_tf_keras.py
11: #
12: # Evaluate the model from pre-trained model weights from a give directory
```

---

[3]Fashion: MNIST official website, https://github.com/zalandoresearch/fashion-mnist, [23 May 2020].

```
13: # python lenet_fashion_mnist_tf_keras.py --weights data/lenet_fashion_
weights.hdf5
14:
15: # first, let's import tensorFlow
16: import tensorflow as tf
17: import numpy as np
18:
19: # import the FASHION_MNIST dataset
20: from tensorflow.keras.datasets import fashion_mnist
21:
22: # imports used to build the deep learning model
23: from tensorflow.keras.optimizers import SGD
24: from tensorflow.keras.models import Sequential
25: from tensorflow.keras.layers import Conv2D
26: from tensorflow.keras.layers import MaxPooling2D
27: from tensorflow.keras.layers import Activation
28: from tensorflow.keras.layers import Flatten
29: from tensorflow.keras.layers import Dense
30:
31: # import the keras util functions
32: import tensorflow.keras.utils as np_utils
33:
34: import argparse
35: import cv2
36: import matplotlib.pyplot as plt
```

We will then define the command line arguments:

```
38: # Setup the argument parser to parse out command line arguments
39: ap = argparse.ArgumentParser()
40: ap.add_argument("-t", "--train-model", type=int, default=-1,
41:                 help="(optional) Whether the model should be trained on
the MNIST dataset. Defaults to no")
42: ap.add_argument("-s", "--save-trained", type=int, default=-1,
43:                 help="(optional) Whether the trained models weights
should be saved." +
```

```
44:                        "Overwrites existing weights file with the same name.
Use with caution. Defaults to no")
45: ap.add_argument("-w", "--weights", type=str, default="data/lenet_
fashion_weights.hdf5",
46:                        help="(optional) Path to the weights file. Defaults to
'data/lenet_fashion_weights.hdf5'")
47: args = vars(ap.parse_args())
```

Then we will load and preprocess the dataset:

```
50: # Getting the FASHION_MNIST dataset from Keras datasets
51: print("[INFO] Loading the FASHION_MNIST dataset...")
52: (trainData, trainLabels), (testData, testLabels) = fashion_mnist.load_
data()
53: # The data is already in the form of numpy arrays,
54: # and already split to training and testing datasets
55:
56: # Rescale the data from values between [0 - 255] to [0 - 1.0]
57: trainData = trainData / 255.0
58: testData = testData / 255.0
59:
60: # Defining the string labels for the classes
61: class_names = ['T-shirt/top', 'Trouser', 'Pullover', 'Dress', 'Coat',
62:                    'Sandal', 'Shirt', 'Sneaker', 'Bag', 'Ankle boot']
63:
64: # Display a sample from the FASHION_MNIST dataset
65: plt.figure(figsize=(16,16))
66: for i in range(25):
67:     plt.subplot(5,5, i+1)
68:     plt.xticks([])
69:     plt.yticks([])
70:     plt.grid(False)
71:     plt.imshow(trainData[i], cmap=plt.cm.binary)
72:     plt.xlabel(class_names[trainLabels[i]])
73: plt.show()
74:
```

```
75: # Reshape the data matrix from (samples, height, width) to (samples,
height, width, depth)
76: # Depth (i.e. channels) is 1 since MNIST only has grayscale images
77: trainData = trainData[:, :, :, np.newaxis]
78: testData = testData[:, :, :, np.newaxis]
79:
80: # The labels comes as a single digit, indicating the class.
81: # But we need a categorical vector as the label. So we transform it.
82: # So that,
83: # '0' will become [1, 0, 0, 0, 0, 0, 0, 0, 0, 0]
84: # '1' will become [0, 1, 0, 0, 0, 0, 0, 0, 0, 0]
85: # '2' will become [0, 0, 1, 0, 0, 0, 0, 0, 0, 0]
86: # and so on...
87: trainLabels = np_utils.to_categorical(trainLabels, 10)
88: testLabels = np_utils.to_categorical(testLabels, 10)
```

Here, we define a list named class_names to house the text labels of the 10 classes of the Fashion-MNIST dataset (line 61). The index of each element of the list is the class ID.

We also load 25 samples from the dataset and display (lines 65–73).

Now we build our model structure. This is the same LeNet model we used for the MNIST dataset:

```
091: def build_lenet(width, height, depth, classes, weightsPath=None):
092:     # Initialize the model
093:     model = Sequential()
094:
095:     # The first set of CONV => RELU => POOL layers
096:     model.add(Conv2D(20, (5, 5), padding="same",
097:                         input_shape=(height, width, depth)))
098:     model.add(Activation("relu"))
099:     model.add(MaxPooling2D(pool_size=(2, 2), strides=(2, 2)))
100:
101:     # The second set of CONV => RELU => POOL layers
102:     model.add(Conv2D(50, (5, 5), padding="same"))
103:     model.add(Activation("relu"))
104:     model.add(MaxPooling2D(pool_size=(2, 2), strides=(2, 2)))
```

```
105:
106:        # The set of FC => RELU layers
107:        model.add(Flatten())
108:        model.add(Dense(500))
109:        model.add(Activation("relu"))
110:
111:        # The softmax classifier
112:        model.add(Dense(classes))
113:        model.add(Activation("softmax"))
114:
115:        # If a weights path is supplied, then load the weights
116:        if weightsPath is not None:
117:            model.load_weights(weightsPath)
118:
119:        # Return the constructed network architecture
120:        return model
```

We also define the graph_training_history() function exactly as before:

```
123: def graph_training_history(history):
124:        plt.rcParams["figure.figsize"] = (12, 9)
125:
126:        plt.style.use('ggplot')
127:
128:        plt.figure(1)
129:
130:        # summarize history for accuracy
131:
132:        plt.subplot(211)
133:        plt.plot(history.history['accuracy'])
134:        plt.plot(history.history['val_accuracy'])
135:        plt.title('Model Accuracy')
136:        plt.ylabel('Accuracy')
137:        plt.xlabel('Epoch')
138:        plt.legend(['Training', 'Validation'], loc='lower right')
139:
```

```
140:        # summarize history for loss
141:
142:        plt.subplot(212)
143:        plt.plot(history.history['loss'])
144:        plt.plot(history.history['val_loss'])
145:        plt.title('Model Loss')
146:        plt.ylabel('Loss')
147:        plt.xlabel('Epoch')
148:        plt.legend(['Training', 'Validation'], loc='upper right')
149:
150:        plt.tight_layout()
151:
152:        plt.show()
```

Also like we did before, we build, compile, and run the training:

```
155: # Build and Compile the model
156: print("[INFO] Building and compiling the LeNet model...")
157: opt = SGD(lr=0.01)
158: model = build_lenet(width=28, height=28, depth=1, classes=10,
159:                     weightsPath=args["weights"] if args["train_model"]
<= 0 else None)
160: model.compile(loss="categorical_crossentropy",
161:               optimizer=opt, metrics=["accuracy"])
162:
163: # Check the argument whether to train the model
164: if args["train_model"] > 0:
165:     print("[INFO] Training the model...")
166:
167:     history = model.fit(trainData, trainLabels,
168:                         batch_size=128,
169:                         epochs=50,
170:                         validation_data=(testData, testLabels),
171:                         verbose=1)
172:
173:     # Use the test data to evaluate the model
174:     print("[INFO] Evaluating the model...")
```

```
175:
176:        (loss, accuracy) = model.evaluate(
177:            testData, testLabels, batch_size=128, verbose=1)
178:
179:        print("[INFO] accuracy: {:.2f}%".format(accuracy * 100))
180:
181:        # Visualize the training history
182:        graph_training_history(history)
```

Here we are setting the number of training epochs to 50 (line 169).

Once training is complete, we save the model weights to a file and select few random images from the test dataset to evaluate the trained model:

```
184: # Check the argument on whether to save the model weights to file
185: if args["save_trained"] > 0:
186:     print("[INFO] Saving the model weights to file...")
187:     model.save_weights(args["weights"], overwrite=True)
188:
189: # Training of the model is now complete
190:
191: # Randomly select a few samples from the test dataset to evaluate
192: for i in np.random.choice(np.arange(0, len(testLabels)), size=(10,)):
193:     # Use the model to classify the digit
194:     probs = model.predict(testData[np.newaxis, i])
195:     prediction = probs.argmax(axis=1)
196:
197:     # Convert the digit data to a color image
198:     image = (testData[i] * 255).astype("uint8")
199:     image = cv2.cvtColor(image, cv2.COLOR_GRAY2RGB)
200:
201:     # The images are in 28x28 size. Much too small to see properly
202:     # So, we resize them to 280x280 for viewing
203:     image = cv2.resize(image, (280, 280), interpolation=cv2.INTER_
LINEAR)
204:
205:     # Add the predicted value on to the image
```

```
206:     cv2.putText(image, str(class_names[prediction[0]]), (20, 40),
207:                 cv2.FONT_HERSHEY_DUPLEX, 1.5, (0, 255, 0), 1)
208:
209:     # Show the image and prediction
210:     print("[INFO] Predicted: \"{}\", Actual: \"{}\"".format(
211:         class_names[prediction[0]], class_names[np.
argmax(testLabels[i])]))
212:     cv2.imshow("Digit", image)
213:     cv2.waitKey(0)
214:
215: cv2.destroyAllWindows()
```

We use the class_names list defined earlier to get the text class name from the predictions (lines 206 and 210).

Running Our Fashion-MNIST Model

When our code is ready, and we have also done the same prechecks we did for the MNIST, we can run our new model:

```
python lenet_fashion_mnist_tf_keras.py --train-model 1 --save-trained 1
```

If you have not used the Fashion-MNIST dataset before, Keras will automatically download it. Once the dataset is loaded, our code will display few samples from the dataset (Figure 4-11).

Figure 4-11. *A few samples from the dataset*

The training will run for 50 epochs, and will take few minutes when running on a GPU.

With our LeNet model you will get around 90% accuracy (Figure 4-12).

```
Epoch 50/50
60000/60000 [==============================] - 2s 32us/sample - loss: 0.2059 - accuracy: 0.9257 - val_loss: 0.2832 - val
_accuracy: 0.9013
[INFO] Evaluating the model...
10000/10000 [==============================] - 0s 17us/sample - loss: 0.2832 - accuracy: 0.9013
[INFO] accuracy: 90.13%
```

Figure 4-12. *Accuracy of our model on Fashion-MNIST*

The training history graph will look something like the one in Figure 4-13.

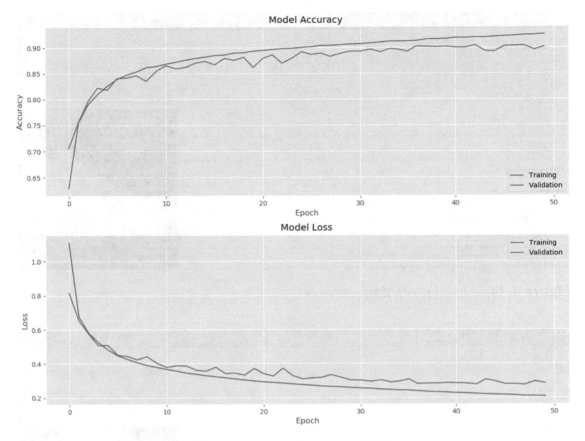

Figure 4-13. *The training history graph of our model*

Our code will then display 10 random samples from the test dataset along with their predicted class from the model (Figures 4-14, 4-15, 4-16).

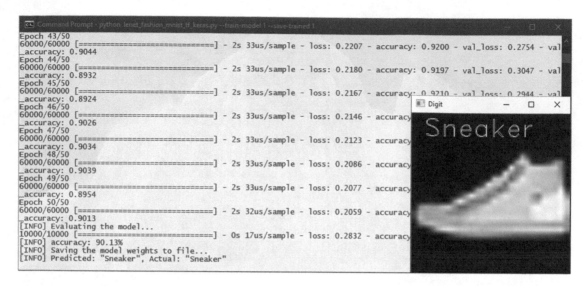

Figure 4-14. *Model prediction: sneaker*

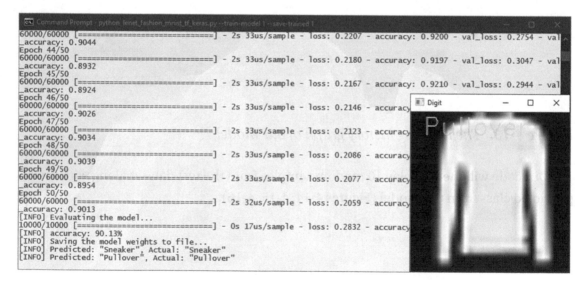

Figure 4-15. *Model prediction: pullover*

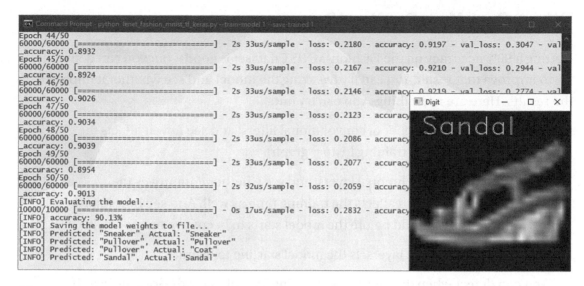

Figure 4-16. *Model prediction: sandal*

Along with showing the results of the samples, the code will also print the predicted and actual values to the console (Figure 4-17).

```
[O]  Command Prompt                                                        —    □    ×
60000/60000 [==============================] - 2s 33us/sample - loss: 0.2146 - accuracy: 0.9219 - val_loss: 0.2774 - val
_accuracy: 0.9026
Epoch 47/50
60000/60000 [==============================] - 2s 33us/sample - loss: 0.2123 - accuracy: 0.9231 - val_loss: 0.2774 - val
_accuracy: 0.9034
Epoch 48/50
60000/60000 [==============================] - 2s 33us/sample - loss: 0.2086 - accuracy: 0.9241 - val_loss: 0.2733 - val
_accuracy: 0.9039
Epoch 49/50
60000/60000 [==============================] - 2s 33us/sample - loss: 0.2077 - accuracy: 0.9246 - val_loss: 0.2940 - val
_accuracy: 0.8954
Epoch 50/50
60000/60000 [==============================] - 2s 32us/sample - loss: 0.2059 - accuracy: 0.9257 - val_loss: 0.2832 - val
_accuracy: 0.9013
[INFO] Evaluating the model...
10000/10000 [==============================] - 0s 17us/sample - loss: 0.2832 - accuracy: 0.9013
[INFO] accuracy: 90.13%
[INFO] Saving the model weights to file...
[INFO] Predicted: "Sneaker", Actual: "Sneaker"
[INFO] Predicted: "Pullover", Actual: "Pullover"
[INFO] Predicted: "Pullover", Actual: "Coat"
[INFO] Predicted: "Sandal", Actual: "Sandal"
[INFO] Predicted: "Shirt", Actual: "Shirt"
[INFO] Predicted: "T-shirt/top", Actual: "T-shirt/top"
[INFO] Predicted: "Trouser", Actual: "Trouser"
[INFO] Predicted: "Sneaker", Actual: "Sneaker"
[INFO] Predicted: "Pullover", Actual: "Pullover"
[INFO] Predicted: "Ankle boot", Actual: "Ankle boot"

(deep-learning) C:\Development\experiments>
```

Figure 4-17. *The predictions and actual values printed on the console*

After the training completes, the model weights will be saved to data/ lenet_fashion_ weights.hdf5 like it did before.

What Can You Do Next?

Getting a 90% accuracy on the Fashion-MNIST dataset is good—but you can definitely try to improve that result. You can try tweaking the model and see whether it improves the results. Here are a few things you can try out:

- Change the number of convolutional filters, and see how it affects the training (via the training history graph).

- Add more convolutional layers, and see whether it improves the model. See how it affects the training time as well. And see how many layers you can add before the model starts to become worse.

- Add more dense layers. Is the model starting to overfit?

You can detect when the model is overfitting by looking at the loss metrics. If the validation loss stops dropping while the training loss continues to drop as the training progresses, then the model is overfitting. This means the model has basically "memorized" our training samples but has not learned to generalize the problem, causing it to fail on the unseen samples (in this case, the validation samples).

We will be talking about how we can handle much more complex datasets and models in later chapters.

CHAPTER 5

Understanding What We Built

Running our first deep learning model gave us a small glimpse of what deep learning can do. There are many exciting projects we can build with deep learning.

But first, it is better to understand what we built, and how it works.

Let us look back at the model we built. We used the LeNet architecture, which looks like this (Figure 5-1):

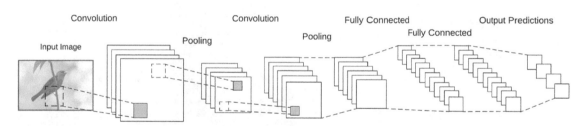

Figure 5-1. *The LeNet model*

Looking through the model architecture and going through our code, we see that the workings of our model is based on few functions:

1. Input: Digital Images

2. Convolutions

3. Nonlinearity function (ReLU)

4. Pooling

5. Classifier (Fully Connected Layer)

Let us see how each of these functions work and how they contribute to our model.

© Thimira Amaratunga 2021
T. Amaratunga, *Deep Learning on Windows*, https://doi.org/10.1007/978-1-4842-6431-7_5

Digital Images

Our input image is the first piece of the process.

Although we consider them as images based on our perception, for a machine, images are just another form of digital data.

A digital image consists of a collection of pixels. Each pixel is defined by the color value of one or more color-channels. A grayscale image has only a single channel. Each pixel in the image has a value from 0 to 255, where 0 indicates black and 255 indicates white (Figure 5-2).

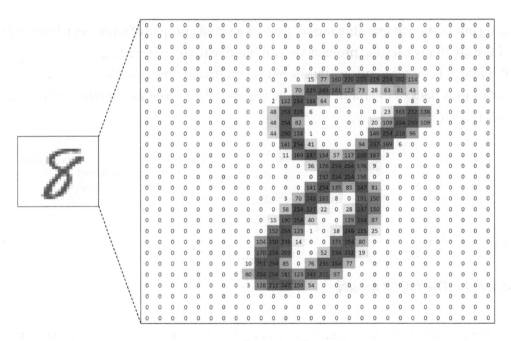

Figure 5-2. *An image is just a matrix of pixel values*

A color image has three channels—red, green, and blue for an RGB image (Figure 5-3).

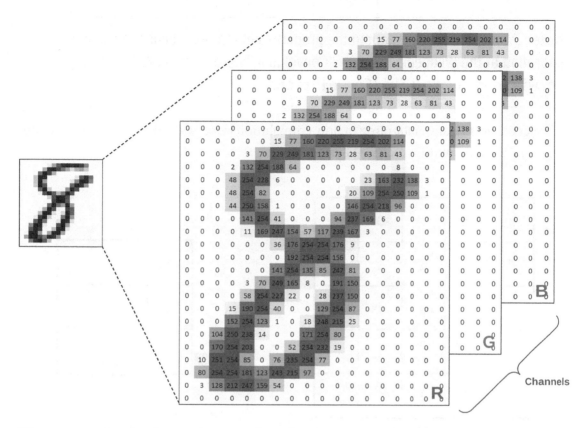

Figure 5-3. *A color image is a set of pixel values per each channel*

Therefore, in mathematical terms, an image is a matrix of pixel values.

The operations in a deep learning model (and in neural networks in general) are performed on these matrices of values.

Convolutions

The mathematical convolution operation on matrices is capable of extracting features from a matrix such as an image, as it preserves the spatial relationship between the elements of the matrix. CNNs extensively use convolution operations, which is where they get the name convolutional neural networks. As we discussed in Chapter 1, the mathematical convolutions on an image work like the receptive fields of the visual cortex in humans and animals. Like the receptive fields, convolutions work by processing small squares of the input at a time.

Note   You can learn more about the properties of mathematical convolution operation at the Wikipedia page for "Convolution" here: `https://en.wikipedia.org/wiki/Convolution`.

To get a simple understanding of how convolutions works, think of two matrices: the input and the convolution matrix (Figure 5-4).

Input Matrix   Convolution Matrix

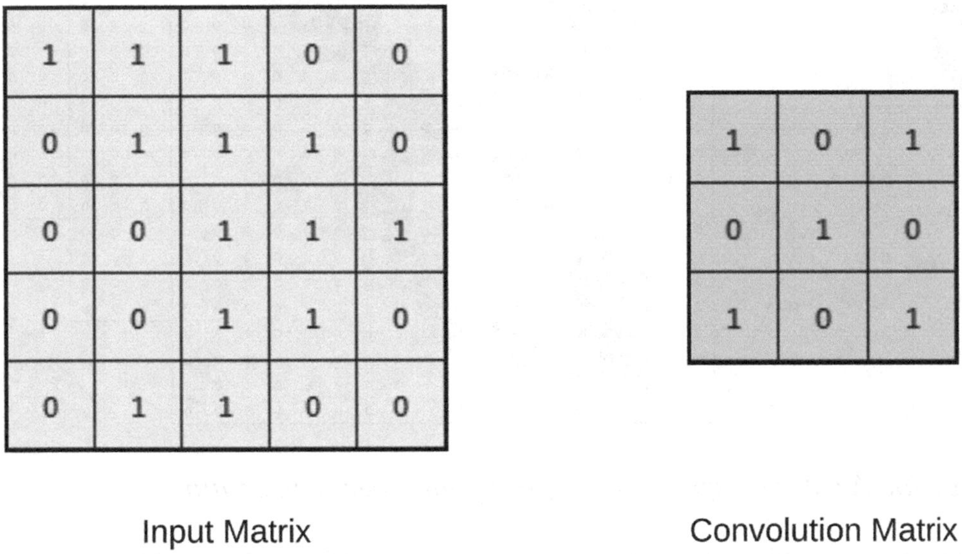

Figure 5-4. *The input and the convolution matrices*

The convolution operation happens by the convolution matrix "sliding on" the input matrix, to produce the convoluted output (Figure 5-5).

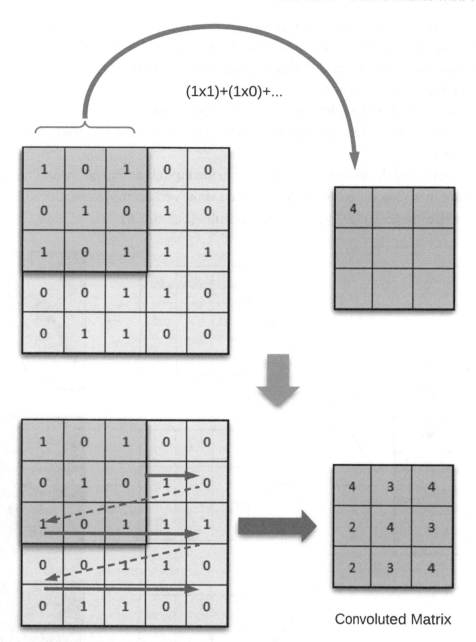

Figure 5-5. *The convolution operation*

As the convolution operation happens, the convolution matrix only sees part of the input matrix, but it maintains the spatial relationship of what it sees. Various different convolution matrices produce different outputs from the input.

What if we apply the same operation to an image?

As we discussed, a digital image is a matrix of pixel values.

Therefore, we should be able to perform the same convolution operations on an image as well.

If we attempted the same operation—where the input is an image—with different convolution matrices, the output of them would show various representations of the features of the image. Following are a few examples (Figure 5-6).

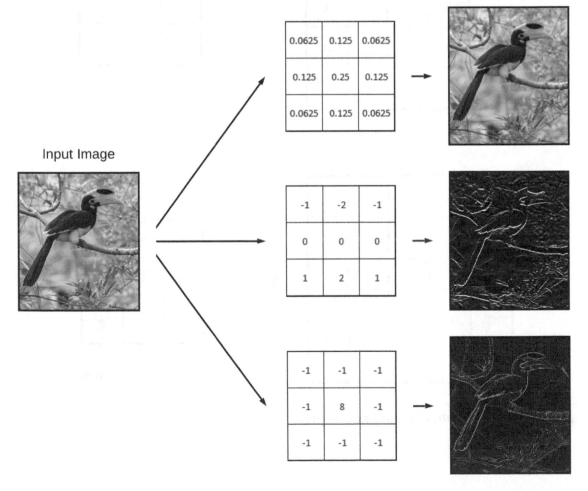

Figure 5-6. *Effects of different convolutions on an image*

As these different convolution operations filter and extract different features of the images, they are typically called "filters."

In a CNN, many filters are used to extract and learn different features from the input images. When using deep learning libraries such as TensorFlow or Keras, we do not need to specify what each of the filters should be. Instead, we only specify the number and the size of the filters. The training process of the library will determine which filters get used. Typically, the more filters you have in a network, the better it is at learning patterns from the input.

Nonlinearity Function

Once the convolution step is complete and the various feature maps of the input image have been generated, a CNN applies a nonlinearity function on the feature maps. Nonlinearity is needed because real-world data is nonlinear, but the convolution function is a linear operation. Therefore, to handle the representation of real-world data, we need to apply a nonlinearity function.

Rectified linear unit, or ReLU, is a commonly used nonlinearity function. Other functions such as tanh or sigmoid can also be used as nonlinearity functions. Which function to use will depend on the architecture of your model. ReLU performs better in most general cases when using backpropagation for training. In most cases, ReLU also performs better with deeper model architectures than sigmoid and tanh. Therefore, ReLU is a good starting point when developing new model architectures.

The ReLU function can be seen in Figure 5-7.

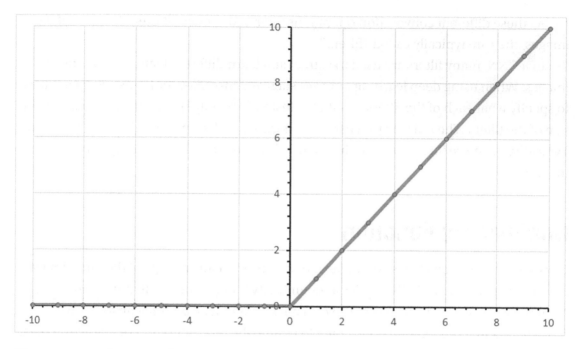

Figure 5-7. *The ReLU function*

This may look complicated, but ReLU is quite simple. It goes through each pixel and sets the negative values to zero, and retains the positive pixel values as they are.

The function can also be shown as:

```
Output = max(0, Input)
```

When applied to a feature map, the results from ReLU looks like this (Figure 5-8):

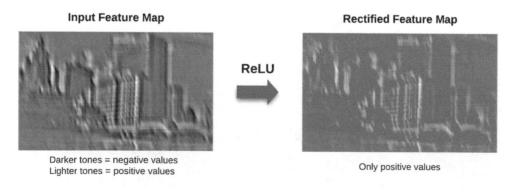

Figure 5-8. *ReLU applied to a feature map*

Pooling

After the nonlinearity is applied, the CNN does a pooling step (also known as spatial pooling, subsampling, or downsampling). Pooling reduces the dimensionality of each feature map by retaining only the most important information. It can be done in several ways, such as max pooling, average pooling, and sum pooling. Out of these, max pooling has shown better results in general.

In max pooling, we define a window (an area of the feature map) and get the max value from the pixels in that area (Figure 5-9).

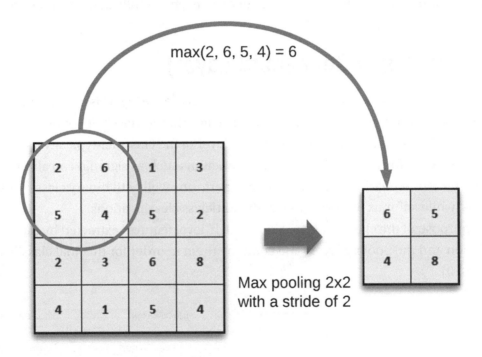

Figure 5-9. *Max pooling*

Pooling gives a CNN several benefits:

1. It makes the feature dimensions smaller and more manageable.

2. It reduces the potential to overfit by reducing the number of parameters and computations needed in the network.

3. It makes the network invariant to small transformations, distortions, and translations in the input, which means that small changes in the input will not significantly affect the output. This allows the network to generalize better.

4. It makes the network scale invariant, allowing objects to be detected wherever they are in the input image.

At this point the work of a single convolution layer of the CNN is complete. The next convolution layers would take the output feature maps of the previous layer, as their inputs and continue the same operation until they reach the fully connected layers.

Classifier (Fully Connected Layer)

The classifier (also known as a fully connected layer or dense layer) is a traditional multilayer perceptron network. Each neuron of a layer in the classifier connects with every neuron in the next layer. The final output layer of the classifier typically uses a softmax activation function. Other activation functions such as sigmoid can also be used for different scenarios. Sigmoid generally performs well with binary classification problems, while softmax performs well with multiclass classifications.

The purpose of the classifier is to take the high-level features extracted by the convolution and the pooling layers and combine them in order for the final classification (Figure 5-10).

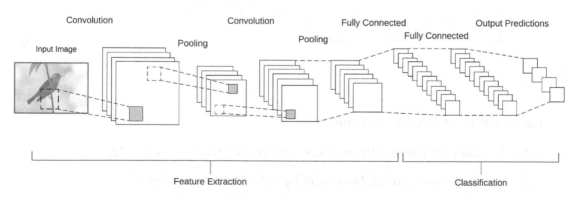

Figure 5-10.   *The feature extraction and classification*

How Does This All Come Together?

How do these elements that we discussed—convolutions, ReLU, pooling, and classifiers—work together to understand the images?

To understand this, let us take an extremely simplified example: let's see how a neural network might learn to recognize a square shape.

Like any other training task, the neural network would need to go through hundreds, or maybe thousands, of training images.

What it needs to learn are the defining features of a square.

For us humans, as we have a firm grasp of visual elements, the defining features of a square would be "lines," "length," and "angles." And we know—that is, our minds have been trained to know—which of the combinations of those features results in a square and what to look for when recognizing one (Figure 5-11).

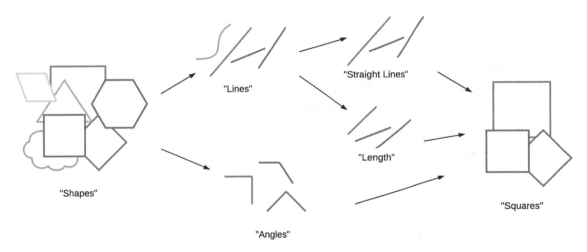

Figure 5-11. *A possible thought process of identifying a square*

But a machine (or an untrained AI) has no concept of what a line, length, or angle is. What the AI (the neural network in this case) would try to do is to look for any common features that can be seen in the provided training set.

The ability to "see" features of a neural network can be greatly increased by using a feature extraction method such as convolutions.

As you can see in the preceding diagram (Figure 5-12), the convolution filters allow to extract out some unique elements out of the images.

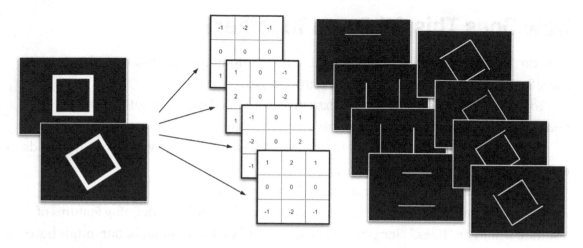

Figure 5-12. *Possible features learned by a model using convolutions*

Using feature extraction flows like this (with convolutions, ReLU, and pooling), a neural network would be able to better generalize the identified features from the input images. As such, it would be able to narrow down the common features of the given data set more easily.

Our handwritten digit classifier works in the same way.

The model we built uses many convolutional filters to identify the common features of the digits and tries to identify which combinations of them contributes to which of the digit classes (Figure 5-13).

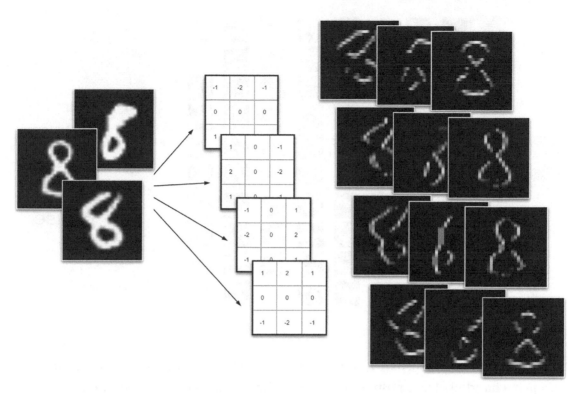

Figure 5-13. *Possible features learned on the digits of the MNIST dataset*

This same concept can be applied to recognize more complex inputs, such as more real-world images, as well. The following diagram shows how an image of a car might be identified with feature extraction in a CNN (Figure 5-14).

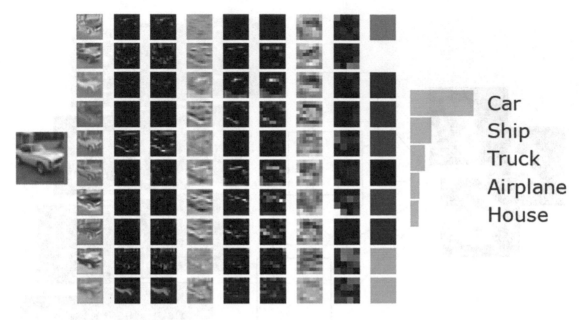

Figure 5-14. *How the filters extract features*

What we talked about here is the flow of our simple convolutional neural network with just a handful of layers. But the concepts within that model—convolutions, regularization, pooling, and so on—are used within more complex models as well. You will notice combinations of these same concepts applied within larger, more complex models as we start to build them.

CHAPTER 6

Visualizing Models

When building a deep learning model, it is often better to be able to visualize the model. Although the model we created—the LeNet model—is simple, it is better if we can see the structure. Especially when we are tweaking or modifying the model, we can easily compare their structures. And when working with more complex models (which we will look at in the next chapter), it is easier to wrap your head around them if you can see their structure visually.

But wouldn't it be better if there was a way to automatically draw the structure of a model?

As it happens, TensorFlow/Keras has just the method for it. But first, we first need to learn how to save our models properly.

Saving Models in Keras

In Chapter 4, when we build our first deep learning model, we learned of a one way to save a Keras model, which is to use the `model.save_weights()` function. This method, as the name suggests, only saves the weights of the model's neurons. The weights of a model are what the model has learned through the training.

But a model is more than just its weights.

In order to use the saved weights, we have to reconstruct the model structure in code, and load the weights into it. Furthermore, the `save_ weights ()` function does not save the optimizer state of the model. Therefore, we cannot use it to resume the training of a model from a previous training state.

For those requirements Keras provides another save option: `model.save()`.

When using model.save() it saves all of the following as a single file:

- The model's structure, architecture, and configuration

- The model's learned weights

© Thimira Amaratunga 2021
T. Amaratunga, *Deep Learning on Windows*, https://doi.org/10.1007/978-1-4842-6431-7_6

- The model's compilation information (configuration used with model.compile())

- The optimizer and its state of the model (allowing you to resume training)

This provides much more versatility to the saved models.

Note   The model.save_weights() function has its own usage as well. In more advanced situations, such as when the learned weights of one model needs to be transferred to a different model architecture, the save_weights() function is highly useful.

Let us add model.save() function to our LeNet model. We will modify the following code segment from our original code (lines 178, 179):

```
173: # Check the argument on whether to save the model weights to file
174: if args["save_trained"] > 0:
175:     print("[INFO] Saving the model weights to file...")
176:     model.save_weights(args["weights"], overwrite=True)
177:
178:     # Save the entire model
179:     model.save('data/lenet_model.h5')
```

Now, if we run training on our model, it will save the full model as lenet_model.h5 in the data directory (Figure 6-1).

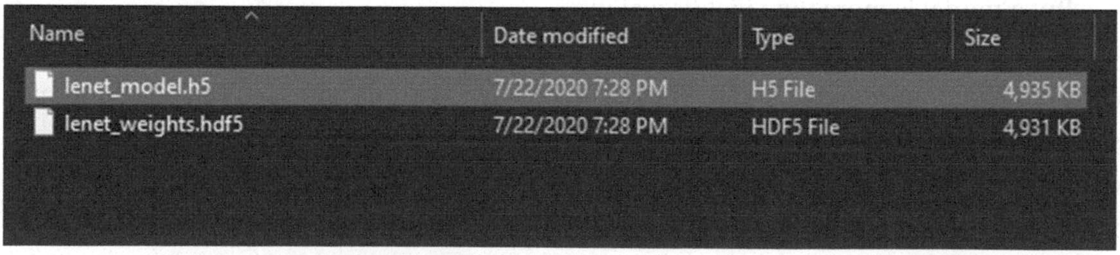

Name	Date modified	Type	Size
lenet_model.h5	7/22/2020 7:28 PM	H5 File	4,935 KB
lenet_weights.hdf5	7/22/2020 7:28 PM	HDF5 File	4,931 KB

Figure 6-1. *The saved model file*

With the full model saved, we can now use the built-in functions of Keras to visualize the model.

Using the plot_model Function of Keras

We can use the `plot_model` function from the `tf.keras.utils` package to plot the structure of a Keras or tf.keras model.

However, to get the plot_model function to work, we will need to install few additional packages:

- **Graphviz library:** an open-source graph visualization library

- **Pydot:** the Python bindings of the Dot language used by Graphviz

We can install both the packages in to our conda environment by running (Figure 6-2):

```
conda install graphviz pydot
```

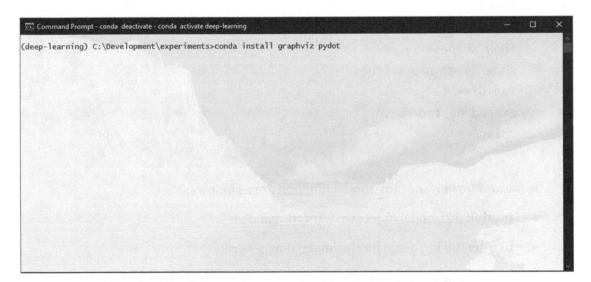

Figure 6-2. *Installing Graphviz and Pydot packages*

Once the packages are installed, we can start a new code file to add our visualization code. We will name it model_visualization.py.

In this new file we will start by importing the necessary packages:

```
1: # Import the packages
2: import tensorflow as tf
3: import numpy as np
4:
5: from tensorflow.keras.models import load_model
6: from tensorflow.keras.utils import plot_model
```

We will use the load_model function to load the LeNet model we saved in the earlier step. The plot_model function is what we will use for the visualization.

We can then load our model by passing the path to our saved model file to the load_model function:

```
8: # Loading the model from saved model file
9: model = load_model('data/lenet_model.h5')
```

Finally, we can generate the model structure visualization by using the plot_model function:

```
11: # Visualizing the model
12: plot_model(
13:     model,
14:     to_file='model.png',
15:     show_shapes=True,
16:     show_layer_names=True,
17:     rankdir='TB',
18:     expand_nested=False,
19:     dpi=96
20: )
```

The parameters for the plot_model function are as follows:

- **model:** the model object we want to visualize

- **to_file:** the file name for the image that generates

- **show_shapes:** whether to show the input and output shapes of the layers

- **show_layer_names:** whether to show the layer names of the model

- **rankdir:** this is an argument passed on to PyDot which determines the format of the generated plot. rankdir is the direction of the plot. TB or Top-to-Bottom will generate a vertical plot, while LR or Left-to-Right will generate a horizontal plot.

- **expand_nested:** if your model has nested models, this will specify whether to expand them in the plot or not

- **dpi:** the resolution of the generated plot in dots-per-inch

When we run our code, the visualization will be saved as model.png on the same folder as the code file, and would look like this (Figure 6-3):

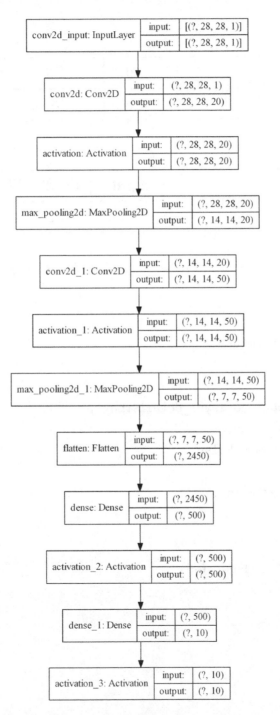

Figure 6-3. *The structure of the LeNet model visualized using plot_model*

The show_shapes and show_layer_names parameters allows you to control the amount of details that will be displayed in the generated plot (Figure 6-4).

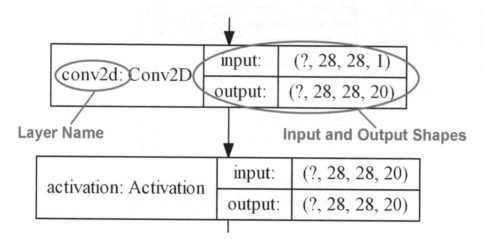

Figure 6-4. *The layer name and the shape in the visualized plot*

You can try turning them off:

```
11: # Visualizing the model
12: plot_model(
13:     model,
14:     to_file='model_no_layer_details.png',
15:     show_shapes=False,
16:     show_layer_names=False,
17:     rankdir='TB',
18:     expand_nested=False,
19:     dpi=96
20: )
```

Which would result in (Figure 6-5):

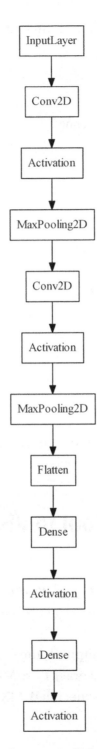

Figure 6-5. *Plot with both show_shapes and show_layer_names off*

Finally, with the rankdir parameter, you can switch to generating a horizontal plot:

```
11: # Visualizing the model
12: plot_model(
13:     model,
14:     to_file='model_horizontal.png',
15:     show_shapes=True,
16:     show_layer_names=True,
17:     rankdir='LR',
18:     expand_nested=False,
19:     dpi=96
20: )
```

This results in a horizontal plot (Figure 6-6).

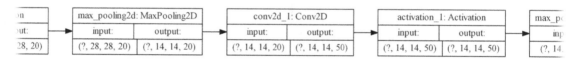

Figure 6-6. *Horizontal plot*

Because of these flexibilities of the plot_model function, it can be an excellent tool when you are building more complex models.

Using an Opensource tool to Visualize Model Structures: Netron

Netron is an opensource visualizer for neural network, deep learning, and machine learning models. Netron has been created by Lutz Roeder,[1] and is available through its GitHub page.[2]

At the time of this writing, Netron supports the following model file formats: ONNX (.onnx, .pb, .pbtxt), Keras (.h5, .keras), Core ML (.mlmodel), Caffe (.caffemodel, .prototxt), Caffe2 (predict_net.pb), Darknet (.cfg), MXNet (.model, -symbol.json),

---

[1]GitHub (Lutz Roeder), `https://github.com/lutzroeder`, [14 Nov, 2020].
[2]Github (Netron), `https://github.com/lutzroeder/netron`, [14 Nov, 2020].

Barracuda (.nn), ncnn (.param), Tengine (.tmfile), TNN (.tnnproto), UFF (.uff), and TensorFlow Lite (.tflite). It also has experimental support for many other formats and is actively being developed to constantly add support to more formats.

Netron has standalone installer packages for MacOS, Linux, and Windows.[3] It also has a browser version.[4]

Once installed (or with the browser version), you just need to open the saved model file from its UI (Figure 6-7).

Figure 6-7. *The Netron UI*

[3]Github (Netron downloads), https://github.com/lutzroeder/netron/releases/latest, [14 Nov, 2020].

[4]Lutz Roeder (Netron browser version), https://www.lutzroeder.com/ai/netron, [14 Nov, 2020].

When the model is loaded, you can select nodes/layers from the visualized graph to view their properties (Figure 6-8).

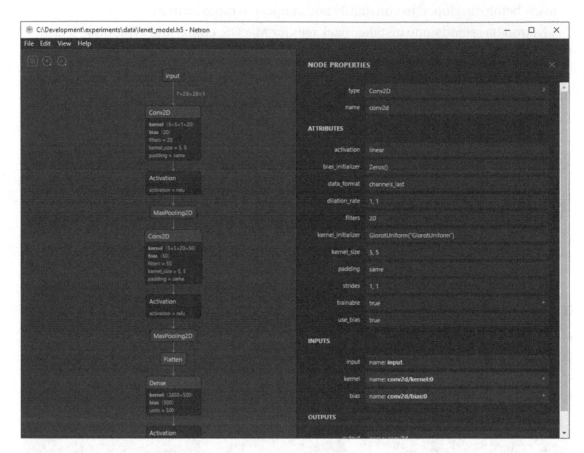

Figure 6-8. *Netron displaying a properties of a layer*

Netron gives many other visualization properties as well as the ability to export the visualized plot.

Visualizing the Features Learned by Convolutional Filters

In the past few chapters, we have been looking into building our first deep learning model and learn how it uses convolutional filters to extract features from the input and procedurally "learn" how to interpret the input using those features.

But what does convolutional filters see? What features do they learn?

We can attempt to see the features learned by the filters by maximizing the activations of them.

Let us attempt it on our LeNet model. We will start with a new code file, which we will name `lenet_filter_visualization.py`.

We start by importing the necessary packages:

```
1: # importing the necessary packages
2: import tensorflow as tf
3: import numpy as np
4: import time
5: import cv2
6:
7: from tensorflow.keras.preprocessing.image import save_img
8: from tensorflow.keras import backend as K
9: from tensorflow.keras.models import load_model
```

For the technique we are going to use, we need to disable eager execution, which is in TensorFlow v2.x:

```
11: # we disable eager execution of TensorFlow v2.x
12: # Ref: https://github.com/tensorflow/tensorflow/issues/33135
13: tf.compat.v1.disable_eager_execution()
```

We then set the parameters for the generated images, and select the layer from the model we are going to visualize:

```
15: # dimensions of the generated pictures for each filter.
16: img_width = 28
17: img_height = 28
18:
19: # the name of the layer we want to visualize
20: # (check the model.summary())
21: layer_name = 'conv2d_1'
```

As the layer name, we need to select a convolutional layer. If we look back at the model structure we visualized earlier, we can see that our LeNet model has two convolutional layers: conv2d and conv2d_1. We will select conv2d_1 here.

We then load our model, using the model file we saved earlier in this chapter:

```
23: # Loading the model from saved model file
24: model = load_model('data/lenet_model.h5')
25:
26: print('Model loaded.')
27:
28: # get the summary of the model
29: model.summary()
```

The model.summary() function will give you a text representation of the model structure. The output would look like this (Figure 6-9):

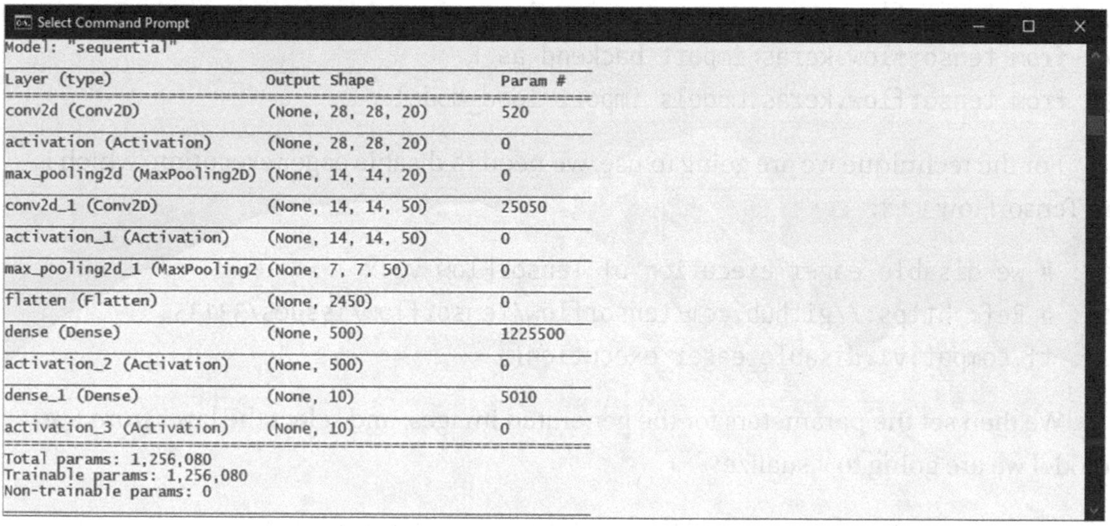

Figure 6-9. *The summary of the LeNet model*

We then define the input data and the dictionary of layers with their names:

```
31: # this is the placeholder for the input images
32: input_img = model.input
33:
34: # get the symbolic outputs of each "key" layer (we gave them unique names).
35: layer_dict = dict([(layer.name, layer) for layer in model.layers[1:]])
```

We then define two utility functions:

```
37: # utility function to normalize a tensor by its L2 norm
38: def normalize(x):
39:     return x / (K.sqrt(K.mean(K.square(x))) + 1e-5)
40:
41: # util function to convert a tensor into a valid image
42: def deprocess_image(x):
43:     # normalize tensor: center on 0., ensure std is 0.1
44:     x -= x.mean()
45:     x /= (x.std() + 1e-5)
46:     x *= 0.1
47:
48:     # clip to [0, 1]
49:     x += 0.5
50:     x = np.clip(x, 0, 1)
51:
52:     # convert to RGB array
53:     x *= 255
54:     if K.image_data_format() == 'channels_first':
55:         x = x.transpose((1, 2, 0))
56:     x = np.clip(x, 0, 255).astype('uint8')
57:     return x
```

The normalize function normalizes a given tensor by its L2-norm to allow a smooth gradient ascent. The deprocess_image transforms a given tensor into a valid image.

Next comes the main chunk of the code. We loop over the 50 filters of the conv2d_1 layer, obtain the loss and gradients of each, and normalize the gradients (using the normalize function defined earlier). We then start with a gray image with random noise and run gradient ascent for 20 steps. 20 was selected here as the number of epochs based on the results from past experiments which resulted in sharper visualizations. You can attempt to change the number of epochs and see how it affects the output.

Finally, the processed filters are converted to images (using the deprocess_image function defined earlier) and added to a list named kept_filters:

```
059: kept_filters = []
060: for filter_index in range(0, 50):
```

```
061:     # we scan through the 50 filters in our model
062:     print('Processing filter %d' % filter_index)
063:     start_time = time.time()
064:
065:     # we build a loss function that maximizes the activation
066:     # of the nth filter of the layer considered
067:     layer_output = layer_dict[layer_name].output
068:     if K.image_data_format() == 'channels_first':
069:         loss = K.mean(layer_output[:, filter_index, :, :])
070:     else:
071:         loss = K.mean(layer_output[:, :, :, filter_index])
072:
073:     # we compute the gradient of the input picture wrt this loss
074:     grads = K.gradients(loss, input_img)[0]
075:
076:     # normalization trick: we normalize the gradient
077:     grads = normalize(grads)
078:
079:     # this function returns the loss and grads given the input picture
080:     iterate = K.function([input_img], [loss, grads])
081:
082:     # step size for gradient ascent
083:     step = 1.
084:
085:     # we start from a gray image with some random noise
086:     input_img_data = np.random.random((1, img_width, img_height, 1))
087:     input_img_data = (input_img_data - 0.5) * 20 + 128
088:
089:     # we run gradient ascent for 20 steps
090:     for i in range(20):
091:         loss_value, grads_value = iterate([input_img_data])
092:         input_img_data += grads_value * step
093:
094:         print('Current loss value:', loss_value)
095:         if loss_value <= 0.:
```

```
096:              # some filters get stuck to 0, we can skip them
097:              break
098:
099:      # decode the resulting input image
100:      if loss_value > 0:
101:          img = deprocess_image(input_img_data[0])
102:          kept_filters.append((img, loss_value))
103:      end_time = time.time()
104:      print('Filter %d processed in %ds' % (filter_index, end_time -
start_time))
```

With the images of the filters ready, we can stitch them into a single 6x6 grid image and enlarge to make it more visible:

```
106: # we will stich the best 36 filters on a 6 x 6 grid.
107: n = 6
108:
109: # the filters that have the highest loss are assumed to be better-looking.
110: # we will only keep the top 36 filters.
111: kept_filters.sort(key=lambda x: x[1], reverse=True)
112: kept_filters = kept_filters[:n * n]
113:
114: # build a black picture with enough space for
115: # our 8 x 8 filters of size 28 x 28, with a 5px margin in between
116: margin = 5
117: width = n * img_width + (n - 1) * margin
118: height = n * img_height + (n - 1) * margin
119: stitched_filters = np.zeros((width, height, 3))
120:
121: # fill the picture with our saved filters
122: for i in range(n):
123:     for j in range(n):
124:         img, loss = kept_filters[i * n + j]
125:         stitched_filters[(img_width + margin) * i: (img_width +
margin) * i + img_width,
126:                          (img_height + margin) * j: (img_height +
margin) * j + img_height, :] = img
```

```
127:
128: # enlarge the resulting image to make it more visible
129: stitched_filters = cv2.resize(stitched_filters, (579, 579),
interpolation=cv2.INTER_LINEAR)
130:
131: # save the result to disk
132: save_img('lenet_filters_%dx%d.png' % (n, n), stitched_filters)
```

The resulting image, named lenet_filters_6x6.png, will be saved in the same folder as the code file, and will look something like this (Figure 6-10):

Figure 6-10. *The visualized activations of convolutional filters of the LeNet model*

While at first glance this may seem like random noise, if you look closely you can see some subtle patterns in the output. These patterns represent attempts in matching lines, edges, and textures of the input images from various directions. As we discussed in the last chapter, the different filters extract different features from the images. Once the filters "learn" the features, a combination of those are used to match the input images to determine what the image is.

CHAPTER 7

Transfer Learning

We saw how exceptionally well deep learning models performed when applied to computer vision and classification tasks. Our LeNet model with the MNIST and Fashion-MNIST datasets was able to achieve 90%–99% accuracy under a very reasonable amount of training time. We have also seen how the ImageNet models have achieved record-breaking accuracy levels in more complex datasets.

Now you might be eager to try out what we learned on a more complex and practical classification task. But what should we consider when we are going to train our own image classification model with our own categories from scratch?

The Problem with Little Data

If you attempted to build such a system, you might find that building a classifications system from scratch—even with deep learning—is not an easy task. To get sufficient accuracy from your model, without overfitting, would require a lot of training data. The ImageNet has millions of data samples, which is why the models trained on them perform so well. But for us to find or build a training dataset of that level for the classification task we plan on building would be practically infeasible.

The problem with having a small dataset to train a model is that when the model sees the same few samples repeatedly through its training epochs, it tends to overfit to those specific samples. And not having a large enough validation dataset makes matters worse.

But do we really need that much of data to get an image classification model working? What can we do with a little amount of data?

One method we can try is the use of data augmentation.

© Thimira Amaratunga 2021
T. Amaratunga, *Deep Learning on Windows*, https://doi.org/10.1007/978-1-4842-6431-7_7

Using Data Augmentation

The idea of augmenting the data is simple: we perform random transformations and normalization on the input data so that the model being trained never sees the same input twice.

When working with limited amounts of training data, this method can significantly reduce the chance of the model overfitting.

But performing such transformations to our input data manually would be a tedious task, which is why TensorFlow/Keras has built-in functions to help with just that.

The Image Preprocessing package of tf.keras has the ImageDataGenerator function, which can be configured to perform the random transformations and the normalization of input images, as needed. This ImageDataGenerator can then be coupled with the `flow()` and `flow_from_directory()` functions to automatically load the data, apply the augmentations, and feed into the model.

Note When using the ImageDataGenerator of tf.keras the output of it will be the augmented dataset. Therefore, when using an ImageDataGenerator to feed the data to a model, the model will only see the augmented dataset. This is the recommended way that will work for many situations. There are other techniques that combine the augmented dataset with the original dataset, but they are used less commonly.

Let us write a small script to see the data augmentation capabilities of ImageDataGenerator.

We will use the following as our input image (Figure 7-1). Create a directory named data at the same place as the script and place this input image in there. Also create a subdirectory named augmented inside this data directory. This will be where the augmented images that are generated will be saved.

Figure 7-1. *The input image bird.jpg*

We will then use the following script to load the image, run data augmentations using ImageDataGenerator on it 20 times, and save the resulting augmented images:

```
01: from tensorflow.keras.preprocessing.image import ImageDataGenerator,
img_to_array, load_img
02:
03: # define the parameters for the ImageDataGenerator
04: datagen = ImageDataGenerator(
05:     rotation_range=40,
06:     width_shift_range=0.2,
07:     height_shift_range=0.2,
08:     shear_range=0.2,
09:     zoom_range=0.2,
10:     horizontal_flip=True,
11:     fill_mode='nearest')
12:
13: img = load_img('data/Bird.jpg')  # this is a PIL image
14:
```

```
15: # convert image to numpy array with shape (3, width, height)
16: img_arr = img_to_array(img)
17:
18: # convert to numpy array with shape (1, 3, width, height)
19: img_arr = img_arr.reshape((1,) + img_arr.shape)
20:
21: # the .flow() command below generates batches of randomly transformed images
22: # and saves the results to the `data/augmented` directory
23: i = 0
24: for batch in datagen.flow(
25:          img_arr,
26:          batch_size=1,
27:          save_to_dir='data/augmented',
28:          save_prefix='Bird_A',
29:          save_format='jpeg'):
30:    i += 1
31:    if i > 20:
32:        break  # otherwise the generator would loop indefinitely
```

Here, we have used the following parameters for our augmentations:

- **rotation_range:** the range (degrees) within which to apply random rotations to the images.

- **width_shift_range:** the range within which to apply random horizontal shifts.

- **height_shift_range:** the range within which to apply random vertical shifts.

- **shear_range:** the range within which to apply random shearing transformations.

- **zoom_range:** the range within which to apply random zooming to the images.

- **horizontal_flip:** whether to apply random horizontal flips to the images.

- **fill_mode='nearest':** the method of which the newly created pixels are filled. Specifying as nearest will fill the new pixels with the same values as the nearest pixels of the input image.

The ImageDataGenerator has several more parameters for augmentations. You can read about them in the official documentation page.[1]

The `flow()` function of the ImageDataGenerator is able to take in the input images, apply the augmentations we defined, and produce batches of augmented data indefinitely on a loop. While in this example we only have one input image, the `flow()` function is really meant to be used with batches of images.

The resulting augmented images are saved into the `data/augmented` directory, and would look something like this (Figure 7-2):

Figure 7-2. *Some of the augmented images*

---

[1]TensorFlow (ImageDataGeneraor parameters), `https://www.tensorflow.org/api_docs/python/tf/keras/preprocessing/image/ImageDataGenerator`, [14 Nov, 2020].

By using data augmentations like these, we should be able to reduce the chance of a deep learning model overfitting when training on a small dataset.

Build an Image Classification Model with Data Augmentation

With our understanding of data augmentations, let us apply it to building a practical model.

But first, we will need an image dataset. For this we will use a bird image dataset from Kaggle.

Kaggle is a community of data scientists and machine learning enthusiasts, and lets you find and publish datasets, experiment and build models in Jupyter notebook environments, and participate in data science and machine learning competitions.

In the vast catalog of datasets of Kaggle, we will use the 225 Bird Species dataset.[2] The dataset is about 1.4GB is size and is downloadable as a zip file (Figure 7-3).

---

[2]Kaggle, "225 Bird Species Dataset," `https://www.kaggle.com/gpiosenka/100-bird-species`, [1 Mar, 2020]. You will need to register for a Kaggle account to download datasets. Registration is free, and gives you many benefits as a machine learning enthusiast.

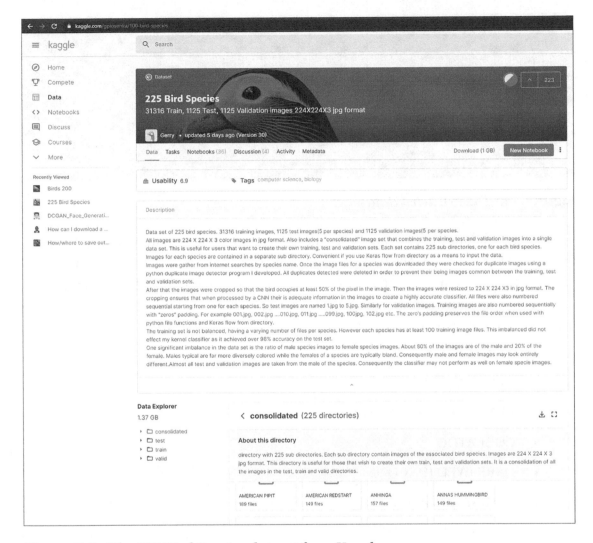

Figure 7-3. *The 225 Bird Species dataset from Kaggle*

Note   This dataset, as with many other datasets in Kaggle, is actively maintained. While there are images of 225 bird species at the time of this writing, more species and categories may have been added to this dataset by the time you read this. You can also select any other dataset with a similar structure.

Once downloaded, you can extract the contents of the zip file. In the extracted directory, you will get 4 subdirectories: consolidated, train, test, and valid (Figure 7-4).

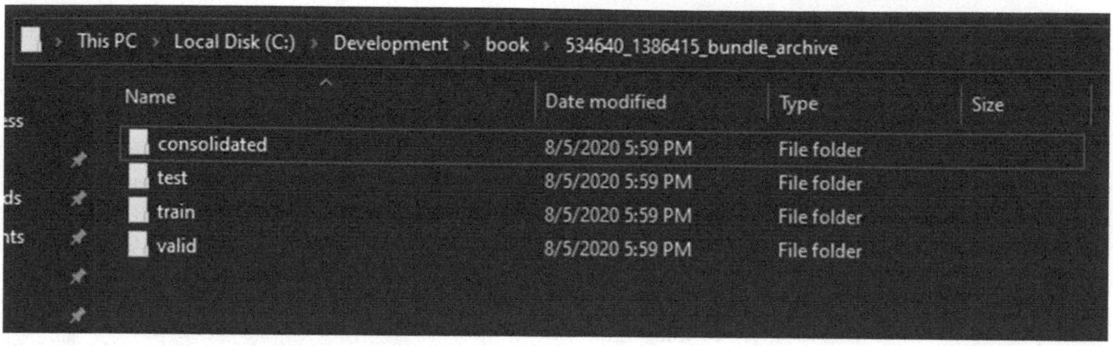

Name	Date modified	Type	Size
consolidated	8/5/2020 5:59 PM	File folder	
test	8/5/2020 5:59 PM	File folder	
train	8/5/2020 5:59 PM	File folder	
valid	8/5/2020 5:59 PM	File folder	

This PC > Local Disk (C:) > Development > book > 534640_1386415_bundle_archive

Figure 7-4. The extracted dataset

The consolidated directory contains the full dataset, organized into subdirectories for each specie/category. The train, test, and valid subdirectories contain the same dataset split into train, test, and validation sets with the same subdirectory structure.

For our experiment, initially we will only select 10 of the categories from the 225. We will select the following 10 as a start:

- ALBATROSS

- BANANAQUIT

- BLACK-THROATED SPARROW

- COCKATOO

- DARK EYED JUNCO

- D-ARNAUDS BARBET

- GOLDEN PHEASANT

- HOUSE FINCH

- ROBIN

- SORA

Note   These 10 categories were selected because they contain different number of samples for each category. We will see how that affects the training accuracy and how to overcome its negative effects.

Create a new directory named data and create two subdirectories named train and validation inside it. Copy over the directories of the preceding selected categories from the train and valid directories of the extracted dataset to the train and validation directories you have created. The final directory structure should be like this (Figure 7-5):

Figure 7-5. *The directory structure of the dataset*

Note   When creating the directory structure, make sure that the subdirectory structure of the validation directory is same as that of the train directory.

Let us start our bird classification model with data augmentation by staring a new code file. We will name it bird_classify_augmented.py.

We will start with importing the necessary packages:

```
1: from tensorflow.keras.preprocessing.image import ImageDataGenerator
2: from tensorflow.keras.models import Sequential
3: from tensorflow.keras.layers import Conv2D, MaxPooling2D
4: from tensorflow.keras.layers import Activation, Dropout, Flatten, Dense
5: from tensorflow.keras import backend as K
6: import matplotlib.pyplot as plt
7: import math
```

We then define our utility function to graph the training history using Matplotlib:

```
09: # utility functions
10: def graph_training_history(history):
11:     plt.rcParams["figure.figsize"] = (12, 9)
12:
13:     plt.style.use('ggplot')
14:
15:     plt.figure(1)
16:
17:     # summarize history for accuracy
18:
19:     plt.subplot(211)
20:     plt.plot(history.history['accuracy'])
21:     plt.plot(history.history['val_accuracy'])
22:     plt.title('Model Accuracy')
23:     plt.ylabel('Accuracy')
24:     plt.xlabel('Epoch')
25:     plt.legend(['Training', 'Validation'], loc='lower right')
26:
27:     # summarize history for loss
28:
29:     plt.subplot(212)
30:     plt.plot(history.history['loss'])
31:     plt.plot(history.history['val_loss'])
32:     plt.title('Model Loss')
33:     plt.ylabel('Loss')
```

```
34:     plt.xlabel('Epoch')
35:     plt.legend(['Training', 'Validation'], loc='upper right')
36:
37:     plt.tight_layout()
38:
39:     plt.show()
```

Then, we define some parameters for the training:

```
41: # dimensions of our images.
42: img_width, img_height = 224, 224
43:
44: train_data_dir = 'data/train'
45: validation_data_dir = 'data/validation'
46:
47: # number of epochs to train
48: epochs = 50
49:
50: # batch size used by flow_from_directory
51: batch_size = 16
```

224x224 pixels is one of the standard sizes used in large-scale image classification models such as ImageNet. We also use it here, as it allows us some flexibility later.

To use automatic data augmentations with our model training we need to define data generator functions, like we did on our previous data augmentation example. Using data generators gives us the added advantage of being able to use the flow_from_directory() function, which loads the data from our directory structure as well as provide category labels using the subdirectory names. Here, we define two data generators: one for training and one for validation:

```
53: # this is the augmentation configuration we will use for training
54: train_datagen = ImageDataGenerator(
55:     rescale=1. / 255,
56:     shear_range=0.2,
57:     zoom_range=0.2,
58:     horizontal_flip=True)
59:
```

```
60: # this is the augmentation configuration we will use for testing:
61: # only rescaling
62: test_datagen = ImageDataGenerator(rescale=1. / 255)
63:
64: train_generator = train_datagen.flow_from_directory(
65:     train_data_dir,
66:     target_size=(img_width, img_height),
67:     batch_size=batch_size,
68:     class_mode='categorical')
69:
70: validation_generator = test_datagen.flow_from_directory(
71:     validation_data_dir,
72:     target_size=(img_width, img_height),
73:     batch_size=batch_size,
74:     class_mode='categorical')
75:
76: # print the number of training samples
77: print(len(train_generator.filenames))
78:
79: # print the category/class labal map
80: print(train_generator.class_indices)
81:
82: # print the number of classes
83: print(len(train_generator.class_indices))
```

As we are building a multiclass image classification model, the class_mode is set to categorical.

The <generator>.filenames contains all the filenames of the training set. By getting its length, we can get the size of the training set.

Likewise, <generator>.class_indices is the map/dictionary for the class names and their indexes. Getting its length gives us the number of classes.

We use these values to calculate the required training and validation steps:

```
85: # the number of classes/categories
86: num_classes = len(train_generator.class_indices)
87:
```

```
88: # calculate the training steps
89: nb_train_samples = len(train_generator.filenames)
90: train_steps = int(math.ceil(nb_train_samples / batch_size))
91:
92: # calculate the validation steps
93: nb_validation_samples = len(validation_generator.filenames)
94: validation_steps = int(math.ceil(nb_validation_samples / batch_size))
```

Now, we can define our model:

```
097: # build the model
098: input_shape = (img_width, img_height, 3)
099:
100: model = Sequential()
101: model.add(Conv2D(32, (3, 3), input_shape=input_shape))
102: model.add(Activation('relu'))
103: model.add(MaxPooling2D(pool_size=(2, 2)))
104:
105: model.add(Conv2D(32, (3, 3)))
106: model.add(Activation('relu'))
107: model.add(MaxPooling2D(pool_size=(2, 2)))
108:
109: model.add(Conv2D(64, (3, 3)))
110: model.add(Activation('relu'))
111: model.add(MaxPooling2D(pool_size=(2, 2)))
112:
113: model.add(Flatten())
114: model.add(Dense(64))
115: model.add(Activation('relu'))
116: model.add(Dropout(0.5))
117: model.add(Dense(num_classes))
118: model.add(Activation('softmax'))
```

This is a slightly deeper model than our LeNet model, but uses the same concepts. This uses three sets of CONV => RELU => POOL layers. Followed by a dense layer and a softmax classifier.

Once we have the model structure defined, we can compile it and run the training. The `model.fit()` function accepts data generators just like it accepts arrays of training data (as well as several other data formats).[3]

```
120: model.compile(loss='categorical_crossentropy',
121:               optimizer='rmsprop',
122:               metrics=['accuracy'])
123:
124: history = model.fit(
125:     train_generator,
126:     steps_per_epoch=train_steps,
127:     epochs=epochs,
128:     validation_data=validation_generator,
129:     validation_steps=validation_steps
130:     )
```

After the training step, we can save the trained model, evaluate it, and graph the training history using the function we defined at the start:

```
132: model.save('bird_classify_augmented.h5')
133:
134: (eval_loss, eval_accuracy) = model.evaluate(
135:     validation_generator, steps=validation_steps)
136:
137: print("\n")
138:
139: print("[INFO] accuracy: {:.2f}%".format(eval_accuracy * 100))
140: print("[INFO] Loss: {}".format(eval_loss))
141:
142: # visualize the training history
143: graph_training_history(history)
```

If we run this code now, we should be getting as accuracy value somewhere between 70% and 85%. The accuracy you will be getting can vary due to the randomness of

---

[3]TensorFlow (Model.fit() function), https://www.tensorflow.org/api_docs/python/tf/keras/Model#fit, [21 Nov, 2020].

the applied data augmentations as well as the dataset being extremely small. For an example, in the following instance we have achieved 82% accuracy (Figure 7-6).

```
Command Prompt                                                          —   □   ×
uracy: 0.8800
Epoch 45/50
110/110 [==============================] - 14s 129ms/step - loss: 0.7042 - accuracy: 0.7994 - val_loss: 0.1313 - val_acc
uracy: 0.9600
Epoch 46/50
110/110 [==============================] - 14s 128ms/step - loss: 0.6525 - accuracy: 0.8068 - val_loss: 0.3606 - val_acc
uracy: 0.9000
Epoch 47/50
110/110 [==============================] - 14s 129ms/step - loss: 0.6968 - accuracy: 0.8239 - val_loss: 0.3346 - val_acc
uracy: 0.9200
Epoch 48/50
110/110 [==============================] - 14s 129ms/step - loss: 0.6398 - accuracy: 0.8205 - val_loss: 0.4138 - val_acc
uracy: 0.8200
Epoch 49/50
110/110 [==============================] - 14s 128ms/step - loss: 0.6512 - accuracy: 0.8216 - val_loss: 0.3677 - val_acc
uracy: 0.9000
Epoch 50/50
110/110 [==============================] - 14s 129ms/step - loss: 0.6737 - accuracy: 0.8017 - val_loss: 1.0177 - val_acc
uracy: 0.8200
WARNING:tensorflow:sample_weight modes were coerced from
  ...
    to
  ['...']
4/4 [==============================] - 0s 18ms/step - loss: 1.0177 - accuracy: 0.8200

[INFO] accuracy: 82.00%
[INFO] Loss: 1.0177310425788164

(deep-learning) C:\Development\deep_learning_on_windows>
```

Figure 7-6. *The accuracy of the model using data augmentations*

If we look at the training history graph, we can see that the accuracy and the loss curves have plateaued (Figure 7-7).

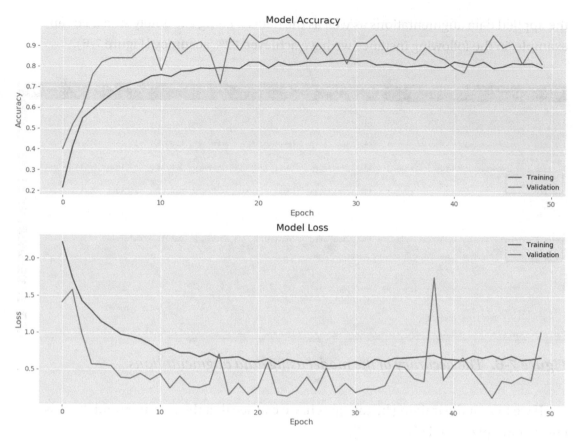

Figure 7-7. *The training history graph of the model using data augmentations*

This usually indicates that the model cannot go further without more data. You may also note that the validation accuracy is higher than training accuracy. This is also usually an indication of insufficient data.

While an accuracy of 82% is not terrible, it is clear that to achieve a better accuracy with the given data, we would need to use more advanced techniques.

Bottleneck Features

Should we accept the 82% accuracy that we achieved, or give up on attempting to build our own bird image classifier?

No. Because deep learning has a solution.

Deep learning supports an immensely useful technique called *transfer learning*. This means that you can take a pretrained deep learning model— trained on a large-scale dataset such as ImageNet—and repurpose it to handle an entirely different problem. Since the model has already learned certain features from a large dataset (think back to hierarchical feature learning), it would be able to use those features as a base to learn the new classification problem we present it with.

The basic technique to get transfer learning working is to get a pretrained model (with the trained model weights loaded) and remove the final fully connected layers from that model. We then use the remaining portion of the model as a feature extractor for our smaller dataset. These extracted features are called *bottleneck features*, which are the last activation maps prior to the fully connected layers in the original model. We then train a small model with fully connected layers on top of those extracted bottleneck features to get the classes we need as outputs for our new classification task. This workflow is shown in Figure 7-8.

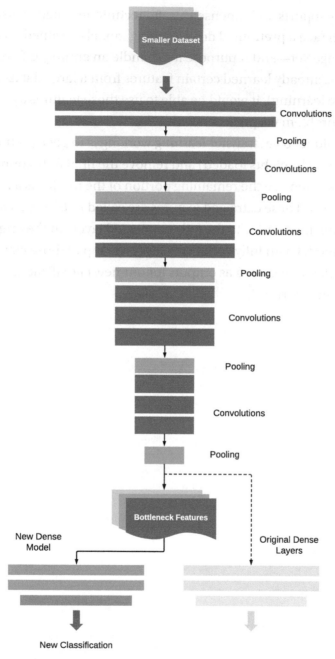

Figure 7-8. *How bottleneck feature extraction works*

As transfer learning is one of the heavily used techniques in building deep learning models, frameworks such as TensorFlow and Keras provides methods to simplify implementing it. TensorFlow and Keras have many of the ImageNet models built in with their trained weights. Their built-in implementations also provide utility functions to remove the original top layers and to build new models around them for transfer learning.

Using Bottleneck Features with a Pretrained VGG16 Model

Let us utilize bottleneck features in our bird image classification model.

We shall use the VGG16 model, with its ImageNet trained weights, as our base model. You can learn more about the VGG16 model and other ImageNet models in Appendix 1.

To train our bird image classifier using bottleneck features we will use the following steps:

1. Create a base model using one of the built-in pretrained ImageNet models without its final dense layers. We will use the VGG16 model for our example.

2. Define a set of new dense layers for classification (which we will refer to as the top model) and create a new model by combining the base model and the top model.

3. "Freeze" the layers of the base model. That is, the weights of the layers in the base model will not be trained, as we do not want to destroy the features already learned by the base model when it was trained on the ImageNet dataset. This allows the base model to reuse those learnings and output the activations—the bottleneck features—to the new dense layers we have added on top.

4. Train the resulting new model with our new categories.

Let us start our bird classification model using bottleneck features by starting a new code file, which we will name bird_classify_bottleneck.py, and importing the necessary packages:

```
01: import tensorflow as tf
02: import numpy as np
03: from tensorflow.keras.preprocessing.image import ImageDataGenerator,
img_to_array, load_img
```

```
04: from tensorflow.keras.models import Sequential, Model, load_model
05: from tensorflow.keras.layers import Dropout, Flatten, Dense,
GlobalAveragePooling2D, Input
06: from tensorflow.keras.applications.vgg16 import VGG16
07: from tensorflow.keras.applications.inception_v3 import InceptionV3
08: from tensorflow.keras import optimizers
09: import matplotlib.pyplot as plt
10: import math
```

Like before, we will define our utility functions:

```
12: # utility functions
13: def graph_training_history(history):
14:     plt.rcParams["figure.figsize"] = (12, 9)
15:
16:     plt.style.use('ggplot')
17:
18:     plt.figure(1)
19:
20:     # summarize history for accuracy
21:
22:     plt.subplot(211)
23:     plt.plot(history.history['accuracy'])
24:     plt.plot(history.history['val_accuracy'])
25:     plt.title('Model Accuracy')
26:     plt.ylabel('Accuracy')
27:     plt.xlabel('Epoch')
28:     plt.legend(['Training', 'Validation'], loc='lower right')
29:
30:     # summarize history for loss
31:
32:     plt.subplot(212)
33:     plt.plot(history.history['loss'])
34:     plt.plot(history.history['val_loss'])
35:     plt.title('Model Loss')
36:     plt.ylabel('Loss')
```

```
37:      plt.xlabel('Epoch')
38:      plt.legend(['Training', 'Validation'], loc='upper right')
39:
40:      plt.tight_layout()
41:
42:      plt.show()
```

The training parameters and data generator definitions would also be the same as before:

```
44: # dimensions of our images.
45: img_width, img_height = 224, 224
46:
47: train_data_dir = 'data/train'
48: validation_data_dir = 'data/validation'
49:
50: # number of epochs to train
51: epochs = 50
52:
53: # batch size used by flow_from_directory
54: batch_size = 16
55:
56: # this is the augmentation configuration we will use for training
57: train_datagen = ImageDataGenerator(
58:      rescale=1. / 255,
59:      shear_range=0.2,
60:      zoom_range=0.2,
61:      horizontal_flip=True)
62:
63: # this is the augmentation configuration we will use for testing:
64: # only rescaling
65: test_datagen = ImageDataGenerator(rescale=1. / 255)
66:
67: train_generator = train_datagen.flow_from_directory(
68:      train_data_dir,
69:      target_size=(img_width, img_height),
```

```
70:        batch_size=batch_size,
71:        class_mode='categorical')
72:
73: validation_generator = test_datagen.flow_from_directory(
74:        validation_data_dir,
75:        target_size=(img_width, img_height),
76:        batch_size=batch_size,
77:        class_mode='categorical')
78:
79: # print the number of training samples
80: print(len(train_generator.filenames))
81:
82: # print the category/class labal map
83: print(train_generator.class_indices)
84:
85: # print the number of classes
86: print(len(train_generator.class_indices))
87:
88: # the number of classes/categories
89: num_classes = len(train_generator.class_indices)
90:
91: # calculate the training steps
92: nb_train_samples = len(train_generator.filenames)
93: train_steps = int(math.ceil(nb_train_samples / batch_size))
94:
95: # calculate the validation steps
96: nb_validation_samples = len(validation_generator.filenames)
97: validation_steps = int(math.ceil(nb_validation_samples / batch_size))
```

Next, we will define the base model. We will load the VGG16 model with its ImageNet weights, but without the top dense layers, by using the include_top=False parameter:

```
100: # create the base pre-trained model
101: base_model = VGG16(weights='imagenet', include_top=False, input_
tensor=Input(shape=(img_width, img_height, 3)))
```

We then define the top model, which is the dense layers and the final classification layer:

```
103: # add a global spatial average pooling layer
104: x = base_model.output
105: x = GlobalAveragePooling2D()(x)
106: x = Dense(512, activation='relu')(x)
107: predictions = Dense(num_classes, activation='softmax')(x)
```

Once both base and the top models are defined, we combine them into a single model:

```
109: # this is the model we will train
110: model = Model(inputs=base_model.input, outputs=predictions)
```

We then set the layers of the base model nontrainable and compile the model. The compiling of the model should only be done after the layers are marked as nontrainable:

```
112: # train only the top layers (which were randomly initialized)
113: # i.e. freeze all convolutional layers
114: for layer in base_model.layers:
115:     layer.trainable = False
116:
117: # compile the model (should be done *after* setting layers to non-
trainable)
118: model.compile(optimizer='rmsprop', loss='categorical_crossentropy',
metrics=['accuracy'])
```

Finally, we run the training, save the model, evaluate, and graph the training history:

```
120: history = model.fit(
121:     train_generator,
122:     steps_per_epoch=train_steps,
123:     epochs=epochs,
124:     validation_data=validation_generator,
125:     validation_steps=validation_steps
126:     )
127:
128: model.save('bird_classify_bottleneck.h5')
129:
```

```
130: (eval_loss, eval_accuracy) = model.evaluate(
131:     validation_generator, steps=validation_steps)
132:
133: print("\n")
134:
135: print("[INFO] accuracy: {:.2f}%".format(eval_accuracy * 100))
136: print("[INFO] Loss: {}".format(eval_loss))
137:
138: # visualize the training history
139: graph_training_history(history)
```

Let us now run the training and see how the bottleneck model compares against the simple model from before.

The accuracy has increased to 94% (Figure 7-9).

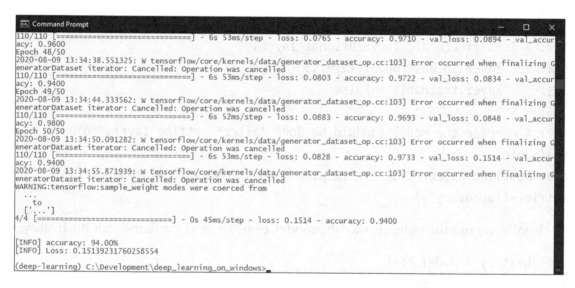

Figure 7-9. *The accuracy of the model using bottleneck features*

The training history graph also shows the improvements. The characteristics of insufficient data which was there before are now gone (Figure 7-10).

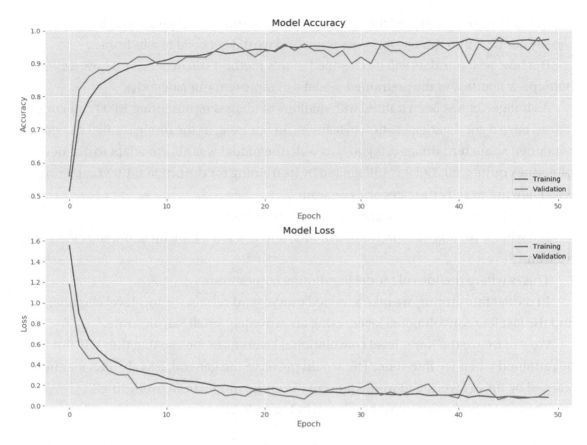

Figure 7-10. *The training history graph of the model using bottleneck features*

Using the bottleneck features, we were able to increase our accuracy on the same dataset from 82% to 94%.

But can we do better?

Going Further with Model Fine-tuning

Getting an accuracy of 94% is great. But we have seen deep learning models achieve far more impressive results.

So, how can we improve our results further?

What we did when using bottleneck features was to take a deep learning model—the VGG16 model in our case—which was already trained using a large dataset—the ImageNet dataset in our case—and used the bottleneck features from it to train a set of dense layers to classify our data into the categories we want. And we did get good results from it.

But how well our data will be classified in this method still depends on how well the bottleneck features of the pretrained model can represent our categories.

As ImageNet has been trained with millions of images representing 1,000 categories, it does have a good generalization of features. In our case, as the original 1,000 categories contained some bird image categories as well, the model was able to adapt to our new categories quite well. But it is still limited by its training for the original 1,000 categories, which are not exactly the categories we want.

This is the reason why our accuracy got limited to 94%.

But what if we take that pretrained model, and teach it a little bit about the categories we want?

This is where the idea of model fine-tuning comes from.

In model fine-tuning, we take a trained model, and retrain the top-level classifier and the last few convolutional layers using an extremely small learning rate.

We still freeze the lower level convolutional layers as before, so that they will not be retrained when we fine-tune. This would preserve the general, less abstract features learned by these layers, and would prevent the entire model from overfitting.

The workflow for fine-tuning is shown in Figure 7-11.

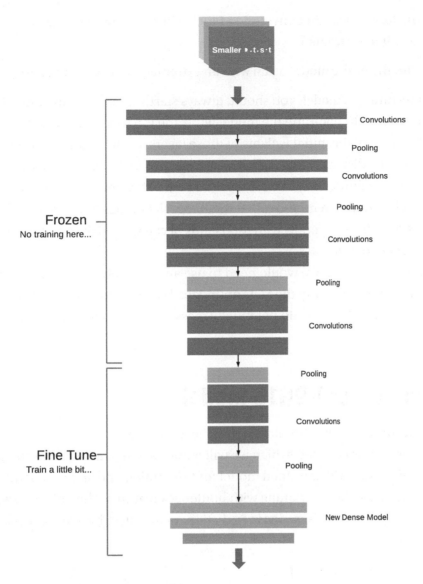

Figure 7-11. *The concept of model fine-tuning*

To fine-tune our model, we will use the following steps:

1. Define the base model (with the pretrained weights) and the top model as before.

2. Train the entire model using the bottleneck features as we did in the earlier section.

3. "Un-freeze" the last convolution block of the base model, that is, allow it to be trained.

4. Train the entire model again with an extremely small learning rate.

When fine-tuning a model, you should always start with an already trained model. If we attempt to fine-tune the model while the top model we added is still untrained, because of the initial weights of those layers it will be randomly initialized, it would potentially disrupt the already learned features of the base model due to back propagation. As the limited data we have would be insufficient to fulfil the high learning capacity of such a model (remember that the ImageNet models are capable of learning from millions of training samples with thousands of categories), it would most definitely cause the model to overfit.

Also, when fine-tuning, we would need to use an extremely small learning rate—such as 0.0001—typically using the SGD optimizer. Using an adaptive learning rate optimizer such as RMSProp could potentially mess up the already learned features of the model.

Fine-tuning our VGG16 Model

Let us add fine-tuning to our bird image classification model.

We will start a new code file, which we will name as bird_classify_finetune.py.

As we need to start with a trained model for fine-tuning, the first part of the code is nearly the same as we did for training with bottleneck features. The only difference is at line 91, where we save the class_indices dictionary to a file. This file will become useful in the later sections:

```
001: import tensorflow as tf
002: import numpy as np
003: from tensorflow.keras.preprocessing.image import ImageDataGenerator,
img_to_array, load_img
004: from tensorflow.keras.models import Sequential, Model, load_model
005: from tensorflow.keras.layers import Dropout, Flatten, Dense,
GlobalAveragePooling2D, Input
006: from tensorflow.keras.applications.vgg16 import VGG16
007: from tensorflow.keras import optimizers
008: from tensorflow.keras.optimizers import SGD
```

```
009: import matplotlib.pyplot as plt
010: import math
011:
012: # utility functions
013: def graph_training_history(history):
014:     plt.rcParams["figure.figsize"] = (12, 9)
015:
016:     plt.style.use('ggplot')
017:
018:     plt.figure(1)
019:
020:     # summarize history for accuracy
021:
022:     plt.subplot(211)
023:     plt.plot(history.history['accuracy'])
024:     plt.plot(history.history['val_accuracy'])
025:     plt.title('Model Accuracy')
026:     plt.ylabel('Accuracy')
027:     plt.xlabel('Epoch')
028:     plt.legend(['Training', 'Validation'], loc='lower right')
029:
030:     # summarize history for loss
031:
032:     plt.subplot(212)
033:     plt.plot(history.history['loss'])
034:     plt.plot(history.history['val_loss'])
035:     plt.title('Model Loss')
036:     plt.ylabel('Loss')
037:     plt.xlabel('Epoch')
038:     plt.legend(['Training', 'Validation'], loc='upper right')
039:
040:     plt.tight_layout()
041:
042:     plt.show()
043:
```

```
044: # dimensions of our images.
045: img_width, img_height = 224, 224
046:
047: train_data_dir = 'data/train'
048: validation_data_dir = 'data/validation'
049:
050: # number of epochs to train
051: epochs = 50
052:
053: # batch size used by flow_from_directory
054: batch_size = 16
055:
056: # this is the augmentation configuration we will use for training
057: train_datagen = ImageDataGenerator(
058:     rescale=1. / 255,
059:     shear_range=0.2,
060:     zoom_range=0.2,
061:     horizontal_flip=True)
062:
063: # this is the augmentation configuration we will use for testing:
064: # only rescaling
065: test_datagen = ImageDataGenerator(rescale=1. / 255)
066:
067: train_generator = train_datagen.flow_from_directory(
068:     train_data_dir,
069:     target_size=(img_width, img_height),
070:     batch_size=batch_size,
071:     class_mode='categorical')
072:
073: validation_generator = test_datagen.flow_from_directory(
074:     validation_data_dir,
075:     target_size=(img_width, img_height),
076:     batch_size=batch_size,
077:     class_mode='categorical')
078:
```

```
079: # print the number of training samples
080: print(len(train_generator.filenames))
081:
082: # print the category/class labal map
083: print(train_generator.class_indices)
084:
085: # print the number of classes
086: print(len(train_generator.class_indices))
087:
088: # the number of classes/categories
089: num_classes = len(train_generator.class_indices)
090:
091: # save the class indices for use in the predictions
092: np.save('class_indices.npy', train_generator.class_indices)
093:
094: # calculate the training steps
095: nb_train_samples = len(train_generator.filenames)
096: train_steps = int(math.ceil(nb_train_samples / batch_size))
097:
098: # calculate the validation steps
099: nb_validation_samples = len(validation_generator.filenames)
100: validation_steps = int(math.ceil(nb_validation_samples / batch_size))
101:
102:
103: # create the base pre-trained model
104: base_model = VGG16(weights='imagenet', include_top=False, input_
tensor=Input(shape=(img_width, img_height, 3)))
105:
106: # add a global spatial average pooling layer
107: x = base_model.output
108: x = GlobalAveragePooling2D()(x)
109: x = Dense(512, activation='relu')(x)
110: predictions = Dense(num_classes, activation='softmax')(x)
111:
112: # this is the model we will train
```

```
113: model = Model(inputs=base_model.input, outputs=predictions)
114:
115: # first: train only the top layers (which were randomly initialized)
116: # i.e. freeze all convolutional layers
117: for layer in base_model.layers:
118:     layer.trainable = False
119:
120: # compile the model (should be done *after* setting layers to non-
trainable)
121: model.compile(optimizer='rmsprop', loss='categorical_crossentropy',
metrics=['accuracy'])
122:
123: history = model.fit(
124:     train_generator,
125:     steps_per_epoch=train_steps,
126:     epochs=epochs,
127:     validation_data=validation_generator,
128:     validation_steps=validation_steps,
129:     max_queue_size=10,
130:     workers=8
131:     )
132:
133: model.save('bird_classify_fine-tune_step_1.h5')
134:
135: (eval_loss, eval_accuracy) = model.evaluate(
136:     validation_generator, steps=validation_steps)
137:
138: print("\n")
139:
140: print("[INFO] accuracy: {:.2f}%".format(eval_accuracy * 100))
141: print("[INFO] Loss: {}".format(eval_loss))
```

Once we have the trained model, we will define the parameters for the fine-tuning, as well as resetting our data generators so that we can reuse them. We are setting the number of epochs to fine-tune as 25:

```
144: # Run Fine-tuning on our model
145:
146: # number of epochs to fine-tune
147: ft_epochs = 25
148:
149: # reset our data generators
150: train_generator.reset()
151: validation_generator.reset()
152:
153: # let's visualize layer names and layer indices to see how many layers
154: # we should freeze:
155: for i, layer in enumerate(base_model.layers):
156:     print(i, layer.name)
```

We will then un-freeze the layers from the last convolutional block of the base model to the classification layers. All other layers in the base model will remain frozen:

```
158: # we chose to train the last convolution block from the base model
159: for layer in model.layers[:15]:
160:     layer.trainable = False
161: for layer in model.layers[15:]:
162:     layer.trainable = True
```

We then recompile the model, to make the modifications take effect, as well as define the SGD optimizer with the low learning rate:

```
164: # we need to recompile the model for these modifications to take
effect
165: # we use SGD with a low learning rate
166: model.compile(
167:     optimizer=optimizers.SGD(lr=0.0001, momentum=0.9),
168:     loss='categorical_crossentropy',
169:     metrics=['acc']
170:     )
```

Finally, we run the training, evaluating, and graphing the training history:

```
172: history = model.fit(
173:     train_generator,
174:     steps_per_epoch=train_steps,
175:     epochs=ft_epochs,
176:     validation_data=validation_generator,
177:     validation_steps=validation_steps,
178:     max_queue_size=10,
179:     workers=8
180:     )
181:
182: model.save('bird_classify_finetune.h5')
183:
184: (eval_loss, eval_accuracy) = model.evaluate(
185:     validation_generator, steps=validation_steps)
186:
187: print("\n")
188:
189: print("[INFO] accuracy: {:.2f}%".format(eval_accuracy * 100))
190: print("[INFO] Loss: {}".format(eval_loss))
191:
192: # visualize the training history
193: graph_training_history(history)
```

Here, we are saving the final trained and fine-tuned model as `bird_classify_finetune.h5`. Keep this file, along with the `class_indices.npy` file we saved earlier in the code, as they will be needed for the later sections.

Let us see how our fine-tuned model performs: our accuracy has increased to 98% (Figure 7-12).

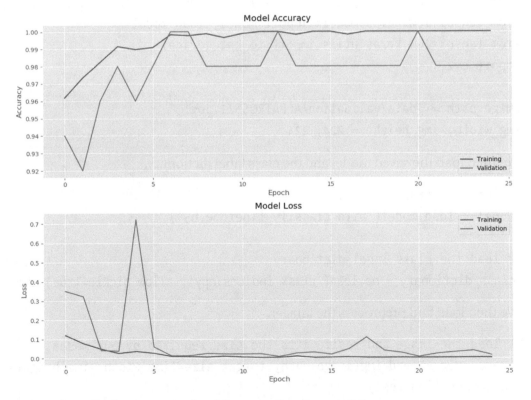

Figure 7-12. *The accuracy of the fine-tuned model*

The graph for the fine-tuning looks good also (Figure 7-13).

Figure 7-13. *The history graph of fine-tuning the model*

With 98% accuracy, we have achieved nearly the limit of what we can do with a tiny dataset.

Making Predictions Using Our Models

We now have a trained model with an excellent accuracy. Now we should look at how we can use it to make predictions and classify images.

Recall that in our fine-tuning code we saved 2 files from the code: the class label dictionary and the trained model file. We can now use those 2 files to rebuild the entire trained model without having to redefine the model structure.

Let us start a new code file. We will name it bird_classify_predict.py.

We will first import the necessary packages and define the path to the test image, as well as the image size parameters:

```
1: import numpy as np
2: import tensorflow as tf
3: from tensorflow.keras.preprocessing.image import img_to_array, load_img
4: from tensorflow.keras.models import Model, load_model
5: from tensorflow.keras.utils import to_categorical
6: import cv2
7:
8: image_path = 'data/validation/ALBATROSS/1.jpg'
9: img_width, img_height = 224, 224
```

We then load the saved model and the class label dictionary.

```
11: # load the trained model
12: model = load_model('bird_classify_finetune.h5')
13:
14: # load the class label dictionary
15: class_dictionary = np.load('class_indices.npy', allow_pickle=True).item()
```

We then load and preprocess the image:

```
17: # load the image and resize itto the size required by our model
18: image_orig = load_img(image_path, target_size=(img_width, img_height),
interpolation='lanczos')
```

```
19: image = img_to_array(image_orig)
20:
21: # important! otherwise the predictions will be '0'
22: image = image / 255.0
23:
24: # add a new axis to make the image array confirm with
25: # the (samples, height, width, depth) structure
26: image = np.expand_dims(image, axis=0)
```

Then, we run the preprocessed image data through the loaded model, decode the predictions, and print the predicted class as well as the confidence to the console:

```
28: # get the probabilities for the prediction
29: probabilities = model.predict(image)
30:
31: # decode the prediction
32: prediction_probability = probabilities[0, probabilities.argmax(axis=1)]
[0]
33: class_predicted = np.argmax(probabilities, axis=1)
34: inID = class_predicted[0]
35:
36: # invert the class dictionary in order to get the label for the id
37: inv_map = {v: k for k, v in class_dictionary.items()}
38: label = inv_map[inID]
39:
40: print("[Info] Predicted: {}, Confidence: {:.5f}%".format(label,
prediction_probability*100))
```

Finally, we use OpenCV to load and display the image, with the label and confidence overlaid on top of it:

```
42: # display the image and the prediction using OpenCV
43: image_cv = cv2.imread(image_path)
44: image_cv = cv2.resize(image_cv, (600, 600), interpolation=cv2.INTER_
LINEAR)
45:
46: cv2.putText(image_cv,
```

```
47:                "Predicted: {}".format(label),
48:                (20, 40), cv2.FONT_HERSHEY_DUPLEX, 1, (0, 0, 255), 2, cv2.
LINE_AA)
49: cv2.putText(image_cv,
50:                "Confidence: {:.5f}%".format(prediction_probability*100),
51:                (20, 80), cv2.FONT_HERSHEY_DUPLEX, 1, (0, 0, 255), 2, cv2.
LINE_AA)
52:
53: cv2.imshow("Prediction", image_cv)
54: cv2.waitKey(0)
55:
56: cv2.destroyAllWindows()
```

Running the prediction code, we would get a result like this (Figure 7-14). As expected, based on the validation accuracy we got, the confidence for the prediction is 99+%.

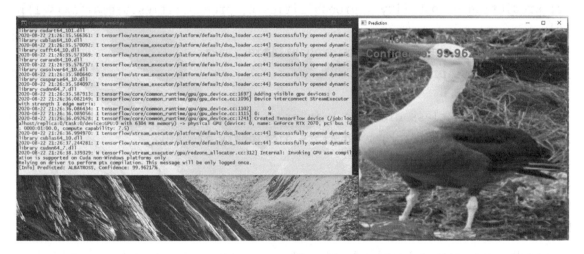

Figure 7-14. *Model prediction and confidence for an image of an albatross*

Following are few more examples of the results (Figures 7-15 and 7-16).

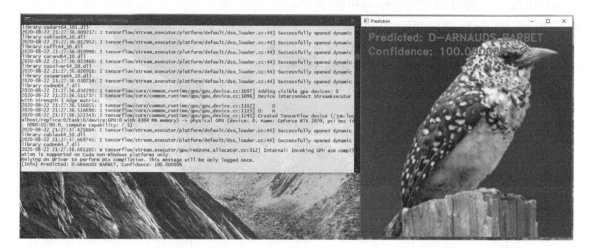

Figure 7-15. *Model prediction and confidence for an image of a d-arnauds barbet*

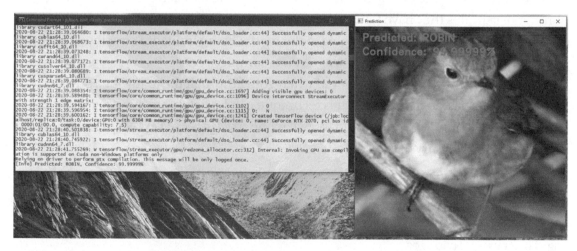

Figure 7-16. *Model prediction and confidence for an image of a robin*

Trying out a Deeper Model: InceptionV3

So far, we have only attempted to run our training on the 10 classes we have selected from the full bird image dataset at the start of the chapter.

What if we need to attempt to build a model for 50, 100, or the full 225 classes of the dataset?

All the transfer learning techniques we have learned here—bottleneck features, finetuning—as well as data augmentation can be applied to a larger set of classes as well.

So far, we have only attempted them with the VGG16 model. When working with larger sets of classes and larger datasets, it is better to try out different pretrained models as the base to find the most optimal model structure.

Here, we will look at how we can apply the same concepts with the InceptionV3 ImageNet model.

Along with using the InceptionV3 model, we will see how we can mitigate the data imbalance of our selected dataset as well.

If you recall, when we selected the 10 classes from the full dataset, we selected them in a way that some of the classes we selected have higher number of samples than others. This is a common problem with real-world datasets that we get to deal with.

When there are large discrepancies in the number of samples presented to a model, it may get more familiar with the features of the classes with the higher number of samples and may undermine the features of less represented classes.

One way to mitigate this by calculating a weight value for each class based on the number of samples they have (giving higher weights to classes with less number of samples) and pass that weight mapping to the model being trained. This allows to model to properly learn features of the classes with less samples.

We will see how this can be achieved when going through the following code for InceptionV3. But keep in mind that this technique can be used with any model.

We will start our new code, which we will name bird_classify_inceptionV3.py, by importing the necessary packages:

```
01: import tensorflow as tf
02: import numpy as np
03: from tensorflow.keras.preprocessing.image import ImageDataGenerator,
img_to_array, load_img
04: from tensorflow.keras.models import Sequential, Model, load_model
05: from tensorflow.keras.layers import Dropout, Flatten, Dense,
GlobalAveragePooling2D, Input
06: from tensorflow.keras.applications.inception_v3 import InceptionV3
07: from tensorflow.keras import optimizers
08: from tensorflow.keras.optimizers import SGD
09: import matplotlib.pyplot as plt
10: import math
```

```
11: import os
12: import os.path
```

Here, we have imported the InceptionV3 model from the built-in models instead of the VGG16 model we used earlier.

We will define our usual utility function to graph the training history:

```
14: # utility functions
15: def graph_training_history(history):
16:     plt.rcParams["figure.figsize"] = (12, 9)
17:
18:     plt.style.use('ggplot')
19:
20:     plt.figure(1)
21:
22:     # summarize history for accuracy
23:
24:     plt.subplot(211)
25:     plt.plot(history.history['accuracy'])
26:     plt.plot(history.history['val_accuracy'])
27:     plt.title('Model Accuracy')
28:     plt.ylabel('Accuracy')
29:     plt.xlabel('Epoch')
30:     plt.legend(['Training', 'Validation'], loc='lower right')
31:
32:     # summarize history for loss
33:
34:     plt.subplot(212)
35:     plt.plot(history.history['loss'])
36:     plt.plot(history.history['val_loss'])
37:     plt.title('Model Loss')
38:     plt.ylabel('Loss')
39:     plt.xlabel('Epoch')
40:     plt.legend(['Training', 'Validation'], loc='upper right')
41:
```

```
42:     plt.tight_layout()
43:
44:     plt.show()
```

We will then define a new utility function to calculate the class weights:

```
46: # util function to calculate the class weights based on the number of
samples on each class
47: # this is useful with datasets that are higly skewed (datasets where
48: # the number of samples in each class differs vastly)
49: def get_class_weights(class_data_dir):
50:     labels_count = dict()
51:     for img_class in [ic for ic in os.listdir(class_data_dir) if ic[0]
!= '.']:
52:         labels_count[img_class] = len(os.listdir(os.path.join(class_
data_dir, img_class)))
53:     total_count = sum(labels_count.values())
54:     class_weights = {cls: total_count / count for cls, count in
55:                         enumerate(labels_count.values())}
56:     return class_weights
```

When called, this function will return a mapping of class weights that looks like the following (Figure 7-17):

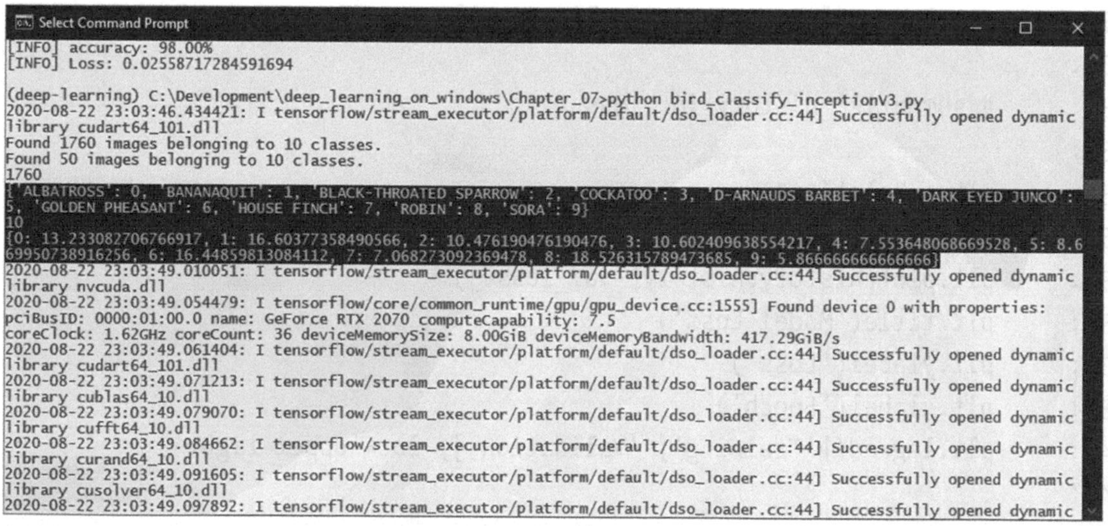

Figure 7-17. *The calculated class weights*

We then define our training parameters and generators, as before:

```
058: # dimensions of our images.
059: img_width, img_height = 224, 224
060:
061: train_data_dir = 'data/train'
062: validation_data_dir = 'data/validation'
063:
064: # number of epochs to train
065: epochs = 50
066:
067: # batch size used by flow_from_directory
068: batch_size = 16
069:
070: # this is the augmentation configuration we will use for training
071: train_datagen = ImageDataGenerator(
072:     rescale=1. / 255,
073:     shear_range=0.2,
074:     zoom_range=0.2,
075:     horizontal_flip=True)
076:
077: # this is the augmentation configuration we will use for testing:
078: # only rescaling
079: test_datagen = ImageDataGenerator(rescale=1. / 255)
080:
081: train_generator = train_datagen.flow_from_directory(
082:     train_data_dir,
083:     target_size=(img_width, img_height),
084:     batch_size=batch_size,
085:     class_mode='categorical')
086:
087: validation_generator = test_datagen.flow_from_directory(
088:     validation_data_dir,
089:     target_size=(img_width, img_height),
090:     batch_size=batch_size,
091:     class_mode='categorical')
```

```
092:
093: # print the number of training samples
094: print(len(train_generator.filenames))
095:
096: # print the category/class labal map
097: print(train_generator.class_indices)
098:
099: # print the number of classes
100: print(len(train_generator.class_indices))
101:
102: # the number of classes/categories
103: num_classes = len(train_generator.class_indices)
104:
105: # calculate the training steps
106: nb_train_samples = len(train_generator.filenames)
107: train_steps = int(math.ceil(nb_train_samples / batch_size))
108:
109: # calculate the validation steps
110: nb_validation_samples = len(validation_generator.filenames)
111: validation_steps = int(math.ceil(nb_validation_samples / batch_size))
```

We load the class weights using the function defined earlier by passing the path to the training directory:

```
113: # get the class weights
114: class_weights = get_class_weights(train_data_dir)
115: print(class_weights)
```

When creating the base model, we will be using InceptionV3 instead of VGG16:

```
118: # create the base pre-trained model
119: base_model = InceptionV3(weights='imagenet', include_top=False, input_
tensor=Input(shape=(img_width, img_height, 3)))
```

The code for defining the top model and compilation remains unchanged:

```
121: # add a global spatial average pooling layer
122: x = base_model.output
```

```
123: x = GlobalAveragePooling2D()(x)
124: x = Dense(512, activation='relu')(x)
125: predictions = Dense(num_classes, activation='softmax')(x)
126:
127: # this is the model we will train
128: model = Model(inputs=base_model.input, outputs=predictions)
129:
130: # first: train only the top layers (which were randomly initialized)
131: # i.e. freeze all convolutional layers
132: for layer in base_model.layers:
133:     layer.trainable = False
134:
135: # compile the model (should be done *after* setting layers to non-trainable)
136: model.compile(optimizer='rmsprop', loss='categorical_crossentropy',
metrics=['accuracy'])
```

At the model training step, we pass the class weights calculated earlier into the class_weight parameter of the model.fit() function:

```
138: history = model.fit(
139:     train_generator,
140:     steps_per_epoch=train_steps,
141:     epochs=epochs,
142:     validation_data=validation_generator,
143:     validation_steps=validation_steps,
144:     class_weight=class_weights
145:     )
```

As before, the trained model is saved and evaluated, and the fine-tuning step begins:

```
147: model.save('bird_classify_fine-tune_IV3_S1.h5')
148:
149: (eval_loss, eval_accuracy) = model.evaluate(
150:     validation_generator, steps=validation_steps)
151:
152: print("\n")
```

```
153:
154: print("[INFO] accuracy: {:.2f}%".format(eval_accuracy * 100))
155: print("[INFO] Loss: {}".format(eval_loss))
156:
157:
158: # Run Fine-tuning on our model
159:
160: # number of epochs to fine-tune
161: ft_epochs = 25
162:
163: # reset our data generators
164: train_generator.reset()
165: validation_generator.reset()
166:
167: # let's visualize layer names and layer indices to see how many layers
168: # we should freeze:
169: for i, layer in enumerate(base_model.layers):
170:     print(i, layer.name)
```

When fine-tuning InceptionV3, the number of layers to freeze is different than VGG16. We will be freezing up to the 249th layer instead of the 15th layer:

```
172: # we chose to train the last convolution block from the base model
173: for layer in model.layers[:249]:
174:     layer.trainable = False
175: for layer in model.layers[249:]:
176:     layer.trainable = True
```

The model is then recompiled, trained and fine-tuned, evaluated, and saved. Here also the class weights are passed to model.fit():

```
178: # we need to recompile the model for these modifications to take
effect
179: # we use SGD with a low learning rate
180: model.compile(
181:     optimizer=optimizers.SGD(lr=0.0001, momentum=0.9),
182:     loss='categorical_crossentropy',
```

```
183:      metrics=['accuracy']
184:      )
185:
186: history = model.fit(
187:      train_generator,
188:      steps_per_epoch=train_steps,
189:      epochs=ft_epochs,
190:      validation_data=validation_generator,
191:      validation_steps=validation_steps,
192:      class_weight=class_weights
193:      )
194:
195: model.save('bird_classify_finetune_IV3_final.h5')
196:
197: (eval_loss, eval_accuracy) = model.evaluate(
198:      validation_generator, steps=validation_steps)
199:
200: print("\n")
201:
202: print("[INFO] accuracy: {:.2f}%".format(eval_accuracy * 100))
203: print("[INFO] Loss: {}".format(eval_loss))
204:
205: # visualize the training history
206: graph_training_history(history)
```

If we run this for the same 10 classes as before, we will see nearly similar results as before (Figure 7-18 and 7-19).

```
Command Prompt - python bird_classify_inceptionV3.py                                    □    ×
eneratorDataset iterator: Cancelled: Operation was cancelled
110/110 [==============================] - 9s 84ms/step - loss: 0.0401 - accuracy: 0.9989 - val_loss: 0.4272 - val_accur
acy: 0.9800
Epoch 23/25
2020-08-22 23:01:13.806231: W tensorflow/core/kernels/data/generator_dataset_op.cc:103] Error occurred when finalizing G
eneratorDataset iterator: Cancelled: Operation was cancelled
110/110 [==============================] - 9s 84ms/step - loss: 0.0515 - accuracy: 0.9977 - val_loss: 0.2017 - val_accur
acy: 1.0000
Epoch 24/25
2020-08-22 23:01:22.999282: W tensorflow/core/kernels/data/generator_dataset_op.cc:103] Error occurred when finalizing G
eneratorDataset iterator: Cancelled: Operation was cancelled
110/110 [==============================] - 9s 84ms/step - loss: 0.0445 - accuracy: 0.9994 - val_loss: 0.3207 - val_accur
acy: 1.0000
Epoch 25/25
2020-08-22 23:01:32.193648: W tensorflow/core/kernels/data/generator_dataset_op.cc:103] Error occurred when finalizing G
eneratorDataset iterator: Cancelled: Operation was cancelled
110/110 [==============================] - 9s 83ms/step - loss: 0.1447 - accuracy: 0.9949 - val_loss: 0.3578 - val_accur
acy: 0.9800
2020-08-22 23:01:41.343898: W tensorflow/core/kernels/data/generator_dataset_op.cc:103] Error occurred when finalizing G
eneratorDataset iterator: Cancelled: Operation was cancelled
WARNING:tensorflow:sample_weight modes were coerced from
  ...
    to
  ['...']
4/4 [==============================] - 1s 294ms/step - loss: 0.0256 - accuracy: 0.9800

[INFO] accuracy: 98.00%
[INFO] Loss: 0.02558717284591694
```

Figure 7-18. *The accuracy of the fine-tuned InceptionV3 model*

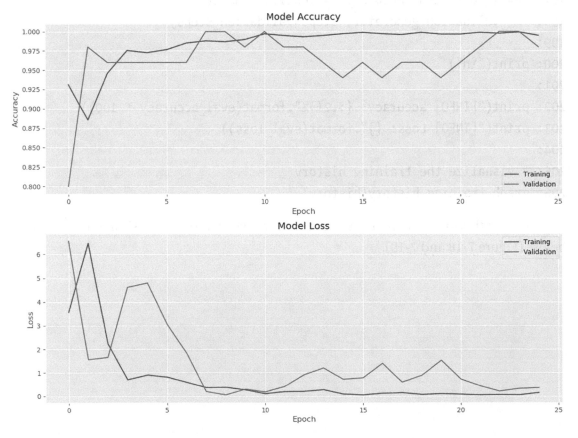

Figure 7-19. *The training history graph of the fine-tuned InceptionV3 model*

However, you will start to see the improvements when you apply this model to larger number of classes or larger datasets.

You can now try applying this to the full 225 Bird Species dataset.

## CHAPTER 8

Starting, Stopping, and Resuming Learning

As you have probably learned by now, training deep learning models can take long times: hours and maybe days, based on how complex the model and how large your dataset.

Sometimes it may not be practical to perform the training in one session.

Power failures, machine becoming unresponsive, OS errors, unplanned reboots, or Windows updates may lead you to lose hours if not days of effort.

How can we mitigate that risk?

One way is to increase the speed of the model training.

Using Multithreading to Increase the Training Speed

When we used the data generators with the model.fit() function for training, by default we were working on a single-threaded mode for the preparation of the data batches. Basically, in this mode, only a single CPU thread is preparing and queuing the batches of data to be sent to the model for training. By default the queue size is set to 10, which may result in the GPU having to wait for more batches to be queued.

While this single-threaded batch preparation mode provides more predictable behavior and is easier to debug, most of the time it slows down the training process.

This is why the model.fit() functions support a multithreaded mode. We can enable it by using the workers parameter to specify the number of worker threads to use, as well as increasing the max_queue_size parameters to increase the number of batches that are queued.

Let us see how much of a speed increase we can achieve by tweaking these parameters.

© Thimira Amaratunga 2021
T. Amaratunga, *Deep Learning on Windows*, https://doi.org/10.1007/978-1-4842-6431-7_8

We'll begin with our bird classification system using the InceptionV3 model from the last chapter, and add few code lines to measure the time taken for training. We will import the time package for this:

```
13: import time
```

We will mark the start time at the beginning of the script just after we defined the utility functions:

```
59: # start time of the script
60: start_time = time.time()
61:
62: # dimensions of our images.
63: img_width, img_height = 224, 224
64:
65: train_data_dir = 'data/train'
66: validation_data_dir = 'data/validation'
67:
```

At the very end of the script we will mark the end time, and calculate the time it took for the training:

```
209: end_time = time.time()
210:
211: training_duration = end_time - start_time
212: print("[INFO] Total Time for training: {} seconds".format(training_
duration))
```

Let us see how much time it takes to run the training (both with bottleneck features and fine-tuning) on our InceptionV3 model in the single-threaded batch mode (Figure 8-1).

```
Command Prompt                                                            —   □   ×
Epoch 20/25
110/110 [==============================] - 15s 133ms/step - loss: 0.0047 - accuracy: 1.0000 - val_loss: 0.3148 - val_acc
uracy: 0.9800
Epoch 21/25
110/110 [==============================] - 14s 131ms/step - loss: 0.0115 - accuracy: 0.9989 - val_loss: 0.1724 - val_acc
uracy: 1.0000
Epoch 22/25
110/110 [==============================] - 15s 133ms/step - loss: 0.0490 - accuracy: 0.9983 - val_loss: 0.2161 - val_acc
uracy: 0.9800
Epoch 23/25
110/110 [==============================] - 15s 132ms/step - loss: 0.0295 - accuracy: 0.9983 - val_loss: 0.4686 - val_acc
uracy: 0.9800
Epoch 24/25
110/110 [==============================] - 15s 132ms/step - loss: 0.0087 - accuracy: 0.9994 - val_loss: 0.5341 - val_acc
uracy: 0.9800
Epoch 25/25
110/110 [==============================] - 14s 130ms/step - loss: 0.0117 - accuracy: 0.9994 - val_loss: 0.6702 - val_acc
uracy: 0.9800
WARNING:tensorflow:sample_weight modes were coerced from
  ...
  to
  ['...']
4/4 [==========================] - 1s 284ms/step - loss: 0.0362 - accuracy: 0.9800

[INFO] accuracy: 98.00%
[INFO] Loss: 0.03617729049046048
[INFO] Total Time for training: 1101.4000144004822 seconds

(deep-learning) C:\Development\deep_learning_on_windows\Chapter_08>
```

Figure 8-1. *Time taken for training in single-threaded batch mode*

It is taking around 1,101 seconds (or 18 minutes 21 seconds) for the full training.

Now let us see whether we can improve it using multithreading.

For both of our model.fit() functions, we will add two more parameters: workers and max_queue_size:

```
142: history = model.fit(
143:     train_generator,
144:     steps_per_epoch=train_steps,
145:     epochs=epochs,
146:     validation_data=validation_generator,
147:     validation_steps=validation_steps,
148:     class_weight=class_weights,
149:     max_queue_size=15,
150:     workers=8
151:     )
...
...
192: history = model.fit(
193:     train_generator,
194:     steps_per_epoch=train_steps,
195:     epochs=ft_epochs,
```

```
196:        validation_data=validation_generator,
197:        validation_steps=validation_steps,
198:        class_weight=class_weights,
199:        max_queue_size=15,
200:        workers=8
201:    )
```

The workers parameter defines how many CPU threads are working in parallel to generate the data batches. The default is 1, so here we have increased it to 8.

The max_queue_size parameters defines how many batches are kept ready in the queue until consumed by the training. The default is 10, and here we have increased it to 15.

Let us see how these parameter values affect our training time (Figure 8-2).

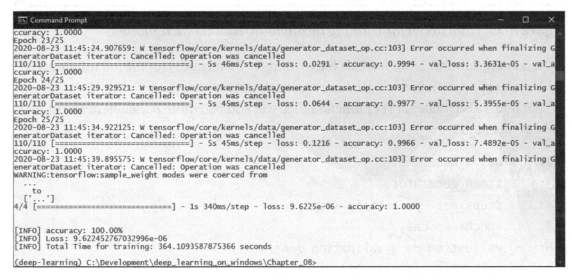

Figure 8-2. *Time taken for training in multithreaded batch mode*

The training time is now decreased to 364 seconds, or just over 6 minutes and 3 seconds. That is about a 300% improvement in the training time.

However, there are few things that you should keep in mind when using this method.

First, the actual increase in speed you will get will depend on the model structure, as well as the dataset you are using.

Secondly, when allocating the number of workers, you should think about the number of threads your CPU supports in parallel. Setting the number of workers to a value too high might lock up or freeze your machine. A good rule of thumb to follow on Windows is to set the number of workers few numbers below the maximum thread count of the CPU. For example, if your CPU supports 12 threads, keep the number of workers at 8. This would allow the OS, background tasks, and the other tasks of the training to run without locking up.

And lastly, in rare situations, you may experience nonstandard behaviors in training. This can be either due to bugs in the version you are using, or in the Windows build of that version. If you are experiencing problems, try disabling the multithreading first before changing anything else in the model.

Note   In some Windows builds of TensorFlow 2.x you may experience an error message such as "tensorflow/core/kernels/data/generator_dataset_op.cc:103] Error occurred when finalizing GeneratorDataset iterator: Cancelled: Operation was cancelled" when running training with multithreading (Figure 8-3). This can be safely ignored and will hopefully be fixed in future builds.

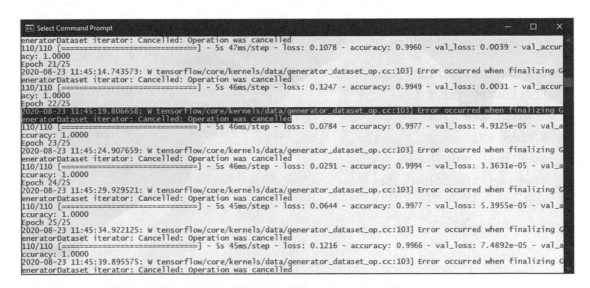

Figure 8-3. *Error message with multithreading*

Using Model Checkpoints

Looking back at our original problem—mitigating potential interruptions to the training—we can see that speeding up the training process solves only part of the problem. Even with the speed-up provided by multithreading, interruptions can still happen and you may lose your progress.

This is where the concept of model checkpoints comes in: saving the state of your model at certain points in the training process so that you can resume or recover the model as at that point later.

We talked about how to save the entire model, including its weights, compilation, and optimizer status, to a file using the `model.save()` function.

Model checkpoints works with the same principle.

But rather than having to save the model manually, you can ask the TensorFlow/Keras framework to save them for you.

In TensorFlow/Keras, the training process supports callback functions. Callbacks allow you to execute functions at certain stages in the training. There are several built-in callbacks in TensorFlow/Keras, while also allowing you to define custom callbacks.

One of these built-in callbacks is ModelCheckpoint.

The ModelCheckpoint callback class allows you to automatically save your model being trained at a given frequency or after a given condition. For example, you can tell ModelCheckpoint to save the model after each training epoch, or after every 5 epochs, or save only if the validation accuracy increases, and so on.

The parameters of ModelCheckpoint are as follows:

```
tensorflow.keras.callbacks.ModelCheckpoint(
    checkpoint_filepath,
    monitor="val_loss",
    verbose=0,
    save_best_only=False,
    save_weights_only=False,
    mode="auto",
    save_freq="epoch"
)
```

- **checkpoint_filepath:** the file path to save the checkpoint. This can take some parameters from the training epoch as formatting options, so that you can inject those values into the filename. We will discuss these options later.

- **monitor:** what training parameter to monitor if save_best_only is set to true.

- **verbose:** the verbosity level, 0 or 1.

- **save_best_only:** whether to only save the checkpoint if the parameter being monitored (specified by the monitor parameter) improves.

- **save_weights_only:** whether to just save the weights (similar to `model.save_weights()`), or the entire model (similar to `model.save()`).

- **mode:** how to monitor the improvement in the parameter being monitored. For example, if monitor is val_acc the mode should be max; if it is val_loss, the mode should be min. If the mode is set to auto, it will try to derive the mode using the name of the parameter being monitored.

- **save_freq:** at what point the checkpoint should be saved. If set to epoch, the checkpoint would be saved after each epoch. If set to a number, the checkpoint would be saved every time that many epochs pass.

Note   On TensorFlow v2.1 or before, use the period parameter instead of save_freq.

Let us add model checkpoints to our bird classification model. We will add a new directory, checkpoints/training, to save the checkpoints. (And potentially a checkpoints/finetune directory, to save the checkpoints in fine-tuning).

We will get a copy of our InceptionV3 fine-tuning code like before, and name it `bird_classify_inceptionV3_checkpoint.py`. We will add the import to the ModelCheckpoint callback in it. We will also make a change to the `model.compile()` call, from `metrics=['accuracy']` to `metrics=['acc']`. This is important to align with some naming conventions that we will be using with ModelCheckpoints:

```
9: from tensorflow.keras.callbacks import ModelCheckpoint
...
...
136: model.compile(optimizer='rmsprop', loss='categorical_crossentropy',
metrics=['acc'])
137:
138: training_checkpoint_dir = 'checkpoints/training'
```

```
139:
140: filepath = training_checkpoint_dir + "/model-{epoch:02d}-{val_
acc:.2f}-{val_loss:.2f}.h5"
141: checkpoint = ModelCheckpoint(
142:                                 filepath,
143:                                 verbose=1,
144:                                 save_best_only=False,
145:                                 save_weights_only=False,
146:                                 save_freq="epoch"
147:                                 )
148:
149: callbacks_list = [checkpoint]
150:
151: history = model.fit(
152:     train_generator,
153:     steps_per_epoch=train_steps,
154:     epochs=epochs,
155:     validation_data=validation_generator,
156:     validation_steps=validation_steps,
157:     class_weight=class_weights,
158:     max_queue_size=15,
159:     workers=8,
160:     callbacks=callbacks_list
161:     )
```

Note   When specifying `metrics=['accuracy']`, the accuracy metrices
will be reported as accuracy and val_accuracy. When specifying them as
`metrics=['acc']` they will be reported as acc and val_acc, which is the naming
convention expected by many of the callback functions. Make sure you also update
the `graph_training_history()` function to update all references of accuracy
to acc, and val_accuracy to val_acc. If not updated, you may receive errors such as
"KeyError: 'acc.'"

Here, we have specified the checkpoint to be saved at each epoch. We are not monitoring any parameters.

Since we have specified the file name pattern as model-{epoch:02d}-{val_acc:.2f}-{val_loss:.2f}.h5, the epoch number, validation accuracy values, and validation loss values will be injected into the file name being saved (Figure 8-4). For example, the filename model-01-0.80-12.06.h5 would indicate that the epoch was 01, validation accuracy was 0.80, and validation loss was 12.06. These values allow you to easily select the best checkpoints just by checking the file name.

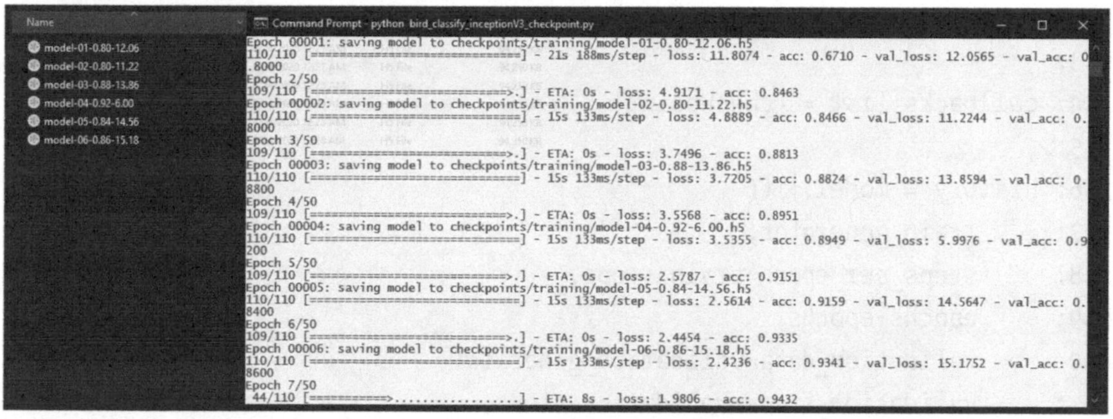

Figure 8-4. *Model checkpoints being saved at each epoch*

While there may be situations where you would need to save every training epoch (such as when training generative adversarial networks, where we cannot rely on the accuracy metrics directly to identify model improvements), in most cases, it is best to only save the checkpoint if the training improves.

Let us now update our code to only save the checkpoints when the validation loss improves (when validation loss minimizes):

```
9: from tensorflow.keras.callbacks import ModelCheckpoint
...
...
130: model.compile(optimizer='rmsprop', loss='categorical_crossentropy',
metrics=['acc'])
131:
132: training_checkpoint_dir = 'checkpoints/training'
133:
```

```
134: filepath = training_checkpoint_dir + "/model-{epoch:02d}-{val_
acc:.2f}-{val_loss:.2f}.h5"
135: checkpoint = ModelCheckpoint(
136:                                   filepath,
137:                                   monitor="val_loss",
138:                                   verbose=1,
139:                                   save_best_only=True,
140:                                   save_weights_only=False,
141:                                   mode="min"
142:                                   )
143:
144: callbacks_list = [checkpoint]
145:
146: history = model.fit(
147:      train_generator,
148:      steps_per_epoch=train_steps,
149:      epochs=epochs,
150:      validation_data=validation_generator,
151:      validation_steps=validation_steps,
152:      class_weight=class_weights,
153:      callbacks=callbacks_list
154:      )
```

Here, we are setting the save_best_only parameter to True, and setting the monitor to val_loss and the mode to min to only save the checkpoint if validation loss gets lower than the previous epoch (Figure 8-5).

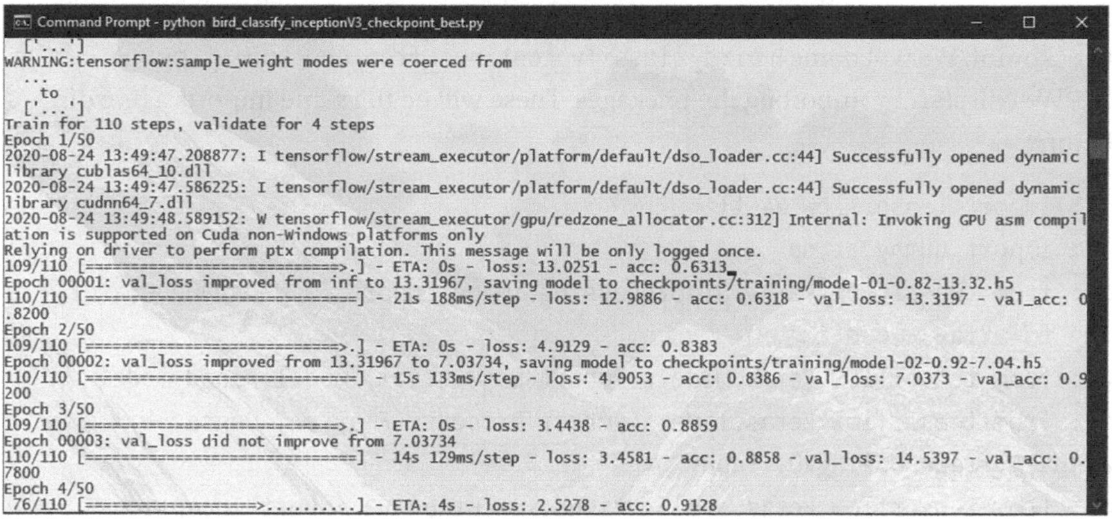

```
[ Command Prompt - python bird_classify_inceptionV3_checkpoint_best.py                    —   □   ×
 ['...']
WARNING:tensorflow:sample_weight modes were coerced from
 ...
   to
 ['...']
Train for 110 steps, validate for 4 steps
Epoch 1/50
2020-08-24 13:49:47.208877: I tensorflow/stream_executor/platform/default/dso_loader.cc:44] Successfully opened dynamic
library cublas64_10.dll
2020-08-24 13:49:47.586225: I tensorflow/stream_executor/platform/default/dso_loader.cc:44] Successfully opened dynamic
library cudnn64_7.dll
2020-08-24 13:49:48.589152: W tensorflow/stream_executor/gpu/redzone_allocator.cc:312] Internal: Invoking GPU asm compil
ation is supported on Cuda non-Windows platforms only
Relying on driver to perform ptx compilation. This message will be only logged once.
109/110 [===========================>.] - ETA: 0s - loss: 13.0251 - acc: 0.6313
Epoch 00001: val_loss improved from inf to 13.31967, saving model to checkpoints/training/model-01-0.82-13.32.h5
110/110 [============================] - 21s 188ms/step - loss: 12.9886 - acc: 0.6318 - val_loss: 13.3197 - val_acc: 0
.8200
Epoch 2/50
109/110 [===========================>.] - ETA: 0s - loss: 4.9129 - acc: 0.8383
Epoch 00002: val_loss improved from 13.31967 to 7.03734, saving model to checkpoints/training/model-02-0.92-7.04.h5
110/110 [============================] - 15s 133ms/step - loss: 4.9053 - acc: 0.8386 - val_loss: 7.0373 - val_acc: 0.9
200
Epoch 3/50
109/110 [===========================>.] - ETA: 0s - loss: 3.4438 - acc: 0.8859
Epoch 00003: val_loss did not improve from 7.03734
110/110 [============================] - 14s 129ms/step - loss: 3.4581 - acc: 0.8858 - val_loss: 14.5397 - val_acc: 0.
7800
Epoch 4/50
 76/110 [===================>..........] - ETA: 4s - loss: 2.5278 - acc: 0.9128
```

Figure 8-5. *Saving only the best checkpoints*

This will reduce the number of checkpoint files being saved, making it easier to pick out the best states of the model.

Based on the requirement of your model, you can do the same for any of the other matrices of the model: acc, loss, val_acc, val_loss.

Now let us imagine that your model training was interrupted, but you have some model checkpoints saved. How can you restart your training from one of those checkpoints?

As an example, let us say that we have the following checkpoints saved (Figure 8-6) and our training was interrupted sometime after epoch 33.

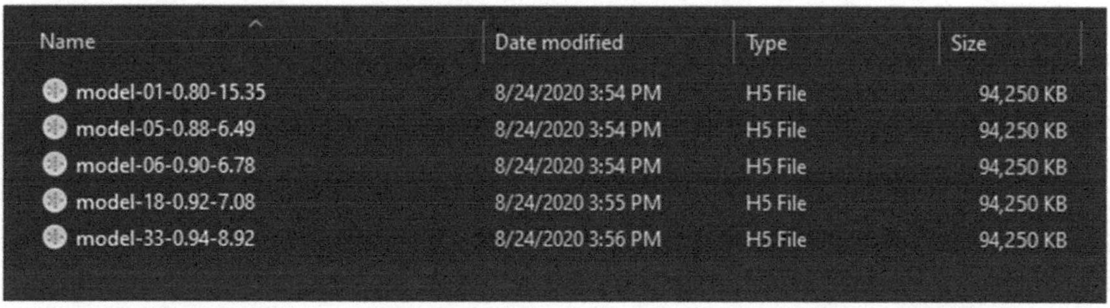

Name	Date modified	Type	Size
model-01-0.80-15.35	8/24/2020 3:54 PM	H5 File	94,250 KB
model-05-0.88-6.49	8/24/2020 3:54 PM	H5 File	94,250 KB
model-06-0.90-6.78	8/24/2020 3:54 PM	H5 File	94,250 KB
model-18-0.92-7.08	8/24/2020 3:55 PM	H5 File	94,250 KB
model-33-0.94-8.92	8/24/2020 3:56 PM	H5 File	94,250 KB

Figure 8-6. *Saved checkpoints*

Let us start a new code file that will allow us to continue the training from a checkpoint. We will name it `bird_classify_continue_from_checkpoint.py`.

We will start by importing the packages. These will be the same imports as we did before:

```
01: import tensorflow as tf
02: import numpy as np
03: from tensorflow.keras.preprocessing.image import ImageDataGenerator,
img_to_array, load_img
04: from tensorflow.keras.models import Sequential, Model, load_model
05: from tensorflow.keras.layers import Dropout, Flatten, Dense,
GlobalAveragePooling2D, Input
06: from tensorflow.keras.applications.inception_v3 import InceptionV3
07: from tensorflow.keras import optimizers
08: from tensorflow.keras.optimizers import SGD
09: from tensorflow.keras.callbacks import ModelCheckpoint
10: import matplotlib.pyplot as plt
11: import math
12: import os
13: import os.path
14: import time
```

We will then define our usual utility functions:

```
16: # utility functions
17: def graph_training_history(history):
18:     plt.rcParams["figure.figsize"] = (12, 9)
19:
20:     plt.style.use('ggplot')
21:
22:     plt.figure(1)
23:
24:     # summarize history for accuracy
25:
26:     plt.subplot(211)
27:     plt.plot(history.history['acc'])
28:     plt.plot(history.history['val_acc'])
```

```
29:     plt.title('Model Accuracy')
30:     plt.ylabel('Accuracy')
31:     plt.xlabel('Epoch')
32:     plt.legend(['Training', 'Validation'], loc='lower right')
33:
34:     # summarize history for loss
35:
36:     plt.subplot(212)
37:     plt.plot(history.history['loss'])
38:     plt.plot(history.history['val_loss'])
39:     plt.title('Model Loss')
40:     plt.ylabel('Loss')
41:     plt.xlabel('Epoch')
42:     plt.legend(['Training', 'Validation'], loc='upper right')
43:
44:     plt.tight_layout()
45:
46:     plt.show()
47:
48: # util function to calculate the class weights based on the number of
samples on each class
49: # this is useful with datasets that are highly skewed (datasets where
50: # the number of samples in each class differs vastly)
51: def get_class_weights(class_data_dir):
52:     labels_count = dict()
53:     for img_class in [ic for ic in os.listdir(class_data_dir) if ic[0]
!= '.']:
54:         labels_count[img_class] = len(os.listdir(os.path.join(class_
data_dir, img_class)))
55:     total_count = sum(labels_count.values())
56:     class_weights = {cls: total_count / count for cls, count in
57:                         enumerate(labels_count.values())}
58:     return class_weights
```

We will then add a new function that will return the epoch number of a given checkpoint:

```
60: # util function to get the initial epoch number from the checkpoint
name
61: def get_init_epoch(checkpoint_path):
62:     filename = os.path.basename(checkpoint_path)
63:     filename = os.path.splitext(filename)[0]
64:     init_epoch = filename.split("-")[1]
65:     return int(init_epoch)
```

Our training parameters will be as same as before:

```
68: # start time of the script
69: start_time = time.time()
70:
71: # dimensions of our images.
72: img_width, img_height = 224, 224
73:
74: train_data_dir = 'data/train'
75: validation_data_dir = 'data/validation'
76:
77: # number of epochs to train
78: epochs = 50
79:
80: # batch size used by flow_from_directory
81: batch_size = 16
```

Then we define the checkpoint to load and get the epoch number of it using the function we defined earlier:

```
83: # the checkpoint to load and continue from
84: checkpoint_to_load = "checkpoints/training/model-33-0.94-8.92.h5"
85: # get the epoch number to continue from
86: init_epoch = get_init_epoch(checkpoint_to_load)
```

Our data generators and parameters will be defined exactly as same as the initial training script:

```
088: # this is the augmentation configuration we will use for training
089: train_datagen = ImageDataGenerator(
090:     rescale=1. / 255,
091:     shear_range=0.2,
092:     zoom_range=0.2,
093:     horizontal_flip=True)
094:
095: # this is the augmentation configuration we will use for testing:
096: # only rescaling
097: test_datagen = ImageDataGenerator(rescale=1. / 255)
098:
099: train_generator = train_datagen.flow_from_directory(
100:     train_data_dir,
101:     target_size=(img_width, img_height),
102:     batch_size=batch_size,
103:     class_mode='categorical')
104:
105: validation_generator = test_datagen.flow_from_directory(
106:     validation_data_dir,
107:     target_size=(img_width, img_height),
108:     batch_size=batch_size,
109:     class_mode='categorical')
110:
111: # the number of classes/categories
112: num_classes = len(train_generator.class_indices)
113:
114: # calculate the training steps
115: nb_train_samples = len(train_generator.filenames)
116: train_steps = int(math.ceil(nb_train_samples / batch_size))
117:
118: # calculate the validation steps
119: nb_validation_samples = len(validation_generator.filenames)
```

```
120: validation_steps = int(math.ceil(nb_validation_samples / batch_size))
121:
122: # get the class weights
123: class_weights = get_class_weights(train_data_dir)
```

Then we use the load_model() function to load the checkpoint. Once loaded it will be our model:

```
125: # load the model state from the checkpoint
126: model = load_model(checkpoint_to_load)
```

The checkpoint definitions will be same as before:

```
128: training_checkpoint_dir = 'checkpoints/training'
129:
130: filepath = training_checkpoint_dir + "/model-{epoch:02d}-
{val_acc:.2f}-{val_loss:.2f}.h5"
131: checkpoint = ModelCheckpoint(
132:                             filepath,
133:                             monitor="val_acc",
134:                             verbose=1,
135:                             save_best_only=True,
136:                             save_weights_only=False,
137:                             mode="max"
138:                             )
139:
140: callbacks_list = [checkpoint]
```

In the model.fit() function we add an additional parameter initial_epoch with the value we derived earlier to specify from which epoch to start the training from:

```
142: history = model.fit(
143:     train_generator,
144:     steps_per_epoch=train_steps,
145:     epochs=epochs,
146:     validation_data=validation_generator,
147:     validation_steps=validation_steps,
148:     class_weight=class_weights,
```

```
149:      initial_epoch=init_epoch,
150:      callbacks=callbacks_list
151:      )
```

The remaining steps of the training will remain same:

```
153: model.save('bird_classify_fine-tune_IV3_S1.h5')
154:
155: (eval_loss, eval_accuracy) = model.evaluate(
156:      validation_generator, steps=validation_steps)
157:
158: print("\n")
159:
160: print("[INFO] accuracy: {:.2f}%".format(eval_accuracy * 100))
161: print("[INFO] Loss: {}".format(eval_loss))
162:
163:
164: # Run Fine-tuning on our model
...

...
```

Running this code, we will see that the training now starts at epoch 34 (Figure 8-7).

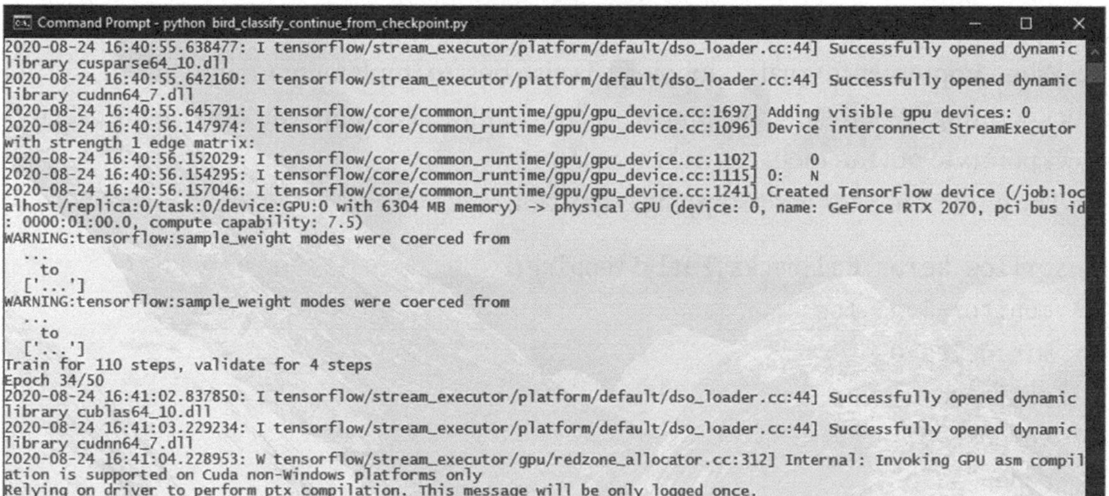

Figure 8-7. *Training continuing from a checkpoint*

With model checkpoints, we can be sure that hours or days of our effort in training a model will not be lost in an event of a failure.

Knowing When to Stop Training

In all the previous models we trained, we specified the number of epochs to train as a fixed number. We used a number that have worked well in similar models in the past.

But how do we determine the best number of epochs to train a model?

Training too much may lead to overfitting. But training too little would not give you the best results. We need to find the best point at which to stop the training for optimal results.

One way we can determine that is to train for different number of epochs and comparing the results. But with deep learning models, each training session can take hours, if not days. Therefore, it may not be practical always to run several training sessions to determine the best.

But what if there is a way to automatically stop the training when it reaches an optimal point?

This is where model early stopping comes in. EarlyStopping is another one of the built-in callbacks in TensorFlow/Keras which can be used with `model.fit()` functions.

The way EarlyStopping works, similar to the way the metric monitoring in model checkpointing worked, is to keep monitoring a given metric and stop the training if it does not improve for a given number of epochs.

When implementing early stopping it is also best to implement model checkpointing. When early stopping stops the training at a point, you can use the saved checkpoints to get the model at its best point.

The parameters for EarlyStopping is as follows:

```
tensorflow.keras.callbacks.EarlyStopping(
    monitor="val_loss",
    min_delta=0,
    patience=0,
    verbose=0,
    mode="auto",
    baseline=None,
    restore_best_weights=False,
)
```

- **monitor:** what metric to monitor, like in model checkpointing.

- **min_delta:** the minimum change in the monitored metric that will
  be considered as an improvement.

- **patience:** how many epochs to wait for an improvement before
  stopping the training.

- **verbose:** the verbosity level

- **mode:** min, max, or auto, as with model checkpoints.

- **baseline:** what the baseline is for the training. The training will stop if
  it does not improve over this baseline.

- **restore_best_weights:** whether to restore the model back to its bast
  point based on the parameter being monitored. If you set this to
  False, then the model will use the weights from the last step that was
  completed before stopping, which may or may not be the best.

Let us add early stopping to our model. We will take a copy of our code from bird_
classify_inceptionV3_checkpoint.py and name it bird_classify_inceptionV3_
early_stopping.py. We will then make the following modifications to it:

```
9: from tensorflow.keras.callbacks import ModelCheckpoint, EarlyStopping
...
...
132: training_checkpoint_dir = 'checkpoints/training'
133:
134: filepath = training_checkpoint_dir + "/model-{epoch:02d}-{val_
acc:.2f}-{val_loss:.2f}.h5"
135: checkpoint = ModelCheckpoint(
136:                             filepath,
137:                             monitor="val_acc",
138:                             verbose=1,
139:                             save_best_only=True,
140:                             save_weights_only=False,
141:                             mode="max"
142:                             )
143:
```

```
144: early_stop = EarlyStopping(
145:                             monitor="val_acc",
146:                             mode="max",
147:                             verbose=1,
148:                             patience=3,
149:                             restore_best_weights=True
150:                             )
151:
152: callbacks_list = [checkpoint, early_stop]
153:
154: history = model.fit(
155:                     train_generator,
156:                     steps_per_epoch=train_steps,
157:                     epochs=epochs,
158:                     validation_data=validation_generator,
159:                     validation_steps=validation_steps,
160:                     class_weight=class_weights,
161:                     max_queue_size=15,
162:                     workers=8,
163:                     callbacks=callbacks_list
164:                     )
```

Here, we are specifying EarlyStopping to monitor the validation accuracy, and stop the training if it does not improve for three consecutive epochs. We also specify that once stopped it should restore the model to the last best state (which would be three epochs before in this case).

When running the model with these configurations, you will see that the training will automatically stop when the training is not improving the model (Figure 8-8).

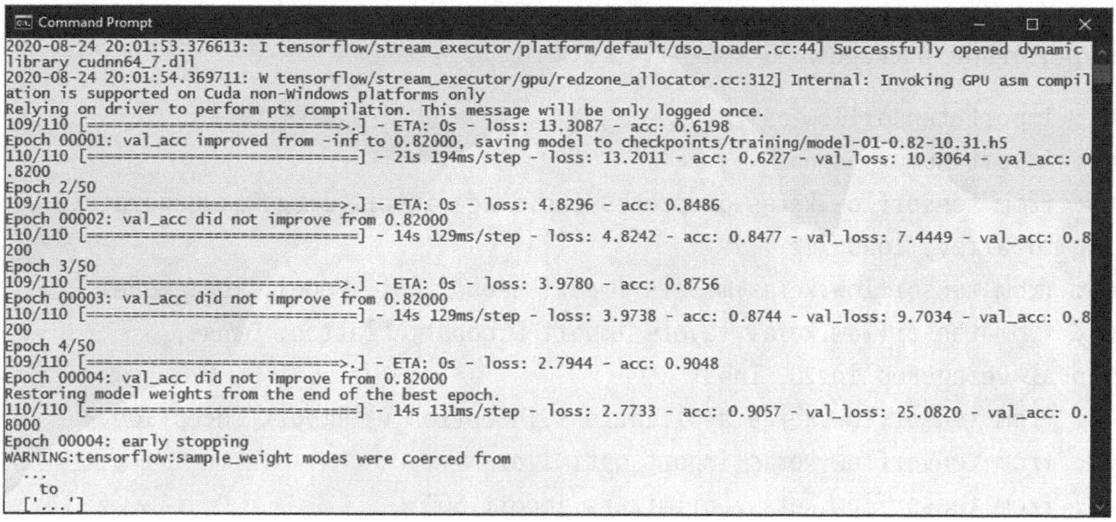

Figure 8-8. *Early stopping the model training*

Building a Robust Training Script

With model checkpoints, we were able to recover our model training state in case of an interruption. With early stopping we were able to automatically stop the training of a model at the right point in training.

Now let us see how we can combine those to build a robust training script—one that you can stop and start any time without losing your progress.

When building a robust training script, we will need to consider the following:

- Training of our module consists of two steps: training the initial model, and fine-tuning the model.

- For each of those steps, we will need to determine whether that step has been completed already, and run the remaining step.

- For each step that needs to run, we will need to determine where the last training stopped, and continue from that epoch.

- When training we need to save checkpoints, so that training of that step can be resumed later from those points.

With these in mind, let us build our robust training script.

We will name our new code file bird_classify_robust_training.py, and start by importing the packages:

```
01: import tensorflow as tf
02: import numpy as np
03: from tensorflow.keras.preprocessing.image import ImageDataGenerator,
img_to_array, load_img
04: from tensorflow.keras.models import Sequential, Model, load_model
05: from tensorflow.keras.layers import Dropout, Flatten, Dense,
GlobalAveragePooling2D, Input
06: from tensorflow.keras.applications.inception_v3 import InceptionV3
07: from tensorflow.keras import optimizers
08: from tensorflow.keras.optimizers import SGD
09: from tensorflow.keras.callbacks import ModelCheckpoint, EarlyStopping
10: import matplotlib.pyplot as plt
11: import math
12: import os
13: import os.path
14: import time
```

Then we will add our utility function definitions. What is new here is that our graph_training_history() function now take two extra parameters to save the figure to a file rather than displaying it:

```
16: # utility functions
17: def graph_training_history(history, save_fig=False, save_path=None):
18:     plt.rcParams["figure.figsize"] = (12, 9)
19:
20:     plt.style.use('ggplot')
21:
22:     plt.figure(1)
23:
24:     # summarize history for accuracy
25:
26:     plt.subplot(211)
27:     plt.plot(history.history['acc'])
28:     plt.plot(history.history['val_acc'])
```

```
29:     plt.title('Model Accuracy')
30:     plt.ylabel('Accuracy')
31:     plt.xlabel('Epoch')
32:     plt.legend(['Training', 'Validation'], loc='lower right')
33:
34:     # summarize history for loss
35:
36:     plt.subplot(212)
37:     plt.plot(history.history['loss'])
38:     plt.plot(history.history['val_loss'])
39:     plt.title('Model Loss')
40:     plt.ylabel('Loss')
41:     plt.xlabel('Epoch')
42:     plt.legend(['Training', 'Validation'], loc='upper right')
43:
44:     plt.tight_layout()
45:
46:     if save_fig:
47:         plt.savefig(save_path, bbox_inches='tight', dpi=300)
48:     else:
49:         plt.show()
50:
51:     # clear and close the current figure
52:     plt.clf()
53:     plt.close()
54:
55: # util function to calculate the class weights based on the number of
samples on each class
56: # this is useful with datasets that are highly skewed (datasets where
57: # the number of samples in each class differs vastly)
58: def get_class_weights(class_data_dir):
59:     labels_count = dict()
60:     for img_class in [ic for ic in os.listdir(class_data_dir) if ic[0]
!= '.']:
```

```
61:            labels_count[img_class] = len(os.listdir(os.path.join(class_
data_dir, img_class)))
62:     total_count = sum(labels_count.values())
63:     class_weights = {cls: total_count / count for cls, count in
64:                       enumerate(labels_count.values())}
65:     return class_weights
66:
67: # util function to get the initial epoch number from the checkpoint name
68: def get_init_epoch(checkpoint_path):
69:     filename = os.path.basename(checkpoint_path)
70:     filename = os.path.splitext(filename)[0]
71:     init_epoch = filename.split("-")[1]
72:     return int(init_epoch)
```

We then check for the existence of the saved model files to determine which step of the training (initial training or fine-tuning) needs to run:

```
74: run_training = True
75: run_finetune = True
76:
77: class_indices_path = 'class_indices.npy'
78: initial_model_path = 'bird_classify_finetune_initial.h5'
79: final_model_path = 'bird_classify_finetune_final.h5'
80:
81: # check which of the training steps still need to complete
82: # if saved model file is already there, then that step is considered
complete
83: if os.path.isfile(initial_model_path):
84:     run_training = False
85:     print("[Info] Initial model exists '{}'. Skipping training
step.".format(initial_model_path))
86:
87: if os.path.isfile(final_model_path):
88:     run_finetune = False
89:     print("[Info] Fine-tuned model exists '{}'. Skipping fine-tuning
step.".format(final_model_path))
```

For each of the steps that need running, we then determine which checkpoint to start from:

```
091: load_from_checkpoint_train = False
092:
093: training_checkpoint_dir = 'checkpoints/training'
094: if run_training and len(os.listdir(training_checkpoint_dir)) > 0:
095:     # the checkpoint to load and continue from
096:     training_checkpoint = os.path.join(training_checkpoint_dir,
os.listdir(training_checkpoint_dir)[len(os.listdir(training_checkpoint_
dir))-1])
097:     load_from_checkpoint_train = True
098:
099: init_epoch_train = 0
100: if load_from_checkpoint_train:
101:     # get the epoch number to continue from
102:     print(training_checkpoint)
103:     init_epoch_train = get_init_epoch(training_checkpoint)
104:     print("[Info] Training checkpoint found for epoch {}. Will
continue from that step.".format(init_epoch_train))
105:
106:
107: load_from_checkpoint_finetune = False
108:
109: finetune_checkpoint_dir = 'checkpoints/finetune'
110: if run_finetune and len(os.listdir(finetune_checkpoint_dir)) > 0:
111:     # the checkpoint to load and continue from
112:     finetune_checkpoint = os.path.join(finetune_checkpoint_dir,
os.listdir(finetune_checkpoint_dir)[len(os.listdir(finetune_checkpoint_
dir))-1])
113:     load_from_checkpoint_finetune = True
114:
115: init_epoch_finetune = 0
116: if load_from_checkpoint_finetune:
117:     # get the epoch number to continue from
118:     init_epoch_finetune = get_init_epoch(finetune_checkpoint)
```

```
119:    print("[Info] Training checkpoint found for epoch {}. Will
continue from that step.".format(init_epoch_finetune))
```

Then, our data generators and training parameters are defined as usual:

```
122: # start time of the script
123: start_time = time.time()
124:
125: # dimensions of our images.
126: img_width, img_height = 224, 224
127:
128: train_data_dir = 'data/train'
129: validation_data_dir = 'data/validation'
130:
131: # number of epochs to train
132: epochs = 50
133:
134: # batch size used by flow_from_directory
135: batch_size = 16
136:
137:
138: # this is the augmentation configuration we will use for training
139: train_datagen = ImageDataGenerator(
140:     rescale=1. / 255,
141:     shear_range=0.2,
142:     zoom_range=0.2,
143:     horizontal_flip=True)
144:
145: # this is the augmentation configuration we will use for testing:
146: # only rescaling
147: test_datagen = ImageDataGenerator(rescale=1. / 255)
148:
149: train_generator = train_datagen.flow_from_directory(
150:     train_data_dir,
151:     target_size=(img_width, img_height),
152:     batch_size=batch_size,
```

```
153:        class_mode='categorical')
154:
155: validation_generator = test_datagen.flow_from_directory(
156:        validation_data_dir,
157:        target_size=(img_width, img_height),
158:        batch_size=batch_size,
159:        class_mode='categorical')
160:
161: # the number of classes/categories
162: num_classes = len(train_generator.class_indices)
163:
164: # save the class indices for use in the predictions
165: np.save(class_indices_path, train_generator.class_indices)
166:
167: # calculate the training steps
168: nb_train_samples = len(train_generator.filenames)
169: train_steps = int(math.ceil(nb_train_samples / batch_size))
170:
171: # calculate the validation steps
172: nb_validation_samples = len(validation_generator.filenames)
173: validation_steps = int(math.ceil(nb_validation_samples / batch_size))
174:
175: # get the class weights
176: class_weights = get_class_weights(train_data_dir)
```

Based on the conditions we checked earlier, we either start training from beginning, start from a checkpoint if checkpoints are already there, or skip the training step if the trained model file is already there:

```
178: if run_training:
179:     if load_from_checkpoint_train:
180:         model = load_model(training_checkpoint)
181:     else:
182:         # create the base pre-trained model
183:         base_model = InceptionV3(
184:             weights='imagenet',
```

```
185:                 include_top=False,
186:                 input_tensor=Input(shape=(img_width, img_height, 3))
187:                 )
188:
189:         # add a global spatial average pooling layer
190:         x = base_model.output
191:         x = GlobalAveragePooling2D()(x)
192:         x = Dense(512, activation='relu')(x)
193:         predictions = Dense(num_classes, activation='softmax')(x)
194:
195:         # this is the model we will train
196:         model = Model(inputs=base_model.input, outputs=predictions)
197:
198:         # first: train only the top layers (which were randomly
initialized)
199:         # i.e. freeze all convolutional layers
200:         for layer in base_model.layers:
201:             layer.trainable = False
202:
203:         # compile the model (should be done *after* setting layers to
non-trainable)
204:         model.compile(optimizer='rmsprop', loss='categorical_
crossentropy', metrics=['acc'])
205:
206:     filepath = training_checkpoint_dir + "/model-{epoch:02d}-{val_
acc:.2f}-{val_loss:.2f}.h5"
207:     checkpoint = ModelCheckpoint(
208:                                 filepath,
209:                                 monitor="val_acc",
210:                                 verbose=1,
211:                                 save_best_only=True,
212:                                 save_weights_only=False,
213:                                 mode="max"
214:                                 )
215:
```

```
216:     early_stop = EarlyStopping(
217:                             monitor="val_acc",
218:                             mode="max",
219:                             verbose=1,
220:                             patience=5,
221:                             restore_best_weights=True
222:                             )
223:
224:     callbacks_list = [checkpoint, early_stop]
225:
226:     history = model.fit(
227:                         train_generator,
228:                         steps_per_epoch=train_steps,
229:                         epochs=epochs,
230:                         validation_data=validation_generator,
231:                         validation_steps=validation_steps,
232:                         class_weight=class_weights,
233:                         max_queue_size=15,
234:                         workers=8,
235:                         initial_epoch=init_epoch_train,
236:                         callbacks=callbacks_list
237:                         )
238:
239:     model.save(initial_model_path)
240:
241:     (eval_loss, eval_accuracy) = model.evaluate(
242:         validation_generator, steps=validation_steps)
243:
244:     print("\n")
245:
246:     print("[INFO] accuracy: {:.2f}%".format(eval_accuracy * 100))
247:     print("[INFO] Loss: {}".format(eval_loss))
248:
249:     graph_training_history(history, save_fig=True, save_
path='training.png')
```

```
250:
251: else:
252:     # training step is already completed
253:     # load the already trained model
254:     model = load_model(initial_model_path)
```

We will then do the same for our fine-tuning step:

```
257: # Run Fine-tuning on our model
258: if run_finetune:
259:     # number of epochs to fine-tune
260:     ft_epochs = 25
261:
262:     # reset our data generators
263:     train_generator.reset()
264:     validation_generator.reset()
265:
266:     if load_from_checkpoint_finetune:
267:         model = load_model(finetune_checkpoint)
268:     else:
269:         # we chose to train the last convolution block from the base
model
270:         for layer in model.layers[:249]:
271:             layer.trainable = False
272:         for layer in model.layers[249:]:
273:             layer.trainable = True
274:
275:         # we need to recompile the model for these modifications to
take effect
276:         # we use SGD with a low learning rate
277:         model.compile(
278:             optimizer=optimizers.SGD(lr=0.0001, momentum=0.9),
279:             loss='categorical_crossentropy',
280:             metrics=['acc']
281:         )
282:
```

```
283:     filepath = finetune_checkpoint_dir + "/model-{epoch:02d}-{val_
acc:.2f}-{val_loss:.2f}.h5"
284:     checkpoint = ModelCheckpoint(
285:                               filepath,
286:                               monitor="val_acc",
287:                               verbose=1,
288:                               save_best_only=True,
289:                               save_weights_only=False,
290:                               mode="max"
291:                               )
292:
293:     early_stop = EarlyStopping(
294:                               monitor="val_acc",
295:                               mode="max",
296:                               verbose=1,
297:                               patience=5,
298:                               restore_best_weights=True
299:                               )
300:
301:     callbacks_list = [checkpoint, early_stop]
302:
303:     history = model.fit(
304:                         train_generator,
305:                         steps_per_epoch=train_steps,
306:                         epochs=ft_epochs,
307:                         validation_data=validation_generator,
308:                         validation_steps=validation_steps,
309:                         class_weight=class_weights,
310:                         max_queue_size=15,
311:                         workers=8,
312:                         initial_epoch=init_epoch_finetune,
313:                         callbacks=callbacks_list
314:                         )
315:
316:     model.save(final_model_path)
```

```
317:
318:     (eval_loss, eval_accuracy) = model.evaluate(
319:         validation_generator, steps=validation_steps)
320:
321:     print("\n")
322:
323:     print("[INFO] accuracy: {:.2f}%".format(eval_accuracy * 100))
324:     print("[INFO] Loss: {}".format(eval_loss))
325:
326:     graph_training_history(history, save_fig=True, save_
path='finetune.png')
327:
328:     end_time = time.time()
329:
330:     training_duration = end_time - start_time
331:     print("[INFO] Total Time for training: {} seconds".
format(training_duration))
```

This script now allows you to resume from any step in the training process
(Figures 8-9 and 8-10).

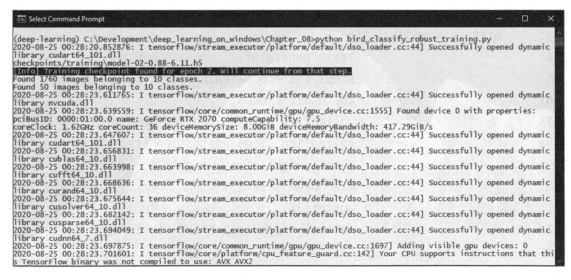

Figure 8-9. *Resuming the training step from a checkpoint*

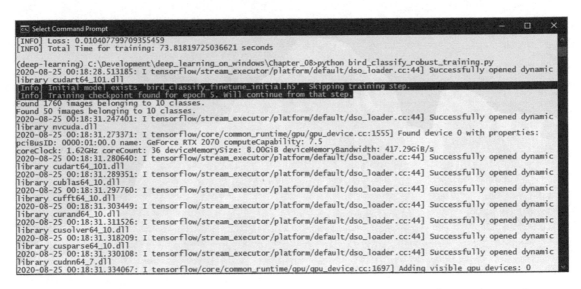

```
Select Command Prompt                                                          —    □    ×
[INFO] Loss: 0.010407799709355459
[INFO] Total Time for training: 73.81819725036621 seconds

(deep-learning) C:\Development\deep_learning_on_windows\Chapter_08>python bird_classify_robust_training.py
2020-08-25 00:18:28.513185: I tensorflow/stream_executor/platform/default/dso_loader.cc:44] Successfully opened dynamic
library cudart64_101.dll
[Info] Initial model exists 'bird_classify_finetune_initial.h5'. Skipping training step.
[Info] Training checkpoint found for epoch 5. Will continue from that step.
Found 1760 images belonging to 10 classes.
Found 50 images belonging to 10 classes.
2020-08-25 00:18:31.247401: I tensorflow/stream_executor/platform/default/dso_loader.cc:44] Successfully opened dynamic
library nvcuda.dll
2020-08-25 00:18:31.273371: I tensorflow/core/common_runtime/gpu/gpu_device.cc:1555] Found device 0 with properties:
pciBusID: 0000:01:00.0 name: GeForce RTX 2070 computeCapability: 7.5
coreClock: 1.62GHz coreCount: 36 deviceMemorySize: 8.00GiB deviceMemoryBandwidth: 417.29GiB/s
2020-08-25 00:18:31.280640: I tensorflow/stream_executor/platform/default/dso_loader.cc:44] Successfully opened dynamic
library cudart64_101.dll
2020-08-25 00:18:31.289351: I tensorflow/stream_executor/platform/default/dso_loader.cc:44] Successfully opened dynamic
library cublas64_10.dll
2020-08-25 00:18:31.297760: I tensorflow/stream_executor/platform/default/dso_loader.cc:44] Successfully opened dynamic
library cufft64_10.dll
2020-08-25 00:18:31.303449: I tensorflow/stream_executor/platform/default/dso_loader.cc:44] Successfully opened dynamic
library curand64_10.dll
2020-08-25 00:18:31.311526: I tensorflow/stream_executor/platform/default/dso_loader.cc:44] Successfully opened dynamic
library cusolver64_10.dll
2020-08-25 00:18:31.318209: I tensorflow/stream_executor/platform/default/dso_loader.cc:44] Successfully opened dynamic
library cusparse64_10.dll
2020-08-25 00:18:31.330108: I tensorflow/stream_executor/platform/default/dso_loader.cc:44] Successfully opened dynamic
library cudnn64_7.dll
2020-08-25 00:18:31.334067: I tensorflow/core/common_runtime/gpu/gpu_device.cc:1697] Adding visible gpu devices: 0
```

Figure 8-10. *Skipping the already completed training step, and continuing from a fine-tuning checkpoint*

With a training script such as this, you can start, stop, and resume training at any time without fear of losing your progress due to an interruption.

CHAPTER 9

Deploying Your Model as a Web Application

Over the past several chapters, we have talked about some techniques to optimize the training of a model. We went through the steps of starting with a small dataset to get results that can be applied in practical scenarios.

You now know the steps needed to train a practical model. Now it is time to talk about how to make your trained model into an application.

In Chapter 7, we briefly talked about how to build a script to run predictions using the trained model (Figure 9-1).

Figure 9-1. *Using a script to run predictions with a model*

---

[1]Flask (handling file uploads), https://flask.palletsprojects.com/en/1.1.x/patterns/fileuploads/#improving-uploads, [Sep 23, 2019].

But using a script like that is not a user-friendly way of making it an application. A better way would be to turn your model into a web application. It would allow for better usability, as well as allowing you to provide your new deep learning application to multiple users.

We can use the Flask Framework to turn our model into a web application.

Setting up Flask

Flask is a lightweight micro web framework for Python, which allows you to build websites, web applications, APIs, and microservices. With only a few base dependencies, you can start building your application with a simple structure and later expand upon it with additional features and scalability using a large library of available extensions.

When we set up our deep learning environment in Chapter 3 with the Anaconda metapackage, we installed the Flask package and few other dependency packages that will aid us in building our application.

If you want to install Flask separately you can simply run:

```
conda install Flask
```

This will install Flask, as well as Werkzeug, Jinja2, MarkupSafe, and ItsDangerous packages (Figure 9-2).

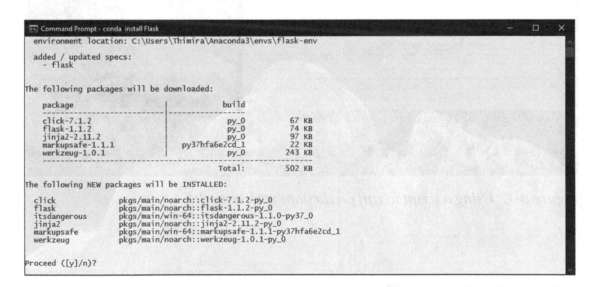

Figure 9-2. *Conda installing Flask and dependencies*

Once installed, we can test Flask by creating a simple application. We will name this file flask-sample.py:

```
01: from flask import Flask
02:
03: header_text = '''
04:     <html>\n<head> <title>Flask Test Application</title> </head>\
n<body>'''
05: page_content = '''
06:     <p>This is a sample webpage generated by Flask.</p>\n'''
07: footer_text = '''</body>\n</html>'''
08:
09: # request handler function for the home/index page
10: def index():
11:   return header_text + page_content + footer_text
12:
13: # setting up the application context
14: application = Flask(__name__)
15:
16: # add a rule for the index page.
17: application.add_url_rule('/', 'index', index, methods=['GET', 'POST'])
18:
19: # run the app.
20: if __name__ == "__main__":
21:     # Setting debug to True enables debug output. This line should be
22:     # removed before deploying a production app.
23:     application.debug = True
24:     application.run()
```

Here, we are importing the Flask package, defining the application context, and running the resulting Flask application. We define a function—index()—and bind it to handle the requests coming to the index route of the application add_url_rule() function. In the index() function, we are simply returning some hardcoded HTML strings for now.

We can run this application by running:

```
python flask-sample.py
```

Flask will spin up a development webserver process to serve your application. By default, it will run on port 5000 on localhost. You can access the application page on http://127.0.0.1:5000/ (Figure 9-3).

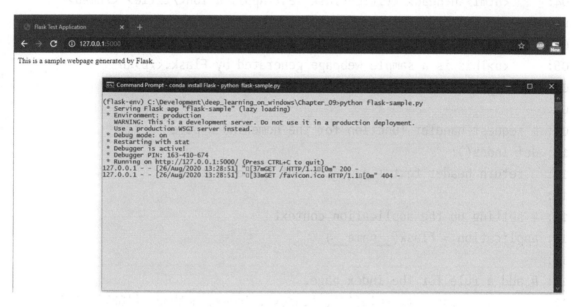

Figure 9-3. *Flask sample Web app running*

With Flask up and running, we are now ready to design our deep learning web application using Flask.

Designing Your Web Application

As we did in Chapter 7, we can use a model file saved using the model.save() function (e.g., the `bird_classify_finetune_IV3_final.h5` file in our fine-tuning of the bird image classification system example). By using the full model file, we can load the model in its trained state without having to redefine the code for the model structure. Along with the model file, we will use the `class_indices.npy` file saved from the same script. The class_indices file contains the dictionary/mapping of the text labels for the classes to their IDs. We will need the label mapping to display the text label for the predicted class (Figure 9-4).

| bird_classify_finetune_IV3_final | 8/22/2020 11:09 PM | H5 File | 137,761 KB |
| class_indices.npy | 8/22/2020 9:03 PM | NPY File | 1 KB |

Figure 9-4. *Model files needed to build the web application*

With our model files at hand, we can start designing the application. We will need to consider the following:

- As the input for our system we will need to have an HTML page with a web form that allows uploading/submitting files.

- The uploaded files need to be placed in a location where the Python code can read them.

- A function is needed to handle the requests which loads the uploaded image file, runs it through the model, and responds with the result/prediction from the model.

- The frontend webpage needs to be able to display the result.

- Loading of the model from file takes time. It is not practical to load the model for every request. Therefore, we need a way to load the model only once (preferably when the application starts).

- Using HTML strings in the code is not practical. We should use a templating engine, which would give us more flexibility in our frontend. Fortunately, the default installation of Flask comes with the Jinja2 template engine.

Based on these considerations, we will define the following structure for our Flask application (Figure 9-5):

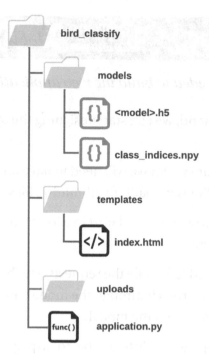

Figure 9-5. *The structure of our application*

Our application will consist of 3 directories: models, templates, and uploads, along with a main application.py file. The models directory will contain our saved model file, as well as the class label dictionary file for that model. The templates directory will contain the Jinja2 template files (the Jinja2 engine expects this directory to be named templates). The uploads directory is for keeping the uploaded files of the application. The application.py will contain the Flask application definitions as well as the functions to process the images and predictions using our trained model.

Following this simple application structure will allow us to extend the capabilities of our application later, as well as allow us to upload and host our application in various services that allow Flask applications.

Building Your Deep Learning Web Application

To build our web application, let us begin with our template file for the main page. In the templates directory of our application structure, create an index.html file.

In this file, start with adding the basic HTML structure of the page. We will be using the Jinja2 templating for this:

```
1: <!doctype html>
2: <html lang="en">
3:     <head>
4:         <title>Bird Image Classification System</title>
5:     </head>
6:     <body>
7:         <h3>Deep Learning Bird Image Identification System</h3>
```

At the top of the page, we will add a section to display any error messages returned from the backend. We will use the Flash messages mechanism from the Flask framework:

```
08:         <!-- show error messages from backend, if any -->
09:         {% with messages = get_flashed_messages() %}
10:           {% if messages %}
11:               <ul>
12:               {% for message in messages %}
13:                   <li>{{ message }}</li>
14:               {% endfor %}
15:               </ul>
16:           {% endif %}
17:         {% endwith %}
```

Next, we will add the main HTML form that allows us to upload the images:

```
18:         <form action="" method="post" enctype="multipart/form-data">
19:           <div>
20:               <label for="bird_image">Select an image to upload
<small>(Supports .jpg, .jpeg, .gif, and .png images.)</small></label>
21:               <input type="file" name="bird_image" id="bird_image"
accept=".jpg,.jpeg,.gif,.png" required="required">
22:           </div>
23:           <div>
24:               <input type="submit" value="Process" name="submit">
25:           </div>
26:         </form>
```

Finally, we will add a section to display the results:

```
27:          {% if label %}
28:          <br/>
29:          <br/>
30:          <div>
31:             {% if image %}
32:            <img src="data:image/jpeg;base64,{{image}}" alt="uploaded image">
33:             {% endif %}
34:             <h3 class="card-title">Identification</h3>
35:             <p class="card-text">Predicted : {{label}}</p>
36:             <p class="card-text">Confidence [0-100]% : {{prob}} %</p>
37:          </div>
38:          {% endif %}
39:       </body>
40: </html>
```

One thing to note here is that we are using Base64 image data in the <img> tag instead of a path to an image file. This allows us to display an image with any image manipulations applied without having to save it as a file.

Note   For simplicity, we will not be adding any style/css here.

Now we can begin the main code of our Flask application.

Start an application.py file in the root of our application structure and import the packages:

```
01: from flask import Flask, request, render_template, url_for, make_
response, send_from_directory, flash, redirect, jsonify
02: from werkzeug.utils import secure_filename
03:
04: import numpy as np
05: import tensorflow as tf
06: from tensorflow.keras.preprocessing.image import img_to_array, load_img
07: from tensorflow.keras.models import Model, load_model
08: from tensorflow.keras.utils import to_categorical
09: from PIL import Image
```

```
10: from io import BytesIO
11: import os
12: import os.path
13: import sys
14: import base64
15: import uuid
16: import time
```

With some versions of TensorFlow there are some incompatibilities of cuDNN and Flask. Therefore, we add the following code to avoid the incompatibilities:

```
18: # avoiding some compatibility problems in TensorFlow, cuDNN, and Flask
19: from tensorflow.compat.v1 import ConfigProto
20: from tensorflow.compat.v1 import InteractiveSession
21: config = ConfigProto()
22: config.gpu_options.allow_growth = True
23: session = InteractiveSession(config=config)
```

Note   You may experience errors such as "BaseCollectiveExecutor::StartAbo rt Unknown: Failed to get convolution algorithm" if you try to run the application without these compatibility fixes. This may be fixed in future releases.

Next, we set the application parameters, and load the model from files:

```
25: # dimensions of our images.
26: img_width, img_height = 224, 224
27: # limiting the allowed filetypes
28: ALLOWED_FILETYPES = set(['.jpg', '.jpeg', '.gif', '.png'])
29:
30: model_path = 'models/bird_classify_finetune_IV3_final.h5'
31:
32: # loading the class dictionary and the model
33: class_dictionary = np.load('models/class_indices.npy',
    allow_pickle=True).item()
34:
35: model = load_model(model_path)
```

Then we will add a function—classify_image()—that will take the image, perform the preprocessing on the image, run it through the model, and return the result:

```
37: # function for classifying the image using the model
38: def classify_image(image):
39:     image = img_to_array(image)
40:
41:     # important! otherwise the predictions will be '0'
42:     image = image / 255.0
43:
44:     # add a new axis to make the image array confirm with
45:     # the (samples, height, width, depth) structure
46:     image = np.expand_dims(image, axis=0)
47:
48:     # get the probabilities for the prediction
49:     # with graph.as_default():
50:     probabilities = model.predict(image)
51:
52:     prediction_probability = probabilities[0, probabilities.
argmax(axis=1)][0]
53:
54:     class_predicted = np.argmax(probabilities, axis=1)
55:
56:     inID = class_predicted[0]
57:
58:     # invert the class dictionary in order to get the label for the id
59:     inv_map = {v: k for k, v in class_dictionary.items()}
60:     label = inv_map[inID]
61:
62:     print("[Info] Predicted: {}, Confidence: {}".format(label,
prediction_probability))
63:
64:     return label, prediction_probability
```

When showing the results for an uploaded image, it is better to show the image in the page as well. Therefore, we will add a utility function to return a thumbnail version of the uploaded image in a Base64 encoded format. Base64 image data can be directly rendered by an HTML <img> tag without needing to supply a file location. Recall that in our template, we specified the <img> tag to use data:image/jpeg;base64:

```
66: # get a thumbnail version of the uploaded image
67: def get_iamge_thumbnail(image):
68:     image.thumbnail((400, 400), resample=Image.LANCZOS)
69:     image = image.convert("RGB")
70:     with BytesIO() as buffer:
71:         image.save(buffer, 'jpeg')
72:         return base64.b64encode(buffer.getvalue()).decode()
```

Then we come to our main request handler, the index() function:

```
074: # request handler function for the home/index page
075: def index():
076:     # handling the POST method of the submit
077:     if request.method == 'POST':
078:         # check if the post request has the submitted file
079:         if 'bird_image' not in request.files:
080:             print("[Error] No file uploaded.")
081:             flash('No file uploaded.')
082:             return redirect(url_for('index'))
083:
084:         f = request.files['bird_image']
085:
086:         # if user does not select a file, some browsers may
087:         # submit an empty field without the filename
088:         if f.filename == '':
089:             print("[Error] No file selected to upload.")
090:             flash('No file selected to upload.')
091:             return redirect(url_for('index'))
092:
093:         sec_filename = secure_filename(f.filename)
094:         file_extension = os.path.splitext(sec_filename)[1]
095:
096:         if f and file_extension.lower() in ALLOWED_FILETYPES:
```

```
097:                file_tempname = uuid.uuid4().hex
098:                image_path = './uploads/' + file_tempname + file_extension
099:                f.save(image_path)
100:
101:                image = load_img(image_path, target_size=(img_width,
img_height), interpolation='lanczos')
102:
103:                label, prediction_probability = classify_
image(image=image)
104:                prediction_probability = np.around(prediction_probability
* 100, decimals=4)
105:
106:                orig_image = Image.open(image_path)
107:                image_data = get_iamge_thumbnail(image=orig_image)
108:
109:                with application.app_context():
110:                    return render_template('index.html',
111:                                           label=label,
112:                                           prob=prediction_probability,
113:                                           image=image_data
114:                                           )
115:        else:
116:            print("[Error] Unauthorized file extension: {}".
format(file_extension))
117:            flash("The file type you selected: '{}' is not supported.
Please select a '.jpg', '.jpeg', '.gif', or a '.png' file.".format(file_
extension))
118:            return redirect(url_for('index'))
119:    else:
120:        # handling the GET, HEAD, and any other methods
121:
122:        with application.app_context():
123:            return render_template('index.html')
```

This index() function handles both the GET request to render the initial page, as well as the POST request from the form submit. When handling the GET requests, the index() function renders the index.html template we defined earlier. The webform in the index page is set to make a POST request (with the submitted file) to itself, which is again picked up by the index() function.

When processing the POST request, we make several checks, such as whether a file was uploaded, does it have an allowed file extension. The flash message mechanism of the Flask framework is used to report any errors to the user. If all checks pass, the uploaded image is then placed in the uploads directory of our application structure, loaded using the load_img() function of Keras, and passed to the classify_image() function we defined earlier. Once results are ready, we render the index.html template again, this time with the result information.

Another utility function is added next to handle the HTTP 413 errors, which are emitted when the uploaded filesize is larger than the MAX_CONTENT_LENGTH of the application:

```
125: # handle 'filesize too large' errors
126: def http_413(e):
127:     print("[Error] Uploaded file too large.")
128:     flash('Uploaded file too large.')
129:     return redirect(url_for('index'))
```

Note   When running our application locally, you may get a "Connection Reset" or a "Connection Aborted" error in the browser instead of the error message we set using the preceding function when uploading files larger than the limit we set. This is a known limitation of the development server of Flask. You can read more about it in the Flask documentation page on handling file uploads.[1]

Finally, the Flask application context, parameters, and URL rules are defined:

```
131: # setting up the application context
132: application = Flask(__name__)
133: # set the application secret key. Used with sessions.
134: application.secret_key = '@#$%^&*@#$%^&*'
135:
```

```
136: # add a rule for the index page.
137: application.add_url_rule('/', 'index', index, methods=['GET', 'POST'])
138:
139: # limit the size of the uploads
140: application.register_error_handler(413, http_413)
141: application.config['MAX_CONTENT_LENGTH'] = 10 * 1024 * 1024
142:
143: # run the app.
144: if __name__ == "__main__":
145:     # Setting debug to True enables debug output. This line should be
146:     # removed before deploying a production app.
147:     application.debug = True
148:     application.run()
```

Like our Flask sample application, we run this as:

```
python application.py
```

When the application starts, it will first load the model from file, before starting the webserver (Figure 9-6).

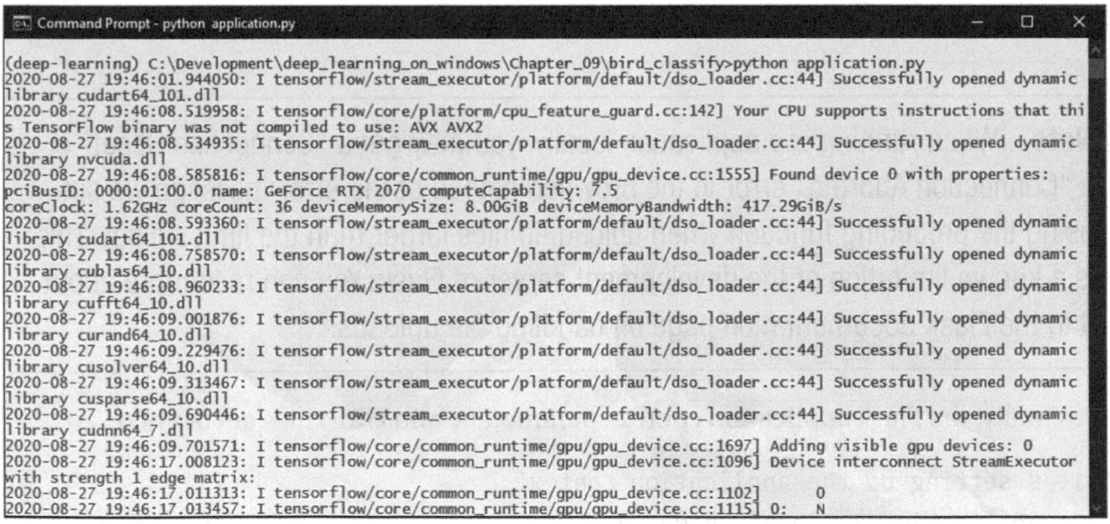

Figure 9-6. *Flask application loading the model*

Once the webserver is started view the webpage in browser, which by default would be running on http://127.0.0.1:5000 (Figure 9-7).

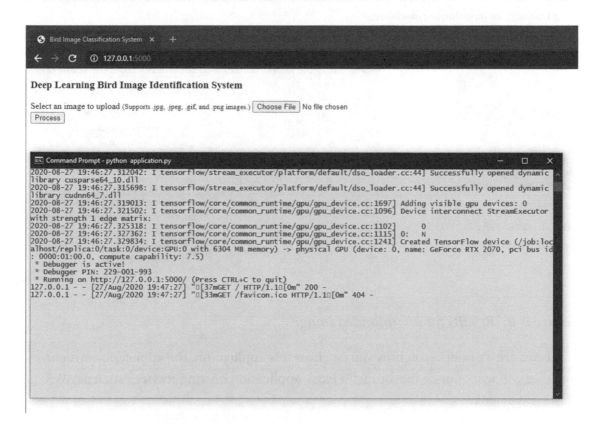

Figure 9-7. *Our bird classification flask application running*

You can now upload an image and see how well our application can recognize it (Figure 9-8). The application will return the predicted label with the confidence for the prediction.

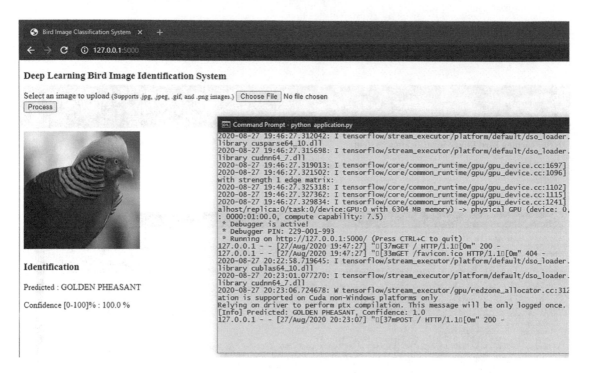

Figure 9-8. *Results for an uploaded image*

If you are wondering on how you can host this application, the application structure we build will work out-of-the-box with Flask application hosting services such as AWS Elastic Beanstalk.[2]

Scaling Up Your Web Application

The application we built here, although functional, if far from an optimal design. There are several areas that we can improve in it, such as:

- The main application handles both the web functions—such as template rendering, request handling—and the deep learning inference tasks as well. This will bottleneck some of the functionality as the same application threads needs to handle both sets of tasks.

---

[2]Elastic Beanstalk (deploying a Flask application to Elastic Beanstalk), [https://docs.aws.amazon.com/elasticbeanstalk/latest/dg/create-deploy-python-flask.html, [22 Nov, 2020].

- Running inferencing is computationally intensive. The same can be said for image preprocessing as well. While the web functions are relatively less complex.

- By having the web and the deep learning components of the application together, we would need to allocate processing/machine resources unnecessarily.

- When implementing computationally intensive functions, it is better to implement limit (or throttle) the number of parallel invocations of such functions as to reduce the resource usage. Think of multiuser scenarios.

- Computationally intensive functions should optimally be done asynchronously.

Considering all these facts, it is better to split the application so that the web components and the deep learning portions are handled by two separate micro-services.

It is also better to implement a job-queue mechanism between the two services as a throttling mechanism.

One possible application design considering these items is shown here (Figure 9-9).

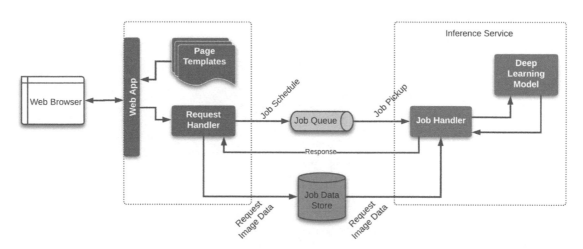

Figure 9-9. *Scaling up the application*

By considering these factors when designing, you can build your application to be able to handle thousands to millions of requests at a time.

## CHAPTER 10

Having Fun with Computer Vision

We have talked about the ways in which deep learning and computer vision go together. In the past few chapters, we have built some computer vision models: deep learning image classification models, from handwritten digit classification to bird identification. In Chapter 3, when we set up our deep learning development environment, we installed several utility libraries that aids in computer vision and image processing tasks.

But other than using OpenCV to load and display the results of our deep learning models, we have not explored many of the functions available in these libraries.

Therefore, in this chapter, let us look at some of those functions and concepts to get you started. While this chapter is not a full computer vision tutorial, this hopes to guide you to start experimenting on your own, and to learn how to couple it with what we have already learned about deep learning.

What We Need

In Chapter 3, "Setting Up Your Tools," we already installed everything we need for computer vision and image processing tasks, which are OpenCV, Dlib, Pillow, and Scikit-Image.

- OpenCV is arguably the best computer vision library out there. It can do simple functions, such as loading and manipulating images, to building complex models, such as deep learning-based image recognition, all on its own.

- Dlib is a machine learning library, which has some optimized and easy-to-use computer vision functions built in.

- Pillow and Scikit-Image allow you to load and handle different formats of images and allow basic manipulations such as color channel handling.

© Thimira Amaratunga 2021
T. Amaratunga, *Deep Learning on Windows*, https://doi.org/10.1007/978-1-4842-6431-7_10

Other than the software libraries, it is best to have a webcam attached to your machine, as we will be looking into some real-time video processing as well.

If you are working on a laptop, then you might already have a built-in webcam, which is sufficient. If not, you can use a USB webcam. For most USB webcams, the default drivers that is installed by Windows will be sufficient.

Note   You can use the Camera app on Windows 10 to check whether the webcam is working and have the working drivers loaded. You also do not need a high-end HD webcam, as we will be working with lower resolutions (640x480).

Basics of Working with Images

The most basic functionality of any image processing task is to load and display images. We have already used this functionality to display the results from our models.

When working with image files, OpenCV has convenient functions to load images and display them. The following code will use the imread function of OpenCV to load the image:

```
01: import numpy as np
02: import cv2
03:
04: # Read the image...
05: # cv2.IMREAD_COLOR - load a color image, without transparency
06: # cv2.IMREAD_GRAYSCALE - load image in grayscale mode
07: # cv2.IMREAD_UNCHANGED - load image as-is, including transparency if it
is there
08: img = cv2.imread('.//images//Bird.jpg', cv2.IMREAD_COLOR)
09:
10: # Display the image
11: cv2.imshow('Image', img)
12:
13: # Wait for a keypress
14: cv2.waitKey(0)
15:
```

```
16: # Close all OpenCV windows
17: cv2.destroyAllWindows()
```

The image will be displayed in a new window by OpenCV (Figure 10-1).

Figure 10-1. *OpenCV loading and displaying an image*

OpenCV can load most image file formats, but the exact format it supports will depend on the version and the build that you have installed.

If you do run into an image file that OpenCV is unable to open, you can always use Pillow to open it. Pillow supports many more formats than OpenCV:

```
01: import numpy as np
02: import cv2
03: from PIL import Image
04:
05: # Read the image...
06: pil_image = Image.open('.//images//Bird.jpg')
07:
08: # Convert image from RGB to BGR
09: opencv_image = cv2.cvtColor(np.array(pil_image), cv2.COLOR_RGB2BGR)
10:
```

```
11: # Display the image
12: cv2.imshow('Image', opencv_image)
13:
14: # Wait for a keypress
15: cv2.waitKey(0)
16:
17: # Close all OpenCV windows
18: cv2.destroyAllWindows()
```

Here, we have loaded the image with Pillow, converted the color format to be compatible with OpenCV, and displayed the image using OpenCV (Figure 10-2).

Figure 10-2. *Loading an image with Pillow and displaying with OpenCV*

When using Pillow with OpenCV we must convert the color formats, because OpenCV uses the BGR format while Pillow uses the more common RGB format. If you forget to convert these color channels, the images will display incorrect colors (Figure 10-3).

Figure 10-3. *Incorrect colors if RGB to BGR color conversion is not performed*

Once you have loaded the image, OpenCV and Pillow allows you to do many transformations to the image, such as resizing, rotating, color conversions, and thresholding. The following code shows how to perform a rotation around the center point of an image using OpenCV:

```
01: import numpy as np
02: import cv2
03:
04: # Read the image...
05: img = cv2.imread('.//images//Bird.jpg', cv2.IMREAD_COLOR)
06:
07: # Perform the rotation around the center point
08: rows,cols,channels = img.shape
09: M = cv2.getRotationMatrix2D((cols/2,rows/2),45,1)
10: dst = cv2.warpAffine(img,M,(cols,rows))
11:
12: # Display the image
13: cv2.imshow('Image', dst)
14:
15: # Wait for a keypress
16: cv2.waitKey(0)
```

```
17:
18: # Close all OpenCV windows
19: cv2.destroyAllWindows()
```

This will result is a 45-degree rotation of the image (Figure 10-4).

Figure 10-4. *Image rotation with OpenCV*

You can read about the full set of available image transformation functions from the OpenCV docs[1] and Pillow docs.[2]

The next most important function you need to learn is extracting out a region of interest from an image. The following code demonstrates how a region from the image can be extracted:

```
01: import numpy as np
02: import cv2
03:
04: # Read the image...
05: img = cv2.imread('.//images//Bird.jpg', cv2.IMREAD_COLOR)
```

[1]OpenCV (image transformations), https://docs.opencv.org/3.4.1/da/d6e/tutorial_py_geometric_transformations.html, [Feb 23, 2018].

[2]Pillow (image transformations), https://pillow.readthedocs.io/en/stable/reference/Image.html, [Jul 24, 2020].

```
06:
07: # Extract the region-of-interest from the image
08: img_roi = img[50:250, 150:300]
09:
10: # Display the extracted region-of-interest
11: cv2.imshow('Image ROI', img_roi)
12:
13: # Wait for a keypress
14: cv2.waitKey(0)
15:
16: # Close all OpenCV windows
17: cv2.destroyAllWindows()
```

This will extract and display a region from the image (Figure 10-5).

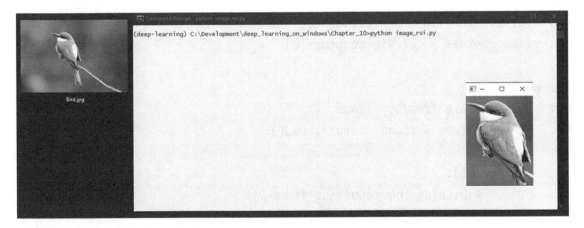

Figure 10-5. *Extracting a region-of-interest from an image*

You can also save the extracted image region using the imwrite function.

```
07: # Extract the region-of-interest from the image
08: img_roi = img[50:250, 150:300]
09:
10: # Save the region-of-interest as an image
11: cv2.imwrite('.//images//Bird_ROI.jpg', img_roi)
```

The ability to extract a region-of-interest is incredibly useful when you are working with object detection and recognition.

Working with Video: Using Webcams

Usually, when working with hardware devices, such as when you are trying to read from a connected camera from code, you would have to fiddle around some camera driver stuff.

But OpenCV has us covered in this instance.

OpenCV can read from any built-in or USB connected camera in the system. A video stream from a camera is just a sequence of images in an order, and OpenCV reads frame-by-frame. Therefore, each frame acts like loading an individual image:

```
01: import numpy as np
02: import cv2
03:
04: # Create the video capture object for camera id '0'
05: video_capture = cv2.VideoCapture(0)
06:
07: while True:
08:     # Capture frame-by-frame
09:     ret, frame = video_capture.read()
10:
11:     if (ret):
12:         # Display the resulting frame
13:         cv2.imshow('Video Feed', frame)
14:
15:     ch = 0xFF & cv2.waitKey(1)
16:
17:     # Press "q" to quit the program
18:     if ch == ord('q'):
19:         break
20:
21: # When everything is done, release the capture
22: video_capture.release()
23: cv2.destroyAllWindows()
```

With this code, OpenCV will open a window—named Video Feed here—and load each frame as it reads them from the camera (Figure 10-6).

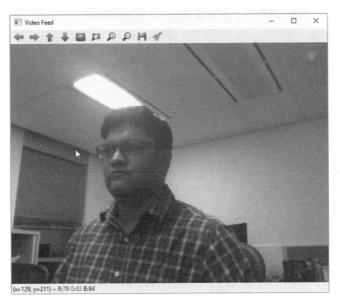

Figure 10-6. *OpenCV loading the video from a webcam*

The code will loop indefinitely, or until you press the q key on the keyboard.

OpenCV uses its HighGUI module (high-level graphical user interface) to access the cameras as well as to display the frames. HighGUI module has three sets of functionalities: hardware, filesystem, and GUI. The hardware part is what handles accessing hardware devices such as cameras. The filesystem part handles the loading and saving of images as well as video files. The GUI part is what generates the windows that display the images or frames, as well as giving you the ability to handle keyboard and mouse events in those windows. The toolbar and the status bar of the window we opened earlier are also components from HighGUI.[3] The HighGUI modlule is installed by default when you are installing OpenCV with conda.

Camera id 0 is your default camera. Typically, this is the built-in camera if you are on a laptop, or whichever camera you have set as default if you have multiple cameras. If you have more than one camera, they would have ids that would be listed as 0, 1, 2, and so on. Just check and set the id to the camera you want. You can use multiple video capture objects to read from multiple cameras (Figure 10-7).

---

[3]OpenCV (HighGUI module), `https://docs.opencv.org/3.4.11/d7/dfc/group__highgui.html`, [Jul 17, 2020].

Figure 10-7. *Reading from multiple cameras in OpenCV*

Once you read the frame from the camera, it acts as an image. Now you can perform any of the image transformations on that frame.

Working with Video: Using Video Files

This is almost identical to reading from a webcam. You just need to pass the path to the video file, instead of the camera id, in the video capture object:

```
01: import numpy as np
02: import cv2
03:
04: # Create the video capture object for a video file
05: cap = cv2.VideoCapture("F:\\GoPro\\Hero7\\GH010038.mp4")
06:
07: while(cap.isOpened()):
08:     # Read frame-by-frame
09:     ret, frame = cap.read()
```

```
10:
11:     if (ret):
12:         # Resize the frame
13:         res = cv2.resize(frame, (960, 540), interpolation = cv2.INTER_
CUBIC)
14:
15:         # Display the resulting frame
16:         cv2.imshow('Video', res)
17:
18:     # Press "q" to quit the program
19:     if cv2.waitKey(1) & 0xFF == ord('q'):
20:         break
21:
22: cap.release()
23: cv2.destroyAllWindows()
```

Just like the webcam code, OpenCV will open a window and load each frame as it reads them from the video file (Figure 10-8).

Figure 10-8. *OpenCV loading a video file*

As with images, the supported video file formats may differ with the exact version/build of the OpenCV you have installed. OpenCV relies on FFmpeg and GStreamer libraries to be able to work with video files, while the DirectShow library is used on Windows to handle video from webcams. These libraries are installed when you install OpenCV with conda. Therefore, opening standard AVI and MP4 files should not be a problem.

You may notice that the playback of the video is either faster or slower than expected. This is because the functions we used are not meant for playing back videos at their natural speed. What we are doing is grabbing each frame of the video—like we did with the webcam—and displaying it in the window with a delay added in between fetching the next frame. That delay is added by the `cv2.waitkey()` function. Here we have set it to 1 millisecond of delay between frames. You can increase or decrease the speed of the video by adjusting this delay.

Detecting Faces in Images

Here we are getting into some of the fun parts of computer vision.

Writing code from scratch to detect faces is a bit of a complex task as the process involved in identifying a face from within an image reliably involves many steps. But libraries such as OpenCV and Dlib already have the complex parts of those algorithms built into them.

To detect any objects (such as faces) in an image, you need to have a trained object detector. Luckily, Dlib already has a pretrained face detector built right into the library. You can load it using `dlib.get_frontal_face_detector()` function.

```
01: import numpy as np
02: import cv2
03: import dlib
04:
05: # Load the built-in face dedector of Dlib
06: detector = dlib.get_frontal_face_detector()
07:
08: # Load the image
```

```
09: img = cv2.imread('.//images//Face.jpg', cv2.IMREAD_COLOR)
10: # Create a grayscale copy of the image
11: img_gray = cv2.cvtColor(img, cv2.COLOR_BGR2GRAY)
12:
13: # Get the detected face bounding boxes, using the grayscale image
14: rects = detector(img_gray, 0)
15:
16: # Loop over the bounding boxes, if there are more than one face
17: for rect in rects:
18:     # Get the OpenCV coordinates from the Dlib rectangle objects
19:     x = rect.left()
20:     y = rect.top()
21:     x1 = rect.right()
22:     y1 = rect.bottom()
23:
24:     # Draw a rectangle around the face bounding box in OpenCV
25:     cv2.rectangle(img, (x, y), (x1, y1), (0, 0, 255), 2)
26:
27: # Display the resulting image
28: cv2.imshow('Detected Faces', img)
29:
30: # Wait for a keypress
31: cv2.waitKey(0)
32:
33: # Close all OpenCV windows
34: cv2.destroyAllWindows()
```

Here, we are using OpenCV to load the image, and then make a grayscale copy of it. We pass this grayscale copy of the image to the Dlib face detector object.

The grayscale image is used as it can increase the detection speed of faces. The Dlib face detector can work with color images as well, but would be slower.

The detector would return an array of Dlib rectangle objects to denote the bounding boxes of all the faces detected. We loop over each of these bounding boxes, extract their coordinates, and use OpenCV to draw a rectangle around the detected face using those coordinates. Finally, we display the resulting image, with the detected faces (Figure 10-9).

Figure 10-9. *Dlib face detection in action*

Detecting Faces in Video

Once we get face detection working with images, getting it to work on a video or a webcam feed is quite simple. All we need to do is to capture the video frame-by-frame and pass each frame to the face detector:

```
01: import numpy as np
02: import cv2
03: import dlib
04:
05: # Create the video capture object for camera id '0'
06: video_capture = cv2.VideoCapture(0)
07: # Load the buil-in face dedector of Dlib
08: detector = dlib.get_frontal_face_detector()
09:
```

```
10: while True:
11:     # Capture frame-by-frame
12:     ret, frame = video_capture.read()
13:
14:     if (ret):
15:         # Create a grayscale copy of the captured frame
16:         gray = cv2.cvtColor(frame, cv2.COLOR_BGR2GRAY)
17:
18:         # Get the detected face bounding boxes, using the grayscale image
19:         rects = detector(gray, 0)
20:
21:         # Loop over the bounding boxes, if there are more than one face
22:         for rect in rects:
23:             # Get the OpenCV coordinates from the Dlib rectangle
objects
24:             x = rect.left()
25:             y = rect.top()
26:             x1 = rect.right()
27:             y1 = rect.bottom()
28:
29:             # Draw a rectangle around the face bounding box in OpenCV
30:             cv2.rectangle(frame, (x, y), (x1, y1), (0, 0, 255), 2)
31:
32:         # Display the resulting frame
33:         cv2.imshow('Video Feed', frame)
34:
35:     ch = 0xFF & cv2.waitKey(1)
36:
37:     # press "q" to quit the program.
38:     if ch == ord('q'):
39:         break
40:
41: # When everything is done, release the capture
42: video_capture.release()
43: cv2.destroyAllWindows()
```

Here we are running the face detection step (as we did with an image) on each frame of the video. On a typical machine, the Dlib's face detector is fast enough to detect faces in real time, allowing us to run it for each frame. You will see the detection box update in real time for each frame (Figure 10-10).

Figure 10-10. *Face detection running on video*

Simple Real-Time Deep Learning Object Identification

Next, we will combine what we learned about deep learning models with the computer vision capabilities of OpenCV and build a rudimentary object identification system.

We will use OpenCV to capture the video stream from a webcam and use the ResNet50 deep learning model from TensorFlow/Keras applications to identify objects in each frame of the video. You can learn more about the ResNet50 model in Appendix 1.

We will start by importing the necessary packages:

```
1: import numpy as np
2: import cv2
3: import tensorflow as tf
4: from tensorflow.keras.applications.resnet50 import ResNet50
```

```
5: from tensorflow.keras.preprocessing import image
6: from tensorflow.keras.applications.resnet50 import preprocess_input,
decode_predictions
```

Apart from OpenCV, numpy, and the ResNet50 model, we also import some image preprocessing functions from Keras.

Next, we load the ResNet50 model with the ImageNet weights and create the video capture object:

```
08: # Load the ResNet50 model with the ImageNet weights
09: model = ResNet50(weights='imagenet')
10: # Create the video capture object
11: video_capture = cv2.VideoCapture(0)
```

In the main loop of the code, we convert the captured frame to RGB (since OpenCV works in BGR) and resize it to 224x224 pixels, which is the input size required by the ResNet50 model:

```
13: while True:
14:     # Capture frame-by-frame
15:     ret, frame = video_capture.read()
16:
17:     if (ret):
18:         # Convert image from BGR to RGB
19:         rgb_im = cv2.cvtColor(frame,cv2.COLOR_BGR2RGB)
20:         # Resize the image to 224x224, the size required by ResNet50 model
21:         res_im = cv2.resize(rgb_im, (224, 224), interpolation = cv2.
INTER_CUBIC)
```

Then we run the image through a set of preprocessing steps, to prepare it to be ingested by the model:

```
23:         # Preprocess image
24:         prep_im = image.img_to_array(res_im)
25:         prep_im = np.expand_dims(prep_im, axis=0)
26:         prep_im = preprocess_input(prep_im)
```

Next we pass the processed image to the model and make the prediction. We also need to decode the prediction—using convenient functions from TensorFlow/Keras—to get the class label for the prediction:

```
28:          # Make the prediction
29:          preds = model.predict(prep_im)
30:
31:          # Decode the prediction
32:          (class_name, class_description, score) = decode_
predictions(preds, top=1)[0][0]
```

Finally, we overlay the predicted label and the confidence score of the prediction on the image itself, and print it on the console, and display the image using OpenCV:

```
34:          # Display the predicted class and confidence
35:          print("Predicted: {0}, Confidence: {1:.2f}".format(class_
description, score))
36:          cv2.putText(frame, "Predicted: {}".format(class_description),
(10, 50),
37:                  cv2.FONT_HERSHEY_PLAIN, 2, (255, 255, 255), 2, cv2.
LINE_AA)
38:          cv2.putText(frame, "Confidence: {0:.2f}".format(score), (10, 80),
39:                  cv2.FONT_HERSHEY_PLAIN, 2, (255, 255, 255), 2, cv2.
LINE_AA)
40:
41:          # Display the resulting frame
42:          cv2.imshow('Video Feed', frame)
43:
44:      ch = 0xFF & cv2.waitKey(1)
45:
46:      # press "q" to quit the program.
47:      if ch == ord('q'):
48:          break
49:
50: # When everything is done, release the capture
51: video_capture.release()
52: cv2.destroyAllWindows()
```

When you run the code, it will pass each frame of the video to the ResNet50 model, which will try to identify the most prominent object in the frame. The code will then display and print out the prediction along with the confidence of the prediction from the ResNet50 model (Figure 10-11).

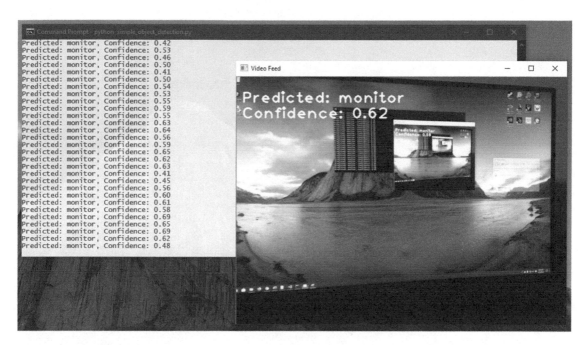

Figure 10-11. *Real-time object detection running*

What we built here is a very rudimentary object identification system that has several limitations. It can only identify one object at a time, as it takes the entire frame as the input. It also cannot identify bounding boxes for the objects it identifies. A true object detection system would be able to identify multiple objects within a frame and identify their boundaries as well.

But with the concepts we learned so far, you can investigate expanding the capabilities of the system.

The same goes for our face detection system.

How would you expand it to perform face recognition on the detected faces as well?

Think of what we learned about extracting a region-of-interest from an image. Can you think of a way to apply that concept to extract out the detected face image and run it through a deep learning model? Can you use the same concept to build the training dataset for the model as well?

## CHAPTER 11

Introduction to Generative Adversarial Networks

Can an AI be creative—can it learn to create art, for example? The traditional answer was no. But lately we are not so sure. Recently, thanks to deep learning, the definition of creativity has been become blurred.

The Story of the Artist and the Art Critic

Let us look at a story.

There once was a novice artist, who was learning to create artwork by taking inspiration from existing art pieces.

The artist created a piece of art and showed it to an art critic.

The critic analyzed the artwork and declared it not good enough. But, being conscientious, the critic also provide feedback to the artist on why it was not considered to be good enough.

The artist absorbed this feedback and attempted again to create another piece of art with changes based on the feedback, and showed it to the critic.

This happened over several cycles.

Every time the critic criticized the artwork, the artist gained experience about how to improve it.

Likewise, every time the artist generated a new artwork, the critic gained experience in how to evaluate it.

After many such iterations, the artist created an artwork that could be considered a masterpiece.

Because of the critic, the artist became a master.

What if we can do the same to an AI?

That is the idea behind generative adversarial networks.

© Thimira Amaratunga 2021
T. Amaratunga, *Deep Learning on Windows*, https://doi.org/10.1007/978-1-4842-6431-7_11

Generative Adversarial Networks

A generative adversarial network (GAN) is a machine learning model where two neural networks contest with each other to generate new data with the same characteristics of a given training set.

- **Generative:** the model generates new data, as opposed to picking the output from a given set.

- **Adversarial:** the two networks are adversaries of each other.

- **Network:** the model is based on neural networks.

Like our story, generative adversarial networks also consists of two elements: a *generator* (the artist) and a *discriminator* (the art critic). The generator is trying to learn to create items that looks "real," while the discriminator is trying to distinguish the generated items from real ones (Figure 11-1).

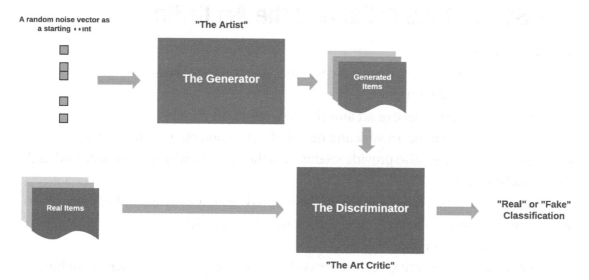

Figure 11-1. *The typical workflow of a GAN*

The items generated can be images, text, videos, sounds, or anything.

In such a system, the generator and the discriminator need to be trained together, as in the artist and the art critic in our story who got experienced together. When we are training such a system, the generator will progressively become better at generating items that look real, and the discriminator will become better at telling them apart from the real ones. After many iterations of training like this, there will come a point where the discriminator may no longer be able to tell the generated items from the real ones (Figure 11-2).

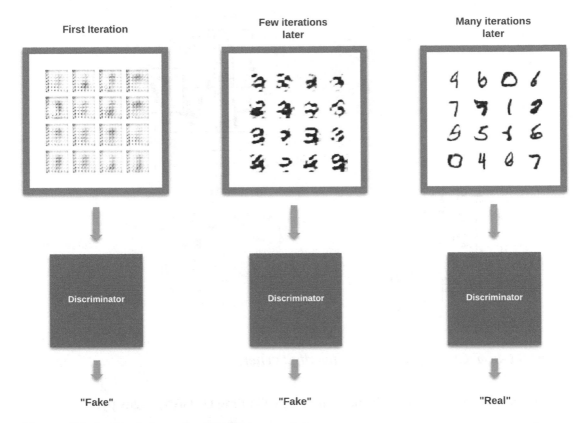

Figure 11-2.   *Training of a GAN*

To simplify the explanation, let us take a GAN than generates images. The generator takes a random noise vector as input, while the discriminator takes a training set of real images belonging to the class of images that we would like to generate.

Generating Handwritten Digits with DCGAN

A DCGAN (deep convolutional generative adversarial network) is one of the simplest GAN implementations. In it we use convolutional layers in the generator and the discriminator, which makes DCGAN models work great with images.

We will use the MNIST dataset as the input. Our target would be to generate images that are indistinguishable from human handwritten digits.

Our workflow would look like the following (Figure 11-3).

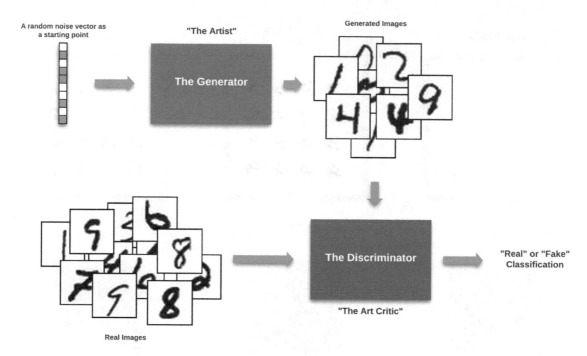

Figure 11-3. *DCGAN for handwritten digit generation*

We will start with a new code file, which we will name DCGAN_Digits.py.

We start our code by importing the necessary packages:

```
01: import tensorflow as tf
02:
03: from tensorflow.keras import layers
04: import glob
05: import imageio
06: import matplotlib.pyplot as plt
07: import numpy as np
08: import os
09: import PIL
10: import time
11: import cv2
```

We then load our dataset and normalize it:

```
13: (train_images, train_labels), (_, _) = tf.keras.datasets.mnist.load_
data()
14:
15: train_images = train_images.reshape(train_images.shape[0], 28, 28,
1).astype('float32')
16: train_images = (train_images - 127.5) / 127.5 # Normalize the images to
[-1, 1]
```

The MNIST pixel values are in the 0–255 range. Here we normalize it to -1–1 range.

Then we define the batch sizes, then shuffle and chunk the dataset for training:

```
18: BUFFER_SIZE = 60000
19: BATCH_SIZE = 256
20:
21: # Batch and shuffle the data
22: train_dataset = tf.data.Dataset.from_tensor_slices(train_images).
shuffle(BUFFER_SIZE).batch(BATCH_SIZE)
```

Next, we need to define the generator and discriminator models.

The Generator

Our generator model takes in a seed of random noise and outputs a 28x28x1 image. The model would look like this (Figure 11-4):

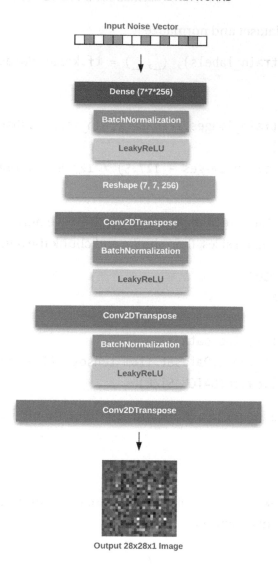

Figure 11-4. *The generator model*

The model uses Conv2DTranspose layers to upsample the input at each layer.
LeakyReLU is used as the regularization, as it allows small amounts of negative values to
go through, as opposed to ReLU, which removes all negatives.

We will define a new function make_generator_model() for the generator model:

```
24: def make_generator_model():
25:     model = tf.keras.Sequential()
26:     model.add(layers.Dense(7*7*256, use_bias=False, input_shape=(100,)))
27:     model.add(layers.BatchNormalization())
```

```
28:      model.add(layers.LeakyReLU())
29:
30:      model.add(layers.Reshape((7, 7, 256)))
31:      assert model.output_shape == (None, 7, 7, 256) # Note: None is the
batch size
32:
33:      model.add(layers.Conv2DTranspose(128, (5, 5), strides=(1, 1),
padding='same', use_bias=False))
34:      assert model.output_shape == (None, 7, 7, 128)
35:      model.add(layers.BatchNormalization())
36:      model.add(layers.LeakyReLU())
37:
38:      model.add(layers.Conv2DTranspose(64, (5, 5), strides=(2, 2),
padding='same', use_bias=False))
39:      assert model.output_shape == (None, 14, 14, 64)
40:      model.add(layers.BatchNormalization())
41:      model.add(layers.LeakyReLU())
42:
43:      model.add(layers.Conv2DTranspose(1, (5, 5), strides=(2, 2),
padding='same', use_bias=False, activation='tanh'))
44:      assert model.output_shape == (None, 28, 28, 1)
45:
46:      return model
```

We can now use this function to create a model instance and generate an initial image:

```
48: generator = make_generator_model()
49:
50: noise = tf.random.normal([1, 100])
51: generated_image = generator(noise, training=False)
52:
53: plt.imshow(generated_image[0, :, :, 0], cmap='gray')
54: plt.show()
55: plt.close()
```

As the generator model is still untrained, the output will look like noise (Figure 11-5).

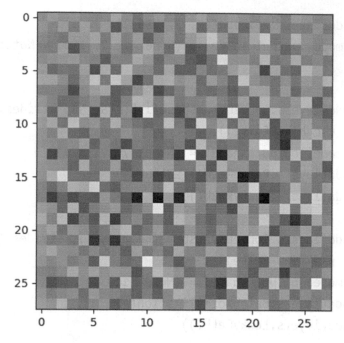

Figure 11-5. *Output from the untrained generator*

The Discriminator

The discriminator is a simple deep learning image classifier (based on a familiar convolutional neural network). It will take a 28x28x1 image as input and classify them as real or fake. The discriminator model would look like this (Figure 11-6):

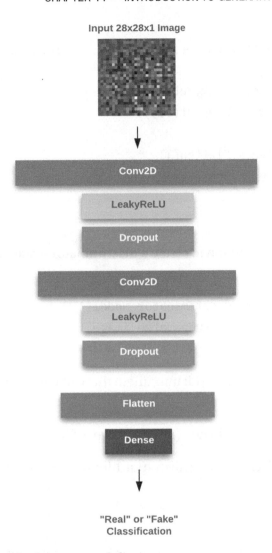

Figure 11-6. *The discriminator model*

We will define the make_discriminator_model() function for the discriminator model. It uses our familiar Conv2D layers:

```
57: def make_discriminator_model():
58:     model = tf.keras.Sequential()
59:     model.add(layers.Conv2D(64, (5, 5), strides=(2, 2), padding='same',
60:                                     input_shape=[28, 28, 1]))
61:     model.add(layers.LeakyReLU())
62:     model.add(layers.Dropout(0.3))
```

```
63:
64:     model.add(layers.Conv2D(128, (5, 5), strides=(2, 2),
padding='same'))
65:     model.add(layers.LeakyReLU())
66:     model.add(layers.Dropout(0.3))
67:
68:     model.add(layers.Flatten())
69:     model.add(layers.Dense(1))
70:
71:     return model
```

We can then use this function to create a discriminator instance and pass the image we generated earlier:

```
73: discriminator = make_discriminator_model()
74: decision = discriminator(generated_image)
75: print (decision)
```

As the discriminator model is still untrained, this will output something like the following:

```
tf.Tensor([[0.00122253]], shape=(1, 1), dtype=float32)
```

Once trained, the discriminator will output 1 for real images and 0 for fake.

The Feedback

Like our story of the artist and the art critic, in order to improve, our generator and discriminator need feedback. Here we are defining the loss values for both the generator and the discriminator, which we will later use to calculate the gradients that will update each of them when training:

```
77: # This method returns a helper function to compute cross entropy loss
78: cross_entropy = tf.keras.losses.BinaryCrossentropy(from_logits=True)
79:
80: def discriminator_loss(real_output, fake_output):
81:     real_loss = cross_entropy(tf.ones_like(real_output), real_output)
82:     fake_loss = cross_entropy(tf.zeros_like(fake_output), fake_output)
```

```
83:        total_loss = real_loss + fake_loss
84:        return total_loss
85:
86: def generator_loss(fake_output):
87:        return cross_entropy(tf.ones_like(fake_output), fake_output)
88:
89: generator_optimizer = tf.keras.optimizers.Adam(1e-4)
90: discriminator_optimizer = tf.keras.optimizers.Adam(1e-4)
```

The discriminator's loss is defined by how well it can distinguish between real images and generated ones. So we take in the predictions from the discriminator for real images (the array of real_output) and for the fake images (the array of fake_output), and compare them against the expected outputs. Once properly trained, the discriminator should yield 1s for the real images, while yielding 0s for the generated or fake images. Therefore, we get the difference between the outputs for the real images with an array of 1s, and the difference between the outputs for fake images with an array of 0s.

Similarly, we expect the generator, once properly trained, to generate images that yields 1s from the discriminator. Like before, we compare the outputs from the generated or fake images to an array of 1s to determine the loss for the generator.

We also define two separate Adam optimizers for the generator and the discriminator, as the two models need to be trained separately while simultaneously.

Since training of GANs can take a long time, we configure model checkpoints to be saved periodically, which would help to recover if the training gets disrupted. Make sure to create a directory named training_checkpoints in the directory where your code file is:

```
92: checkpoint_dir = './training_checkpoints'
93: checkpoint_prefix = os.path.join(checkpoint_dir, "ckpt")
94: checkpoint = tf.train.Checkpoint(generator_optimizer=generator_optimizer,
95:                                  discriminator_optimizer=discriminator_
optimizer,
96:                                  generator=generator,
97:                                  discriminator=discriminator)
```

The Training

Next, we define the training parameters and the random seed for the training:

```
100: EPOCHS = 1000
101: noise_dim = 100
102: num_examples_to_generate = 16
103:
104: # We will reuse this seed overtime (so it's easier)
105: # to visualize progress in the animated GIF)
106: seed = tf.random.normal([num_examples_to_generate, noise_dim])
```

We will reuse the same seed throughout the training epochs to better visualize how each generated sample improves over the epochs (as the same seed results in same digits to be generated).

We then define the function for the training step:

```
108: # Notice the use of `tf.function`
109: # This annotation causes the function to be "compiled".
110: @tf.function
111: def train_step(images):
112:     noise = tf.random.normal([BATCH_SIZE, noise_dim])
113:
114:     with tf.GradientTape() as gen_tape, tf.GradientTape() as disc_
tape:
115:         generated_images = generator(noise, training=True)
116:
117:         real_output = discriminator(images, training=True)
118:         fake_output = discriminator(generated_images, training=True)
119:
120:         gen_loss = generator_loss(fake_output)
121:         disc_loss = discriminator_loss(real_output, fake_output)
122:
123:     gradients_of_generator = gen_tape.gradient(gen_loss, generator.
trainable_variables)
124:     gradients_of_discriminator = disc_tape.gradient(disc_loss,
discriminator.trainable_variables)
```

```
125:
126:        generator_optimizer.apply_gradients(zip(gradients_of_generator,
generator.trainable_variables))
127:        discriminator_optimizer.apply_gradients(zip(gradients_of_
discriminator, discriminator.trainable_variables))
```

In each training step we pass a random noise vector to the generator, which generates a set of images using it as the input. These generated images, as well as a set of real images, are then passed through the discriminator to get their outputs. These outputs are the predictions/classifications from the discriminator as to whether it thinks they are real or fake. Using the loss functions we defined earlier, the loss values are calculated for the generator and discriminator and the gradients of the loss values are used to update them. Think of it as the "feedback" that nudges them to train in the correct direction.

Next is the function for the main training loop:

```
129: def train(dataset, epochs):
130:     train_start = time.time()
131:     for epoch in range(epochs):
132:         start = time.time()
133:
134:         for image_batch in dataset:
135:             train_step(image_batch)
136:
137:         # Produce images for the GIF as we go
138:         generate_and_save_images(generator,
139:                                  epoch + 1,
140:                                  seed,
141:                                  display = True)
142:
143:         # Save the model every 15 epochs
144:         if (epoch + 1) % 15 == 0:
145:             checkpoint.save(file_prefix = checkpoint_prefix)
146:
147:         print ('Time for epoch {} is {} sec'.format(epoch + 1, time.
time()-start))
```

```
148:
149:    print ('Time for total training is {} sec'.format(time.time()-
train_start))
```

Here, we are basically running through each of the training batches through number of epochs we defined. And at the end of each training epoch, we use the seed we defined earlier to generate a set of samples and save those images files.

The function is defined as follows, which is mainly postprocessing of the generated images. Make sure to create a directory named output in the directory where your code file is located:

```
151: def generate_and_save_images(model, epoch, test_input, display =
False):
152:    # Notice `training` is set to False.
153:    # This is so all layers run in inference mode.
154:    predictions = model(test_input, training=False)
155:
156:    fig = plt.figure(figsize=(4,4), facecolor='black')
157:
158:    for i in range(predictions.shape[0]):
159:        plt.subplot(4, 4, i+1)
160:        image = predictions[i, :, :, 0] * 127.5 + 127.5
161:        plt.imshow(image, cmap='gray')
162:        plt.axis('off')
163:
164:    plt.savefig('output/image_at_epoch_{:04d}.png'.format(epoch),
facecolor=fig.get_facecolor())
165:    plt.close()
166:    disp_image = cv2.imread('output/image_at_epoch_{:04d}.png'.
format(epoch))
167:    disp_image = cv2.bitwise_not(disp_image)
168:    cv2.imwrite('output/image_at_epoch_{:04d}.png'.format(epoch),
disp_image)
169:    if (display):
170:        cv2.imshow("Results", disp_image)
171:        cv2.waitKey(100)
```

Once all the training utility functions are defined, we call the main training function:

```
173: train(train_dataset, EPOCHS)
```

At the end of the training we do some cleanup steps, and then combine all the generated output images into an animated GIF file:

```
175: checkpoint.restore(tf.train.latest_checkpoint(checkpoint_dir))
176: cv2.destroyAllWindows()
177:
178: anim_file = 'dcgan.gif'
179:
180: with imageio.get_writer(anim_file, mode='I') as writer:
181:     filenames = glob.glob('output/image*.png')
182:     filenames = sorted(filenames)
183:     last = -1
184:     for i,filename in enumerate(filenames):
185:         frame = 2*(i**0.5)
186:         if round(frame) > round(last):
187:             last = frame
188:         else:
189:             continue
190:         image = imageio.imread(filename)
191:         writer.append_data(image)
192:         cv2.imshow("Results", image)
193:         cv2.waitKey(100)
194:     image = imageio.imread(filename)
195:     writer.append_data(image)
```

Running the Training

With our DCGAN model ready, we can start the training by running:

```
Python DCGAN_Digits.py
```

The script will display the time taken for each epoch in the console, as well as the results from each epoch in an OpenCV window (Figure 11-7).

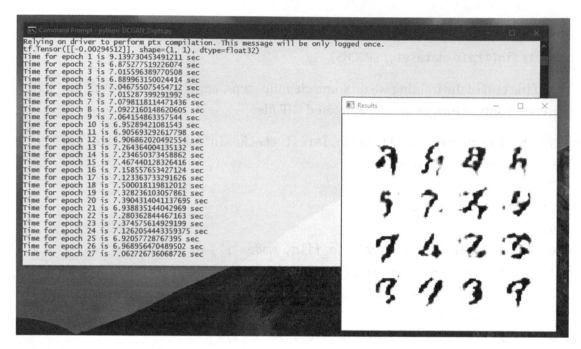

Figure 11-7.   *Training running for DCGAN digit generation*

When running on GPU on an RTX2070 the training took about 2 hours for 1,000 epochs (Figure 11-8).

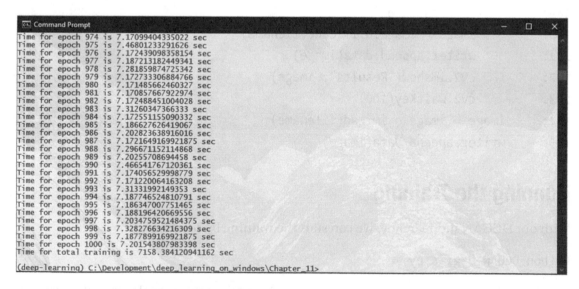

Figure 11-8.   *DCGAN training completed*

Note   Training of GANs can take a long time. Our DCGAN model may take hours to train based on the processing power of the machine being run, as well as whether you are running the model on CPU or GPU. Typically, it may take 7 to 10 seconds per epoch to run on a GPU. Running GAN training on CPU may not be practical due to the time it might take to complete the training.

If you are unsure, run the training for a smaller number of epochs first to get an idea of how long it might take.

Tip   If the training seems to get stuck after the initial noise image is displayed, you can try commenting out the lines 53 to 55. This can happen because our GAN training can take large amounts of system resources and may occasionally exhaust the resources of the machine when attempting to visualize the results. Similarly, you can set the display parameter to False on line 141.

You can use Kaggle notebooks[1] to run your code if you are having issues running in your local machine. Kaggle provides free access to NVIDIA TESLA P100 GPUs in their notebooks/kernels,[2] which can greatly accelerate training complex models such as GANs.

At the start of the training, the results would look like random noise (Figure 11-9).

---

[1]Kaggle, "Notebooks Guide," https://www.kaggle.com/docs/notebooks, [24 Nov, 2020].
[2]Kaggle, "GPU Usage," https://www.kaggle.com/docs/efficient-gpu-usage, [24 Nov, 2020].

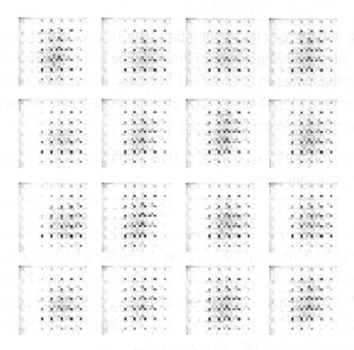

Figure 11-9. *Images generated at epoch 1*

After 100 epochs the distinct shapes of digits are starting to show (Figure 11-10).

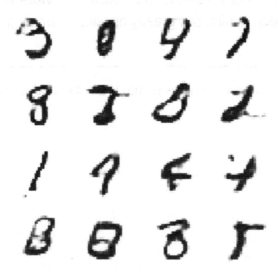

Figure 11-10. *Images generated at epoch 100*

After 200 epochs, the shapes are a bit more refined (Figure 11-11).

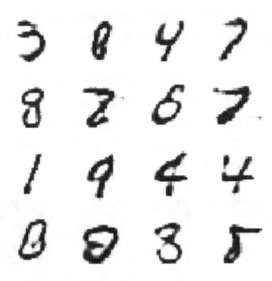

Figure 11-11. *Images generated at epoch 200*

After 1,000 epochs, the images are almost indistinguishable from human handwritten digits (Figure 11-12).

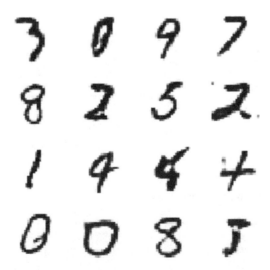

Figure 11-12. *Images generated at epoch 1,000*

You can also view the generated dcgan.gif file for the amination of how the generated results improved over the training.

Can We Generate Something More Complex?

We have now seen how our DCGAN model can generate handwritten digits that are nearly indistinguishable from ones drawn by humans. But can GANs generate something more complex?

To find out, let us try to apply what we learned from our DCGAN_Digits model on to something much more complex: generating images of human faces.

For that, we will need a large dataset with images of human faces to train our discriminator model. We will use the CelebFaces Attributes (CelebA) dataset from Kaggle for that purpose (Figure 11-13).

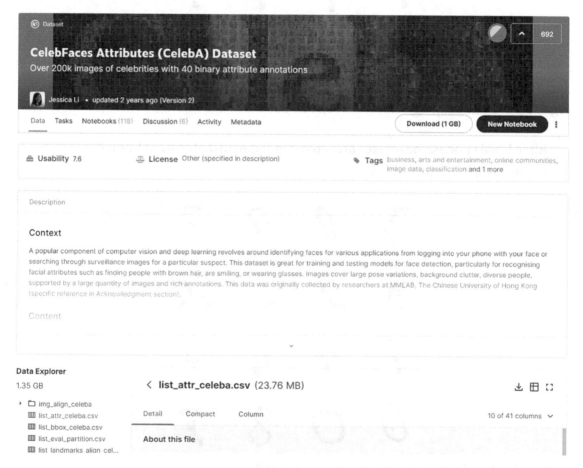

Figure 11-13. *CelebFaces attributes (CelebA) dataset from Kaggle*

The CelebA dataset is about 1.4GB is size.[3] Once downloaded, extract the zip file and rename the top-level directory to celeba-dataset. You should end up with the following folder structure (Figure 11-14):

Figure 11-14. *Folder structure of the uncompressed CelebA dataset*

With the dataset ready, let us start a new code file for our face generator, which we will name DCGAN_Faces.py. Like before, remember to create the training_checkpoints and output directories where your code file is located.

We will start by importing the necessary packages:

```
01: import tensorflow as tf
02:
03: from tensorflow.keras import layers
04: import glob
05: import imageio
06: import matplotlib.pyplot as plt
07: import numpy as np
08: import os
09: import PIL
10: import time
11: import cv2
```

We will then define a helper function to load each face image and crop only the face part of it. As the images in the CelebA dataset is already aligned, we can use hard-coded values to crop the faces:

```
13: # Load the image, crop just the face, and return image data as a numpy array
14: def load_image(image_file_path):
15:     img = PIL.Image.open(image_file_path)
```

---

[3]You can download the CelebA dataset from Kaggle (CelebA dataset), https://www.kaggle.com/jessicali9530/celeba-dataset, [2 June, 2018].

```
16:     img = img.crop([25,65,153,193])
17:     img = img.resize((64,64))
18:     data = np.asarray( img, dtype="int32" )
19:     return data
```

We then load our dataset image paths, and define the batch parameters:

```
21: dataset_path = "celeba-dataset/img_align_celeba/img_align_celeba/"
22:
23: # load the list of training images
24: train_images = np.array(os.listdir(dataset_path))
25:
26: BUFFER_SIZE = 2000
27: BATCH_SIZE = 8
28:
29: # shuffle and list
30: np.random.shuffle(train_images)
31: # chunk the training images list in to batches
32: train_images = np.split(train_images[:BUFFER_SIZE],BATCH_SIZE)
```

We then define our generator model:

```
34: def make_generator_model():
35:     model = tf.keras.Sequential()
36:
37:     model.add(layers.Dense(4*4*1024, use_bias = False, input_shape =
(100,)))
38:     model.add(layers.BatchNormalization())
39:     model.add(layers.LeakyReLU())
40:
41:     model.add(layers.Reshape((4,4,1024)))
42:     assert model.output_shape == (None, 4, 4, 1024) # Note: None is the
batch size
43:
44:     model.add(layers.Conv2DTranspose(512, (5, 5), strides = (2,2),
padding = "same", use_bias = False))
45:     assert model.output_shape == (None, 8, 8, 512)
```

```
46:      model.add(layers.BatchNormalization())
47:      model.add(layers.LeakyReLU())
48:
49:      model.add(layers.Conv2DTranspose(256, (5,5), strides = (2,2),
padding = "same", use_bias = False))
50:      assert model.output_shape == (None, 16, 16, 256)
51:      model.add(layers.BatchNormalization())
52:      model.add(layers.LeakyReLU())
53:
54:      model.add(layers.Conv2DTranspose(128, (5,5), strides = (2,2),
padding = "same", use_bias = False))
55:      assert model.output_shape == (None, 32, 32, 128)
56:      model.add(layers.BatchNormalization())
57:      model.add(layers.LeakyReLU())
58:
59:      model.add(layers.Conv2DTranspose(3, (5,5), strides = (2,2), padding
= "same", use_bias = False, activation = "tanh"))
60:      assert model.output_shape == (None, 64, 64, 3)
61:
62:      return model
63:
64: generator = make_generator_model()
65:
66: noise = tf.random.normal([1,100])
67: generated_image = generator(noise, training = False)
68: plt.imshow(generated_image[0], interpolation="nearest")
69: plt.show()
70: plt.close()
```

This uses the same concepts as the generator in our DCGAN_Digits model. But we are using a deeper model here, as our data is more complex.

The image generated from the untrained generator will look something like this (Figure 11-15):

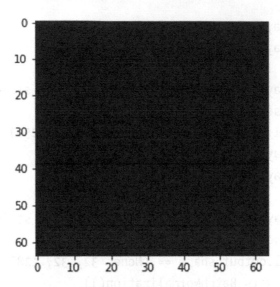

Figure 11-15. *Output from the untrained generator*

We then define our discriminator model, a little deeper than our DCGAN_Digits model:

```
72: def make_discriminator_model():
73:     model = tf.keras.Sequential()
74:     model.add(layers.Conv2D(64, (5, 5), strides=(2, 2), padding='same',
input_shape=[64, 64, 3]))
75:     model.add(layers.LeakyReLU())
76:     model.add(layers.Dropout(0.3))
77:
78:     model.add(layers.Conv2D(512, (5, 5), strides=(2, 2),
padding='same'))
79:     model.add(layers.LeakyReLU())
80:     model.add(layers.Dropout(0.3))
81:
82:     model.add(layers.Conv2D(128, (5, 5), strides=(2, 2),
padding='same'))
83:     model.add(layers.LeakyReLU())
84:     model.add(layers.Dropout(0.3))
85:
86:     model.add(layers.Flatten())
87:     model.add(layers.Dense(1))
```

```
88:
89:     return model
90:
91: discriminator = make_discriminator_model()
92: decision = discriminator(generated_image)
93: print (decision)
94: # output will be something like tf.Tensor([[-6.442342e-05]], shape=(1,
1), dtype=float32)
```

The loss functions, checkpoints, and training parameters are exactly as we used before:

```
096: # This method returns a helper function to compute cross entropy loss
097: cross_entropy = tf.keras.losses.BinaryCrossentropy(from_logits=True)
098:
099: def discriminator_loss(real_output, fake_output):
100:     real_loss = cross_entropy(tf.ones_like(real_output), real_output)
101:     fake_loss = cross_entropy(tf.zeros_like(fake_output), fake_output)
102:     total_loss = real_loss + fake_loss
103:     return total_loss
104:
105: def generator_loss(fake_output):
106:     return cross_entropy(tf.ones_like(fake_output), fake_output)
107:
108: generator_optimizer = tf.keras.optimizers.Adam(1e-4)
109: discriminator_optimizer = tf.keras.optimizers.Adam(1e-4)
110:
111: checkpoint_dir = './training_checkpoints'
112: checkpoint_prefix = os.path.join(checkpoint_dir, "ckpt")
113: checkpoint = tf.train.Checkpoint(generator_optimizer=generator_optimizer,
114:                                  discriminator_
optimizer=discriminator_optimizer,
115:                                  generator=generator,
116:                                  discriminator=discriminator)
117:
118:
119: EPOCHS = 1000
120: noise_dim = 100
```

```
121: num_examples_to_generate = 16
122:
123: # setting the seed for the randomization, so that we can reproduce the
results
124: tf.random.set_seed(1234)
125: # We will reuse this seed overtime (so it's easier)
126: # to visualize progress in the animated GIF)
127: seed = tf.random.normal([num_examples_to_generate, noise_dim])
```

In the train step function, we use the helper function load_image to preprocess our images. The rest of the steps are same as before:

```
129: # Notice the use of `tf.function`
130: # This annotation causes the function to be "compiled".
131: @tf.function
132: def train_step(images):
133:     noise = tf.random.normal([BATCH_SIZE, noise_dim])
134:
135:     # pre-process the images
136:     new_images = []
137:     for file_name in images:
138:         new_pic = load_image(dataset_path + file_name)
139:         new_images.append(new_pic)
140:
141:     images = np.array(new_images)
142:     images = images.reshape(images.shape[0], 64, 64,
3).astype('float32')
143:     images = (images - 127.5) / 127.5 # Normalize the images to [-1, 1]
144:
145:     with tf.GradientTape() as gen_tape, tf.GradientTape() as disc_tape:
146:         generated_images = generator(noise, training=True)
147:
148:         real_output = discriminator(images, training=True)
149:         fake_output = discriminator(generated_images, training=True)
150:
151:         gen_loss = generator_loss(fake_output)
```

```
152:        disc_loss = discriminator_loss(real_output, fake_output)
153:
154:     gradients_of_generator = gen_tape.gradient(gen_loss, generator.
trainable_variables)
155:     gradients_of_discriminator = disc_tape.gradient(disc_loss,
discriminator.trainable_variables)
156:
157:     generator_optimizer.apply_gradients(zip(gradients_of_generator,
generator.trainable_variables))
158:     discriminator_optimizer.apply_gradients(zip(gradients_of_
discriminator, discriminator.trainable_variables))
159:
160:     images = None
```

Finally, the functions for the main training loop, saving the generated images, and generating the animation all use the same steps as we used in our DCGAN_Digits model:

```
162: def train(dataset, epochs):
163:     tf.print("Starting Training")
164:     train_start = time.time()
165:
166:     for epoch in range(epochs):
167:         start = time.time()
168:         tf.print("Starting Epoch:", epoch)
169:
170:         batch_count = 1
171:         for image_batch in dataset:
172:             train_step(image_batch)
173:             batch_count += 1
174:
175:         # Produce images for the GIF as we go
176:         generate_and_save_images(generator,
177:                                     epoch + 1,
178:                                     seed)
179:
180:         tf.print("Epoch:", epoch, "finished")
```

```
181:          tf.print()
182:          tf.print('Time for epoch {} is {} sec'.format(epoch + 1, time.
time()-start))
183:          tf.print()
184:
185:      # Save the model every epoch
186:      checkpoint.save(file_prefix = checkpoint_prefix)
187:
188:      print ('Time for total training is {} sec'.format(time.time()-
train_start))
189:
190:
191: def generate_and_save_images(model, epoch, test_input):
192:      # Notice `training` is set to False.
193:      # This is so all layers run in inference mode.
194:      predictions = model(test_input, training=False).numpy()
195:
196:      fig = plt.figure(figsize=(4,4))
197:
198:      for i in range(predictions.shape[0]):
199:          plt.subplot(4, 4, i+1)
200:          image = predictions[i]
201:          plt.imshow(image)
202:          plt.axis('off')
203:
204:      plt.savefig('output/image_at_epoch_{:04d}.png'.format(epoch))
205:      plt.show()
206:
207: train(train_images, EPOCHS)
208:
209: checkpoint.restore(tf.train.latest_checkpoint(checkpoint_dir))
210: cv2.destroyAllWindows()
211:
212: anim_file = 'dcgan_faces.gif'
```

```
213:
214: with imageio.get_writer(anim_file, mode='I') as writer:
215:     filenames = glob.glob('output/image*.png')
216:     filenames = sorted(filenames)
217:     last = -1
218:     for i,filename in enumerate(filenames):
219:         frame = 2*(i**0.5)
220:         if round(frame) > round(last):
221:             last = frame
222:         else:
223:             continue
224:         image = imageio.imread(filename)
225:         writer.append_data(image)
226:         cv2.imshow("Results", image)
227:         cv2.waitKey(100)
228:     image = imageio.imread(filename)
229:     writer.append_data(image)
```

So, how well does our face generator perform?

At the start of the training, the generator produces pure black images (Figure 11-16).

Figure 11-16. *Images generated at epoch 1*

After 100 epochs, some shapes are starting to appear in the output (Figure 11-17).

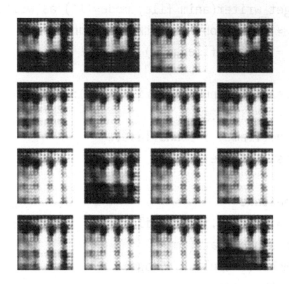

Figure 11-17. *Images generated at epoch 100*

After 1,000 epochs, some facial feature–like shapes are being generated (Figure 11-18).

Figure 11-18. *Images generated at epoch 1,000*

While not life-like, it is quite remarkable that our generator was able to learn to generate features that we can associate with human faces.

To improve our model further, you can try training for a longer number of epochs. Or try combinations of deeper models for the generator and the discriminator.

However, keep in mind that training this model for 1,000 epochs took over seven hours on a GPU. You should plan ahead when attempting to push further.

What Else Can GANs Do?

As we discussed earlier, DCGAN is one of the simplest implementations of GANs. And here we have only scratched the surface of what GANs can do.

Generative adversarial networks are one of the latest research areas within deep learning and AI. It is also one of the areas that is most actively developed in the past few years. Many innovative GAN architectures have recently been proposed and implemented, with more and more innovation happening in that area daily. Following are just a few of notable GAN architectures:

- **CycleGAN (Cycle-Consistent GANs):** able to learn to transform between images of different styles, without needing to have paired image data for training.

- **StyleGAN (style-based GANs):** able to generate high resolution images, by having a stacked model where the lower layers generate lower-resolution images that are progressively enhanced by the higher layers of the model.

- **cGAN (conditional GANs):** able to utilize additional available information (e.g., labels for images) to learn rather than relying on just the raw image data.

- **lsGAN (least-squares GANs):** uses the least-squares loss function for the discriminator instead of the traditional cross-entropy loss function, resulting in higher-quality images.

- **DiscoGAN (discover cross-domain relations with GANs):** able to learn cross-domain relationships between related sets of images in an unsupervised manner.

With these, and many more novel architectures, GANs have been able to produce some groundbreaking results.

A project from NVIDIA named "This Person Does Not Exist"[4] is able to use a StyleGAN to generate photo-realistic images of human faces (Figure 11-19).

Figure 11-19. *Some samples from "This Person Does Not Exist" by NVIDIA*

The GauGAN project,[5] also by NVIDIA, can convert rough sketches into photo-realistic images (Figure 11-20).

---

[4]This Person Does Not Exist, https://thispersondoesnotexist.com, [23 Mar, 2020].
[5]NVIDIA, "The GauGAN Project," http://nvidia-research-mingyuliu.com/gaugan, [18 Oct, 2019].

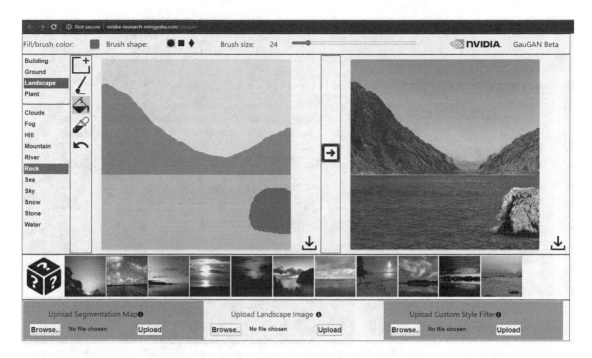

Figure 11-20. *NVIDIA GauGAN in action*

GANs are not just for image generation. The OpenAI Jukebox project[6] can generate music as well as singing using GAN models (Figure 11-21).

---

[6]OpenAI, "The OpenAI Jukebox Project," https://openai.com/blog/jukebox, [30 Apr, 2020].

Figure 11-21. The OpenAI Jukebox Project

With the rapid advancement of GANs, there may come a day when human creativity will be challenged.

CHAPTER 12

Basics of Reinforcement Learning

In Chapter 1, we briefly touched upon the concept of reinforcement learning. As we discussed there, reinforcement learning is one of the methods in which machine learning models are trained.

Reinforcement learning is the main concept behind game AI programming and models like AlphaZero and OpenAI Five (see Appendix 1), as well as applications in the robotics field.

In reinforcement learning, the AI system—typically referred to as the *agent*—is introduced to an environment and is given a goal to achieve. The agent is also given a set of possible actions that can be taken to change the state of the environment. The task of the agent is to use those actions to achieve the desired goal state. The agent is allowed to make any of those possible actions. Based on how appropriate that action is toward achieving the desired goal, the agent will be given a reward or a penalty. By learning to maximize the reward or minimize the penalty, the agent will eventually learn the steps needed to achieve the goal (Figure 12-1).

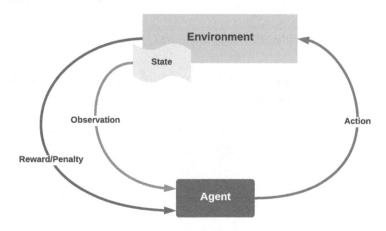

Figure 12-1. *The workflow of a reinforcement learning system*

© Thimira Amaratunga 2021
T. Amaratunga, *Deep Learning on Windows*, https://doi.org/10.1007/978-1-4842-6431-7_12

Because the agent is not given a full set of labeled data to train on, as well as given some feedback on the actions, reinforcement learning falls in between supervised and unsupervised learning.

If we are to experiment with reinforcement learning, we need a framework that can define an environment, a goal to achieve, actions, and a reward mechanism for the actions.

Luckily, there is a framework developed just for that: OpenAI Gym.

What is OpenAI Gym?

OpenAI Gym is an open-source framework developed by OpenAI, to provide tools to train reinforcement learning algorithms.

OpenAI provides a set of built-in environments with classic reinforcement learning problems with their defined actions, states, and reward mechanisms (Figure 12-2). Gym also allows you to add third-party or custom environments as well.

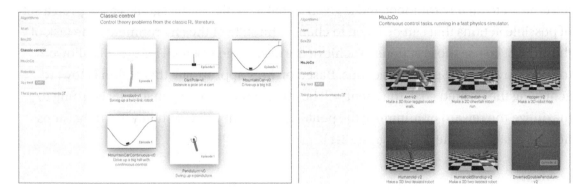

Figure 12-2. *Some available environments in OpenAI Gym*

For the built-in environments, Gym also provides rendering/visualization of the environment, actions, and outcomes (Figure 12-3).

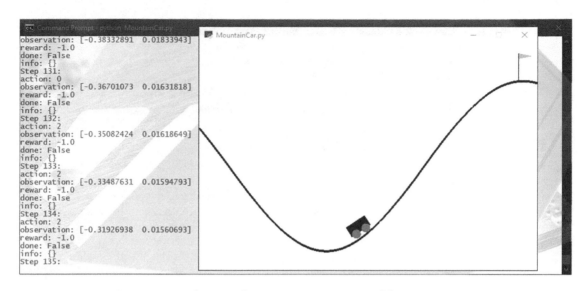

Figure 12-3. *OpenAI rendering the MountainCar problem*

While providing the environments, OpenAI Gym does not limit you to use any framework for the actual training of your reinforcement learning model. Therefore, you can use TensorFlow/Keras, or any other machine learning framework you are familiar with, to train out models with it.

Setting up OpenAI Gym

OpenAI Gym is available as a PIP package. Although originally OpenAI Gym was only meant to support Linux and Mac OS, the Windows support is now better. Most built-in Gym environments now work on Windows.

Note   Some advanced environments, such as the MuJoCo (**Mu**lti-**Jo**int dynamics with **Co**ntact) environments, require extremely specific dependency setups as well as proprietary licenses to use. So we will skip them here.

We will first install the minimal package using pip (Figure 12-4):

```
pip install gym
```

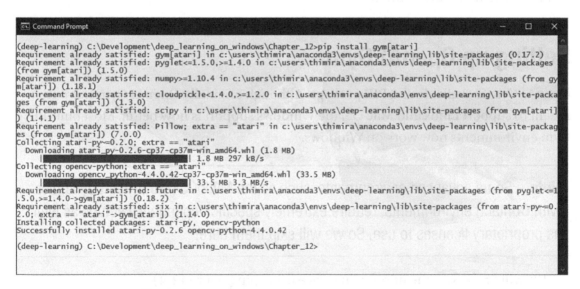

Figure 12-4. *Installing the minimal package of Gym*

This will give you access to the Algorithms, Toy Text, and Classic Control environments.[1] Next, we can install the Atari environments by running (Figure 12-5):

```
pip install gym[atari]
```

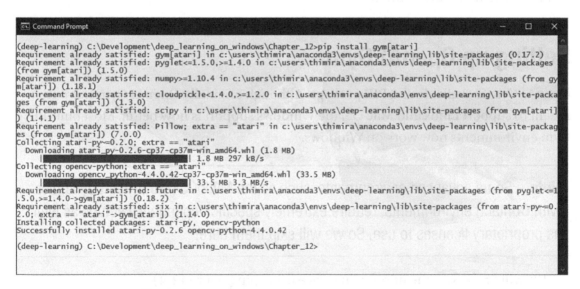

Figure 12-5. *Installing the Atari environments*

---

[1]Gym (OpenAI Gym environments), https://gym.openai.com/envs/#classic_control, [2 Apr, 2020].

Finally, let us get the Box2D environments installed.

To get Box2D working, we need to have the Swig binaries installed. We can install it using conda (Figure 12-6):

```
conda install swig
```

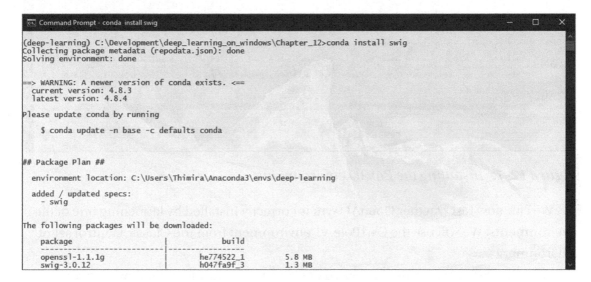

Figure 12-6.   *Installing the swig binaries using Conda*

This allows us to install the Box2D environments (Figure 12-7):

```
pip install gym[box2d]
```

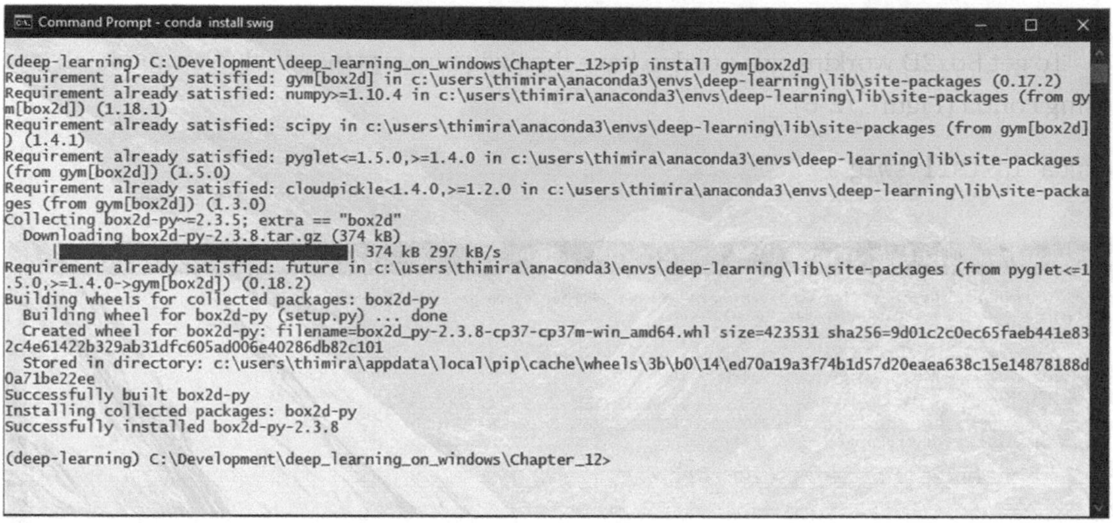

Figure 12-7.   *Installing the Box2D environments*

We can now test whether OpenAI Gym is correctly installed by launching one of the environments. We will use the CartPole-v1 environment from the Classic Control set of environments.

We will create a new code file named CartPole.py, and add the following code:

```
01: import gym
02: env = gym.make('CartPole-v1')
03: observation = env.reset()
04: for step_index in range(1000):
05:     env.render()
06:     action = env.action_space.sample() # take a random action
07:     observation, reward, done, info = env.step(action)
08:     print("Step {}:".format(step_index))
09:     print("Action: {}".format(action))
10:     print("Observation: {}".format(observation))
11:     print("Reward: {}".format(reward))
12:     print("Is Done?: {}".format(done))
13:     print("Info: {}".format(info))
14: observation = env.reset()
15: env.close()
```

Here we are initializing the CartPole-v1 environment and running it for 1,000 steps.

The `env.action_space.sample()` function will return a random action from the list of permitted actions for that environment. We perform this action by passing it to the `env.step()` function, which will return four parameters:

- **observation:** the current state of the environment

- **reward:** the reward or the penalty for the action

- **done:** whether the simulation has reached a done state; either the goal is reached, or the task has failed and need to restart

- **info:** any additional information provided by the environment for debugging purposes (the agent should not use this information for training)

Running this code will result in the CartPole-v1 environment being rendered and the results from each step being printed in the console (Figure 12-8).

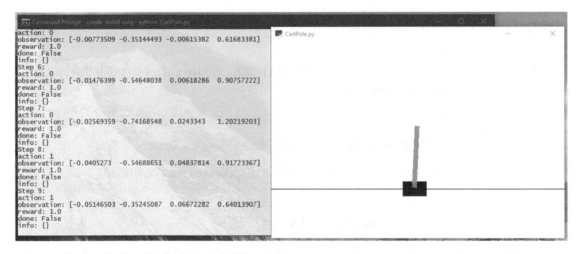

Figure 12-8. *Testing OpenAI Gym by running the CartPole environment*

Solving the CartPole Problem

Let us now take a closer look at the CartPole problem and see how we can build a reinforcement learning model to solve it.

In the CartPole problem there is a friction-less track, and on this track there is a cart. A pole is attached to this cart in a way that the pole can freely rotate around the pivot point where it attaches to the cart. The goal of the CartPole problem is to prevent the pole from falling over by changing the velocity of the cart (Figure 12-9).

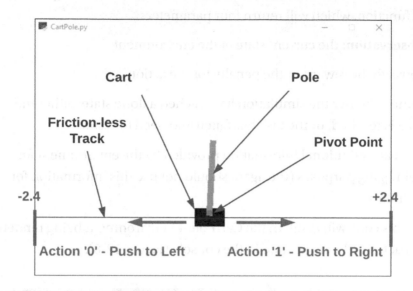

Figure 12-9. *The elements of the CartPole environment*

The only two actions you can take on the environment are either 0 (push the cart to the left) or 1 (push the cart to the right).

The simulation will fail if:[2]

- the angle of the pole goes beyond ±12°

- the position of the cart goes beyond the displayed area (position is more than ±2.4)

- the number of steps goes beyond 500.

The observations return an array of four values, which are cart position (-2.4 to +2.4), cart velocity (-Infinity to +Infinity), pole angle (-41.8° to + 41.8°), and pole velocity at the tip (-Infinity to +Infinity) (Figure 12-10).

---

[2]Github, "CartPole Overview," https://github.com/openai/gym/wiki/CartPole-v0, [8 Feb, 2020].

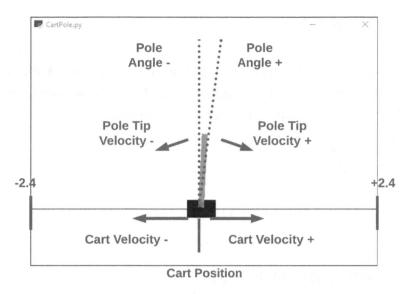

Figure 12-10. *Observations from the CartPole environment*

The reward will be +1 for every step (i.e., the longer you can hold the pole vertical, the better).

With all these in mind let us start building a model.

We will start with a new code file, which we will name CartPole_Train.py, and import the necessary packages:

```
1: import gym
2: import random
3: import numpy as np
4: import tensorflow as tf
5: from tensorflow.keras.models     import Sequential
6: from tensorflow.keras.layers     import Dense
7: from tensorflow.keras.optimizers import Adam
8: import tensorflow.keras.utils as np_utils
9: import matplotlib.pyplot as plt
```

We will then define our training parameters:

```
11: env = gym.make('CartPole-v1')
12: env.reset()
13: goal_steps = 500
```

```
14: score_requirement = 50
15: intial_games = 20000
```

Here, we will initially play 20,000 games and shortlist the actions that resulted in at least 50 steps in the simulation before failing. We will define a function model_data_preparation() to iterate through and gather those step data:

```
17: def model_data_preparation():
18:     training_data = []
19:     accepted_scores = []
20:     for game_index in range(intial_games):
21:         score = 0
22:         game_memory = []
23:         previous_observation = []
24:         for step_index in range(goal_steps):
25:             action = random.randrange(0, 2)
26:             observation, reward, done, info = env.step(action)
27:
28:             if len(previous_observation) > 0:
29:                 game_memory.append([previous_observation, action])
30:
31:             previous_observation = observation
32:             score += reward
33:             if done:
34:                 break
35:
36:         if score >= score_requirement:
37:             accepted_scores.append(score)
38:             for data in game_memory:
39:                 output = np_utils.to_categorical(data[1], 2)
40:                 training_data.append([data[0], output])
41:
42:         env.reset()
43:
44:     print(accepted_scores)
45:
```

```
46:       return training_data
47:
48: training_data = model_data_preparation()
```

We then build a simple model, and train it by using the step-sequences from those successful initial games:

```
50: def build_model(input_size, output_size):
51:       model = Sequential()
52:       model.add(Dense(128, input_dim=input_size, activation='relu'))
53:       model.add(Dense(52, activation='relu'))
54:       model.add(Dense(output_size, activation='linear'))
55:       model.compile(loss='mse', optimizer=Adam())
56:
57:       return model
58:
59: def train_model(training_data):
60:       data_x = np.array([i[0] for i in training_data]).reshape(-1,
len(training_data[0][0]))
61:       data_y = np.array([i[1] for i in training_data]).reshape(-1,
len(training_data[0][1]))
62:       model = build_model(input_size=len(data_x[0]), output_
size=len(data_y[0]))
63:
64:       model.fit(data_x, data_y, epochs=20)
65:       return model
66:
67: trained_model = train_model(training_data)
```

When trained, the model will be able to predict the next step to be taken, based on a sequence of previous steps as input.

We then take this trained model and run 100 games on it. If the model was able to run the game past 400 steps without failing, we will consider it as a successful run:

```
069: scores = []
070: choices = []
071: success_count = 0
```

```
072: for each_game in range(100):
073:     score = 0
074:     prev_obs = []
075:     print('Game {} playing'.format(each_game))
076:     for step_index in range(goal_steps):
077:         # Keep the below line uncommented if you want to see how our
bot is playing the game.
078:         env.render()
079:         if len(prev_obs)==0:
080:             action = random.randrange(0,2)
081:         else:
082:             action = np.argmax(trained_model.predict(prev_obs.
reshape(-1, len(prev_obs)))[0])
083:
084:         choices.append(action)
085:         new_observation, reward, done, info = env.step(action)
086:         prev_obs = new_observation
087:         score += reward
088:         if done:
089:             print('Final step count: {}'.format(step_index + 1))
090:             if (step_index + 1) > 400:
091:                 # if achieved more than 400 steps, consider successful
092:                 success_count += 1
093:             break
094:
095:     env.reset()
096:     scores.append(score)
097: env.close()
098:
099: print(scores)
100: # since we ran 100 games, success count is equal to percentage
101: print('Success percentage: {}%'.format(success_count))
102:
103: print('Average Score:',sum(scores)/len(scores))
```

```
104: print('choice 1:{}   choice 0:{}'.format(choices.count(1)/
len(choices),choices.count(0)/len(choices)))
105:
106: # draw the histogram of scores
107: plt.hist(scores, bins=5)
108: plt.show()
```

At the end of the 100-game run we will print out the success percentage and the average scores, and display the histogram of the scores for the 100 games.

Note   Using env.render() significantly slows down the simulation. Therefore, if you do not need to visually inspect the simulation, it is better to not call the render method.

Running our code, we will be able to see that the trained model is able to achieve the goal by keeping the pole straight by applying the appropriate velocity changes to the cart (Figure 12-11).

Figure 12-11.   *The trained CartPole model*

Out of the 100 games, 51% have achieved our success condition of 400 or more steps, with an average score of 351.77 (Figure 12-12).

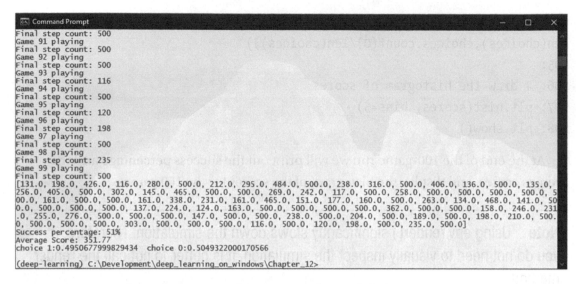

Figure 12-12.   The success rate of our CartPole model

While at first glance this may seem like not such a great result, looking at the histogram of scores shows that our model is skewing towards the success criteria (Figure 12-13).

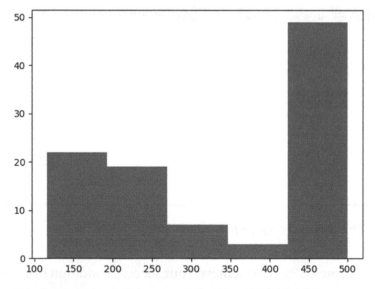

Figure 12-13.   The histogram of scores of our CartPole model

Since we used an initial set of games to retrieve the step sequences as the training data, it is normal for the models not to achieve higher success rates with just one round of training. You can attempt to increase the success rate using several different methods:

1. increasing the initial game count used to gather the training data

2. adjusting the score requirements of the initial training data

3. adjusting or trying a different model structure

4. usin the outputs from the first round of training as training data to train a new model

5. going further by training for multiple rounds.

Solving the MountainCar Problem

The CartPole problem we just solved is one of the simplest problems in reinforcement learning. Let us now step it up a bit and attempt a slightly more complex one: the MountainCar problem.

Let us create a script to first look at the MountainCar environment:

```
01: import gym
02: env = gym.make('MountainCar-v0')
03: observation = env.reset()
04: for step_index in range(1000):
05:     env.render()
06:     action = env.action_space.sample()
07:     observation, reward, done, info = env.step(action)
08:     print("Step {}:".format(step_index))
09:     print("action: {}".format(action))
10:     print("observation: {}".format(observation))
11:     print("reward: {}".format(reward))
12:     print("done: {}".format(done))
13:     print("info: {}".format(info))
14:     if done:
15:         break
16: observation = env.reset()
17: env.close()
```

This is like what we did for the CartPole environment, the difference being that MountainCar-v0 is used as the environment name. This will render the MountainCar environment with random actions as we did before (Figure 12-14).

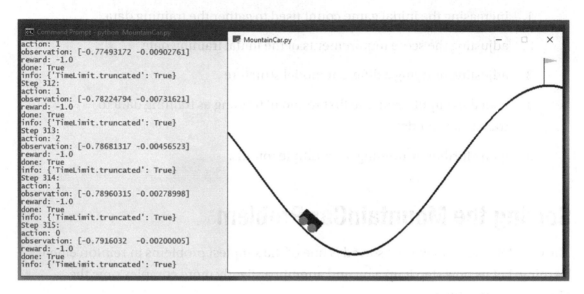

Figure 12-14. *Testing the MountainCar environment*

In the MountainCar problem, you need to push a car up the top of a steep hill marked by the flag. The car starts close to the bottom of the valley. There is a less steep hill to the left of the environment that you can use to gather enough momentum to climb the steeper hill.

The actions you can take are push left (0), push right (2), or not push (1). The position of the goal is 0.5 (Figure 12-15).

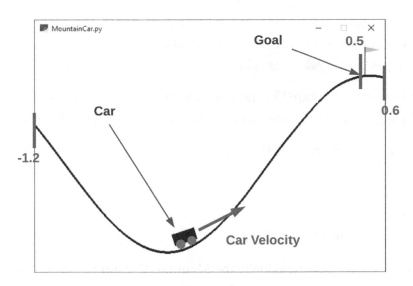

Figure 12-15. *The elements of the MountainCar environment*

The simulation will fail if you take more than 200 steps to reach the goal.[3]

The observations return an array of 2 values, which are the position of the car (-1.2 to +0.6) and the velocity of the car (-0.07 to +0.07).

At the beginning of the simulation the car will be at a random position between -0.6 and -0.4, with no initial velocity.

The reward would be -1 for every step (i.e., the fewer the steps taken to reach the goal, the better). There will be no penalty for climbing the left hill, as it is needed sometimes to achieve the goal.

Let us start a new code file, which we will name MountainCar_Train.py, and import the necessary packages:

```
1: import gym
2: import random
3: import numpy as np
4: import tensorflow as tf
5: from tensorflow.keras.models    import Sequential
6: from tensorflow.keras.layers    import Dense
```

---

[3]Github, "MountainCar Overview," https://github.com/openai/gym/wiki/MountainCar-v0, [1 May, 2020].

```
7: from tensorflow.keras.optimizers import Adam
8: import tensorflow.keras.utils as np_utils
9: import matplotlib.pyplot as plt
```

Our training parameters are like those we used for the CartPole problem. But here, we are specifying the score requirement as -198. We will see why in the next step:

```
11: env = gym.make('MountainCar-v0')
12: env.reset()
13: goal_steps = 200
14: score_requirement = -198
15: intial_games = 20000
```

As we discussed, the reward value in the MountainCar problem is -1 for every step taken. Therefore, the minimum score a MountainCar game can have is -199 (as the game will end if 200 steps are reached). To shortlist the acceptable step data from the initial games we need a way to determine the games that has progressed towards the goal. As the position of the goal is 0.5, and the initial position of the car is between -0.6 and -0.4, we chose games that have achieved the position -0.2 (which is partway up the large hill) at least once. This makes our score requirement -198 or greater.

The data preparation function therefore would look like this:

```
17: def model_data_preparation():
18:     training_data = []
19:     accepted_scores = []
20:     for game_index in range(intial_games):
21:         score = 0
22:         game_memory = []
23:         previous_observation = []
24:         for step_index in range(goal_steps):
25:             action = random.randrange(0, 3)
26:             observation, reward, done, info = env.step(action)
27:
28:             if len(previous_observation) > 0:
29:                 game_memory.append([previous_observation, action])
30:
31:             previous_observation = observation
```

```
32:
33:                if observation[0] > -0.2:
34:                    reward = 1
35:
36:                score += reward
37:                if done:
38:                    break
39:
40:            if score >= score_requirement:
41:                accepted_scores.append(score)
42:                for data in game_memory:
43:                    output = np_utils.to_categorical(data[1], 3)
44:                    training_data.append([data[0], output])
45:
46:            env.reset()
47:
48:        print(accepted_scores)
49:
50:        return training_data
51:
52: training_data = model_data_preparation()
```

The model building and training steps are identical to what we did on the CartPole problem:

```
54: def build_model(input_size, output_size):
55:     model = Sequential()
56:     model.add(Dense(128, input_dim=input_size, activation='relu'))
57:     model.add(Dense(52, activation='relu'))
58:     model.add(Dense(output_size, activation='linear'))
59:     model.compile(loss='mse', optimizer=Adam())
60:
61:     return model
62:
63: def train_model(training_data):
```

```
64:      data_x = np.array([i[0] for i in training_data]).reshape(-1,
len(training_data[0][0]))
65:      data_y = np.array([i[1] for i in training_data]).reshape(-1,
len(training_data[0][1]))
66:      model = build_model(input_size=len(data_x[0]), output_
size=len(data_y[0]))
67:
68:      model.fit(data_x, data_y, epochs=20)
69:      return model
70:
71: trained_model = train_model(training_data)
```

Like before, we run 100 games using the step predictions from the trained model. If the game was able to achieve the goal in less than 200 steps, we consider it to be successful:

```
073: scores = []
074: choices = []
075: success_count = 0
076: for each_game in range(100):
077:      score = 0
078:      prev_obs = []
079:      print('Game {} playing'.format(each_game))
080:      for step_index in range(goal_steps):
081:           # Uncomment below line if you want to see how our bot is
playing the game.
082:           # env.render()
083:           if len(prev_obs)==0:
084:                action = random.randrange(0, 3)
085:           else:
086:                action = np.argmax(trained_model.predict(prev_obs.
reshape(-1, len(prev_obs)))[0])
087:
088:           choices.append(action)
089:           new_observation, reward, done, info = env.step(action)
090:           prev_obs = new_observation
```

```
091:            score += reward
092:           if done:
093:                print('Final step count: {}'.format(step_index + 1))
094:                if (step_index + 1) < 200:
095:                    # if goal achieved in less than 200 steps, consider
successful
096:                    success_count += 1
097:                break
098:
099:       env.reset()
100:       scores.append(score)
101:
102: print(scores)
103:
104: # since we ran 100 games, success count is equal to percentage
105: print('Success percentage: {}%'.format(success_count))
106: print('Average Score:', sum(scores)/len(scores))
107: print('choice 0:{}   choice 1:{}   choice 2:{}'.format(choices.
count(0)/len(choices), choices.count(1)/len(choices), choices.count(2)/
len(choices)))
108:
109: # draw the histogram of scores
110: plt.hist(scores, bins=5)
111: plt.show()
```

If we run our model, you can see that once trained it can push the car to the desired goal position (Figure 12-16).

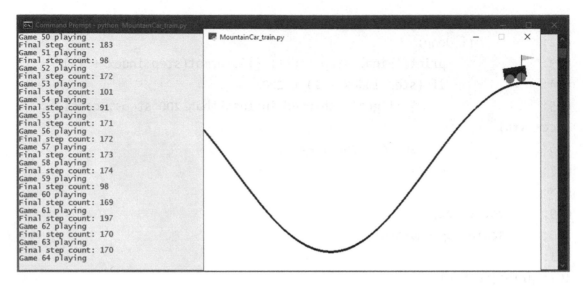

Figure 12-16. *MountainCar reaching the goal*

The score histogram shows that a significant portion of games reached the goal around the 120-step range, a much better score than our target 198 (Figure 12-17).

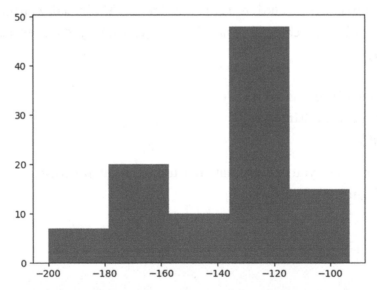

Figure 12-17. *The histogram of scores of our MountainCar model*

We are now achieving a success percentage of 99% (Figure 12-18).

```
Command Prompt                                                    —   □   ×
Game 91 playing
Final step count: 118
Game 92 playing
Final step count: 121
Game 93 playing
Final step count: 114
Game 94 playing
Final step count: 119
Game 95 playing
Final step count: 154
Game 96 playing
Final step count: 114
Game 97 playing
Final step count: 114
Game 98 playing
Final step count: 116
Game 99 playing
Final step count: 161
[-158.0, -116.0, -118.0, -114.0, -156.0, -120.0, -121.0, -115.0, -161.0, -93.0, -121.0, -178.0, -186.0, -177.0, -164.0,
-115.0, -153.0, -115.0, -116.0, -114.0, -196.0, -117.0, -116.0, -165.0, -169.0, -115.0, -161.0, -163.0, -121.0, -163.0,
-122.0, -116.0, -114.0, -119.0, -115.0, -114.0, -114.0, -156.0, -114.0, -160.0, -114.0, -156.0, -157.0, -167.0, -153.0,
-121.0, -98.0, -116.0, -121.0, -117.0, -115.0, -116.0, -114.0, -164.0, -163.0, -158.0, -116.0, -121.0, -116.0, -119.0, -
153.0, -154.0, -116.0, -115.0, -118.0, -163.0, -119.0, -118.0, -120.0, -182.0, -116.0, -119.0, -161.0, -99.0, -118.0, -1
87.0, -179.0, -183.0, -116.0, -153.0, -114.0, -119.0, -174.0, -119.0, -118.0, -118.0, -172.0, -116.0, -115.0, -200.0, -1
15.0, -118.0, -121.0, -114.0, -119.0, -154.0, -114.0, -114.0, -116.0, -161.0]
Success percentage: 99%
Average Score: -134.63
choice 0:0.3603208794473743   choice 1:0.12582633885463865   choice 2:0.5138527816979871

(deep-learning) C:\Development\deep_learning_on_windows\Chapter_12>
```

Figure 12-18. *The success rate of our MountainCar model*

What Can You Do Next?

We have now explored the basics of how to apply reinforcement learning in two
environments of OpenAI Gym: CartPole and MountainCar. Although these two are some
of the simplest problems to solve with reinforcement learning, the concepts that we
learned to apply here are the same for much more complex problems. The cutting-edge
models like OpenAI Five (see Appendix 1) were built upon the same concepts.

There are many other environments available in OpenAI Gym. Once you have
gone through the Classic Control environments, try out some of the other sets of
environments we installed, such as Atari (Figure 12-19).

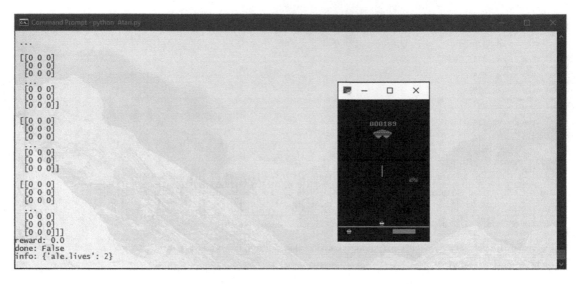

Figure 12-19. *The Atari Assault-v0 Environment*

Another option is one of the Box2D environments (Figure 12-20).

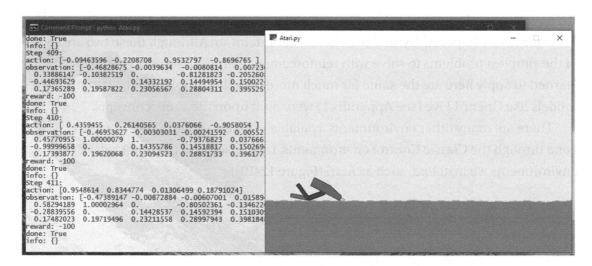

Figure 12-20. *The Box2D BipedalWalker-v3 environment*

A History Lesson: Milestones of Deep Learning

Deep learning has been around for over a decade now. Since its inception, it has taken the world by storm due to its success. To understand how deep learning got to where it is today, we should look at some of its more significant achievements through the years.

When looking at the achievements of deep learning we should also talk about the ImageNet Challenge.

What is the ImageNet Challenge (The ILSVRC)?

The ImageNet Large Scale Visual Recognition Challenge (ILSVRC) is the annual computer vision challenge conducted by the ImageNet project. The ImageNet project was started around 2007, with the intention of providing a complete and easily accessible image database for visual object recognition research. ImageNet organizes the images based on WordNet, a lexical database for the English language, which groups English words into sets of synonyms called synsets. The ImageNet project aims at providing at least 1,000 images for each synset, and has about 14 million images as of now, all of which are hand-annotated and with bounding boxes.

The ILSVRC is held annually by the ImageNet project, where institutions and research groups both from the industry and academia compete against each other with their machine learning and computer vision algorithms. The task is to correctly classify over 100,000 images into 1,000 categories, with a training set of about a million labeled images. The objective of the competition is to allow the competitors to measure and

© Thimira Amaratunga 2021
T. Amaratunga, *Deep Learning on Windows*, https://doi.org/10.1007/978-1-4842-6431-7

compare their applications and algorithms. A secondary objective is to measure and document the progress of machine learning for computer vision at a higher level over the years.

In 2017, as the models from 29 of the 38 teams competing gained greater than 95% accuracy, ImageNet started to build a more difficult challenge and a dataset. Therefore, the last formal ImageNet Challenge happened in 2017. The ImageNet challenge is still available to be participated to those who are interested at the Kaggle ImageNet Object Localization Challenge.[1]

The original ImageNet dataset is also available—both via the ImageNet downloads pages,[2] and through the Kaggle competition mentioned earlier—if you are interested in trying it out yourself.

Over the years, there were many achievements in deep learning that were directly related to the ImageNet challenge. Some of those milestones are presented here.

AlexNet: 2012

AlexNet marked the start of an era, by popularizing the success of deep learning among the AI enthusiasts. It is notable for the following:

- Proved that Convolutional Neural Networks work practically. AlexNet is commonly considered to be what brought deep learning into the mainstream.[3]

- Won 2012 ILSVRC (ImageNet Large-Scale Visual Recognition Challenge) with a 15.3% error rate. (For reference, the second-best entry at ILSVRC had a 26.2% error rate.)

- 8 layers: 5 convolutional, 3 fully connected.

---

[1]Kaggle, "Kaggle ImageNet Object Localization Challenge," https://www.kaggle.com/c/imagenet-object-localization-challenge, [March 26, 2020].

[2]ImageNet, (downloads pages), http://image-net.org/download-imageurls, [7 April, 2017].

[3]See Alex Krizhevsky, Ilya Sutskever, and Geoffrey E. Hinton, "ImageNet Classification with Deep Convolutional Neural Networks," *Advances in Neural Information Processing Systems* 25(2) (January 2012), doi 10.1145/3065386.

- Used ReLU for the nonlinearity function rather than the conventional tanh function used until then.

- Introduced the use of dropout layers, and data augmentation to overcome overfitting.

The Alexnet architecture is shown in Figure A1-1.

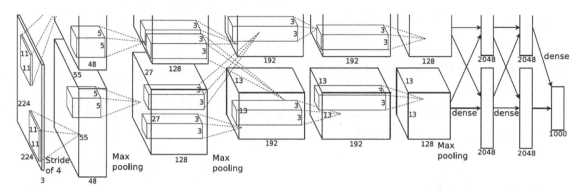

Figure A1-1. *The AlexNet architecture*

ZF Net: 2013

With AlexNet starting the trend, ZF Net kept it going. While continuing the success of AlexNet, the ZFNet attempted to answer the question of why convolutional neural networks perform so well.[4] ZFNet was notable for the following:

- Won the ILSVRC 2013 with error rates from 14.7 to 11.2%.

- Similar to the AlexNet architecture, with some tweaks and fine-tuning to improve the performance.

- Introduced the deconvolutional network (DeConvNet), a visualization technique for viewing the inner workings of a CNN, which allowed better understanding of why CNNs perform well.

[4]Zeiler M.D., Fergus R. (2014) Visualizing and Understanding Convolutional Networks. In: Fleet D., Pajdla T., Schiele B., Tuytelaars T. (eds) Computer Vision – ECCV 2014. ECCV 2014. Lecture Notes in Computer Science, vol 8689. Springer, Cham. https://doi.org/10.1007/978-3-319-10590-1_53.

The ZF Net architecture is shown in Figure A1-2.

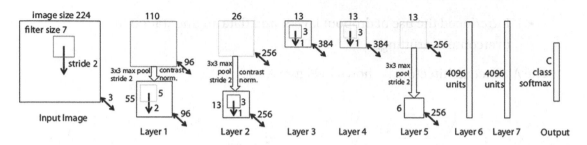

Figure A1-2. *The ZF Net architecture*

The Deconvolutional technique is still used today to view how the internal convolutions perform in a network.

VGG Net: 2014

VGG Net was one of the most popular deep learning architectures, due to its simplicity.[5] It is notable for the following:

- Won the Classification + localization category of the ILSVRC 2014 (not the overall winner), with an error rate of 7.3%.

- The VGG architecture worked well with both image classification and localization.

- Had 2 variations: VGG16 (16 layers), and VGG19 (19 layers).

- Used 3x3 filters (compared to 11x11 filters of AlexNet, and 7x7 filters of ZF Net).

- Proved that simple deep structures work for hierarchical feature extraction.

The VGG16 architecture is shown in Figure A1-3.

---

[5]Simonyan, K. and Zisserman, A., "Very Deep Convolutional Networks for Large-Scale Image Recognition", *arXiv e-prints*, 2014.

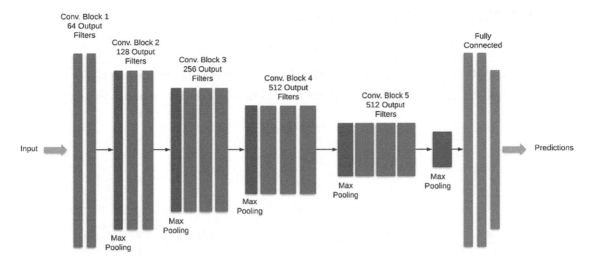

Figure A1-3. *The VGG Net architecture*

The VGG Net architectures are still popular, as they are easy to construct and the training time is less compared to more complex models. They are good candidates for experimenting with transfer learning.

GoogLeNet/Inception: 2014/2015

This is where deep learning became creative in terms of network architectures. The authors of GoogLeNet introduced a unique architecture to increase the computational efficiency,[6] which disrupted the idea that deep learning models need to always be sequential (Figure A1-4).

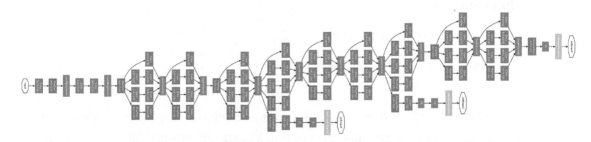

Figure A1-4. *The GoogLeNet architecture*

---

[6]C. Szegedy, et al., "Going deeper with convolutions," in 2015 IEEE Conference on Computer Vision and Pattern Recognition (CVPR), Boston, MA, USA, 2015 pp. 1-9. doi: 10.1109/CVPR.2015.7298594.

GoogLeNet was notable for the following:

- Won the ILSVRC 2014, with an error rate of 6.7%.

- Introduced the inception module (Figure A1-5), which emphasized that the layers of a CNN need not always be stacked up sequentially.

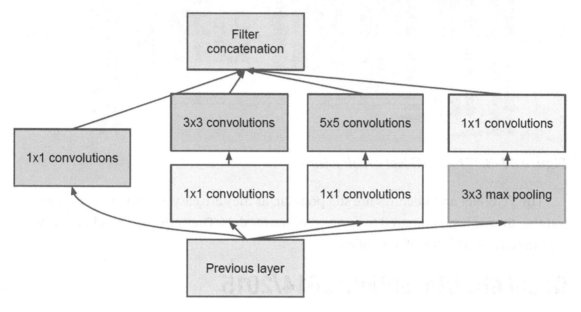

Figure A1-5. *The inception module*

- Had 22 blocks of layers (over 100 layers when considered individually).

- Had no fully connected layers.

- Proved that optimized nonsequential structures may work better than sequential ones.

While the original architecture was named GoogLeNet, two improved models were released subsequently and were named Inception V2, and Inception V3.

Microsoft ResNet: 2015

Typically, if you keep adding layers sequentially to a model, they tend to worsen after a certain point, as the model starts to overfit. ResNet (Figure A1-6) was an attempt to overcome this limitation by introducing the Residual Block, which resulted in an impressively deep network and even more impressive accuracy.[7]

Figure A1-6. *The ResNet architecture*

ResNet was notable for the following:

- ResNet50 won ILSVRC 2015.

- With an error rate of 3.6%, the ResNet had a higher accuracy rate than a human being (a typical human is said to have an error rate of 5 to 10%).

- Ultra-deep (quoting the authors) architecture with 152 layers.

- Introduced the Residual Block, to reduce overfitting (Figure A1-7), which gave the name to the network Residual Network (ResNet).

---

[7]K. He, X. Zhang, S. Ren and J. Sun, "Deep Residual Learning for Image Recognition," 2016 IEEE Conference on Computer Vision and Pattern Recognition (CVPR), Las Vegas, NV, 2016, pp. 770-778, doi: 10.1109/CVPR.2016.90.

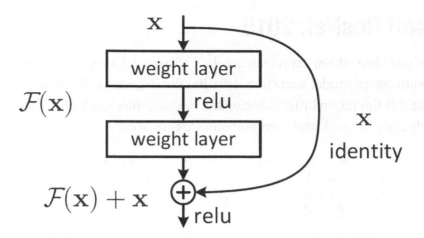

Figure A1-7. *The residual block*

The ResNet architecture is proven to be scalable. There have been successful attempts to increase up to 1,000 layers.

DenseNet: 2017

With ResNet attempting to go deeper using the Residual Block, why would not one attempt to go even further? DenseNet[8] takes it to the extreme (Figure A1-8).

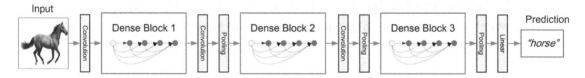

Figure A1-8. *The DenseNet architecture*

The DenseNet architecture consists of several Dense Blocks within which each of the layers are connected to every other layer in that block in a feed forward manner (Figure A1-9).

---

[8]G. Huang, Z. Liu, L. Van Der Maaten and K. Q. Weinberger, "Densely Connected Convolutional Networks," 2017 IEEE Conference on Computer Vision and Pattern Recognition (CVPR), Honolulu, HI, 2017, pp. 2261-2269, doi: 10.1109/CVPR.2017.243.

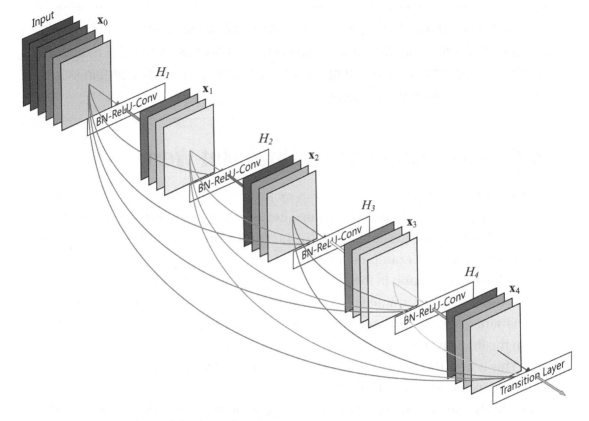

Figure A1-9. *A dense block with 5 layers*

DenseNet is notable for the following:

- In each dense block, the input feature maps are passed to each layer in the block, and the feature maps from each layer also gets passed to all subsequent layers.

- On smaller datasets like CIFAR10 or CIFAR100, DenseNet yields state-of-the-art accuracies: a 3.46% error rate on CIFAR10 and 17.18% on CIFAR100 (with data augmentation), which is a higher accuracy than ResNet.

- On ImageNet dataset, the DenseNet achieves a similar accuracy to that of ResNet, but utilizes less than half the number of parameters and FLOPs (FLoating-point OPerations).

> **Tip** FLOPs is often used as a performance indicator of machine learning models. FLOPs are the number of floating-point operations performed within the model. The fewer the number of floating-point operations required to perform a certain task, the model is considered more optimized.

Why Simply Going Deeper Does Not Work

If you look at the deep learning architectures we just reviewed, you might notice that after a certain point the architectures stopped becoming directly deep, instead starting to come up with more unique structures. The Inception Module, the Residual Block, and the Dense Block are good examples of these.

This is due to a limitation in the method used to train neural networks. A deep neural network is typically trained using a method called backpropagation, where, when a batch of training data gets passed through the network, a gradient signal is passed back from the final layer to the first layer, adjusting the weights of each layer as it passes through. This is how the network "learns" of a batch of training data. The gradient signal reduces as it passes through each layer.

While this is practical in networks with just a couple of layers, when it comes to deep networks with 20+ layers, it becomes harder for backpropagation to keep up, as the gradient signal diminishes to nothing before it reaches the layers at the start.

To overcome this, the Inception Modules, Residual Block, and Dense Blocks all provide shortcuts in the architecture for the gradient signal to propagate back more efficiently. We can expect similar techniques in future deep learning architectures as well.

AlphaGo from DeepMind

AlphaGo—developed by the DeepMind team of Google—is an AI program that plays the board game Go.

The Go board game is an abstract strategy game that was invented in China more than 2,500 years ago. Despite its simple set of rules, Go is considered to be much more complex than Chess and is one of the most studied strategy games of all time.

The AlphaGo uses a Monte Carlo tree search algorithm to find moves using the trained deep neural network, which works as its knowledge core. AlphaGo was initially trained on a training set of over 30 million go piece moves data from human

Go matches. It was then further trained by letting it compete against copies of itself using reinforcement learning.

AlphaGo's first victory was in October 2015. It was against three-time European champion, Fan Hui, on a full-sized (19x19 grid) board. AlphaGo won with a score of 5–0, and became the first computer Go program to beat a human professional.

In March 2016 AlphaGo competed against Lee Sedol, an 18-time world champion and a 9-dan professional (highest professional rank) Go player. In this five-game match AlphaGo won 4–1, earning it an honorary 9-dan title.

In January 2017, an improved version of AlphaGo called AlphaGo Master was set up (without revealing its identity) to compete in an online series of Go games against some of the top international Go players, and it managed to win at 60–0.

At the "*Future of Go*" summit in May 2017, AlphaGo competed against Ke Jie, the world's number-1 ranked player at the time. AlphaGo won 3–0 in this three-game match. The Chinese Weiqi Association awarded the professional 9-dan status to AlphaGo after this victory.

Ke Jie later praised AlphaGo's unique play style, and has stated: "After humanity spent thousands of years improving our tactics, computers tell us that humans are completely wrong . . . I would go as far as to say not a single human has touched the edge of the truth of Go."[9]

After the win with Ke Jie, AlphaGo retired from the Go arena.

In October 2017, DeepMind introduced AlphaGo Zero. While being the latest version of AlphaGo, AlphaGo Zero has been built from scratch. Rather than training it on data from millions of moves from human matches, AlphaGo Zero was trained to play by competing against copies of itself by starting with random play.

Using this technique, AlphaGo Zero surpassed the level of AlphaGo Master in just 21 days and achieved superhuman-level in 40 days.

In December 2017, DeepMind generalized the algorithm of AlphaGo Zero and introduced AlphaZero, which has achieved superhuman levels of gameplay in Chess, Go, and Shogi, with just 24 hours of training.

These generalizations allow AlphaZero to learn and master anything, even beyond games.

By December 2018, the final version of AlphaZero competed against Stockfish v8 (then considered to be the strongest open-source chess engine in the world) on Chess,

---

[9]"Ke Jie vs. AlphaGo: 8 things you must know". 27 May 2017 http://chuansong.me/n/1840585451964.

and Elmo (a world champion Shogi program) on Shogi. Against Stockfish, AlphaZero managed to achieve 155 wins and 6 losses in a 1,000-game chess tournament, with all the other matches resulting in draws. Against Elmo, AlphaZero achieved a 91.2% win rate on Shogi.

DeepMind published the next generation of the algorithm in 2019 named MuZero, which was able to play Atari games in addition to Chess, Go, and Shogi.

Dota 2 Bot from OpenAI

OpenAI—a nonprofit AI research company founded by Elon Musk and Sam Altman, which focuses on developing friendly AI—unveiled their Dota 2 AI Bot in 2013, capable of defeating top Dota professional players.

Dota 2 is a multiplayer online battle arena (MOBA) game developed by the Valve Corporation. First released in July 2013, the game is a sequel to the community game Defence of the Ancients (DotA), which was released back in 2003 as a mod for the game Warcraft III.

A typical match of Dota 2 is played by five-verses-five (5v5), although other variations of the game such as 1v1 exist. Each of the players chooses a hero from 115 playable characters, each with its strengths and weaknesses, various abilities, and powers. The game is played in a real-time strategy manner, where each team battles the other and attempts to destroy the Ancient (large structure on the base) of the opposing team while defending their own.

The diverse characters available, their abilities, strengths, weaknesses, and the real-time way the game is played makes Dota 2 one of the most complex and competitive multiplayer games available. The required permutations of moves to program a bot manually makes it impractical, which makes Dota 2—quoting the engineers of OpenAI—"the perfect test bed for AI."[10]

So how did OpenAI achieve their Dota 2 bot?

OpenAI has used self-play (playing against a copy of itself) to entirely train the bot from scratch. They have not used imitation learning or tree search mechanisms in any way. It is worth noting that creating a dataset for any other types of training might also not be practical due to the complexities we discussed earlier.

---

[10]"OpenAI reveals self-play information after successful Dota 2 test" August 16, 2017
`https://www.teslarati.com/openai-self-play-dota-2-musk/`.

Quoting the engineers of OpenAI: "Supervised deep learning systems can only be as good as their training datasets, but in self-play systems, the available data improves automatically as the agent gets better."[11]

The bot training uses completely random moves and by competing with a copy of itself. As part of "coaching" for the training of the bot, the team has added a set of white-listed item builds (part of the gameplay of Dota 2) into the training. The training of the bot began in March 2017, and by July, it was starting to beat top-level professionals.

On August 7, 2017, the bot competed against three professional pros—Blitz, Pajkatt, CC&C—and won 3–0, 2–1, and 3–0, respectively.

On August 9, 2017, the bot took on Arteezy, the top overall Dota 2 player in the world, and won 10–0.

On August 10, 2017, the bot won against SumaiL, the top 1v1 Dota 2 player in the world, by 6–0 (Figure A1-10). SumaiL then played against the Aug 9 version of the bot and won 2–1, showcasing how the bot had advanced with just one day's training.

Figure A1-10. *Screencap from the Game Between the Bot and SumaiL*

On August 11, 2017, the bot won against Dendi, the former world champion, by 2–0.

---

[11]"OpenAI reveals self-play information after successful Dota 2 test" August 16, 2017 https://www.teslarati.com/openai-self-play-dota-2-musk/.

Most of these players have expressed that the bot felt unbeatable, and that they have learned new moves from the games with the bot.

OpenAI's next goal was to train a set of 5 AI bots that could take on a professional Dota 2 team on a 5v5 match. This was a massive task, as the five bots not only needed to be individually skilled, but they would also need to coordinate with each other to entertain hopes of winning.

It would not be a case of just adding four more bots to the game. The bots need to work as a team, in other words.

Dota 2 is a team game. It is won by coordination, and not by the skill of any single player. Typically, each player needs to bring a different set of skills and tactics to the team.

It seems that OpenAI has tackled that problem as well.

By January 2018, their set of five bots—named the OpenAI Five—managed to win against a set of scripted bots.

By April 2018, OpenAI Five managed to win against OpenAI's in-house human Dota team on a restricted match.

By June 2018, OpenAI Five continued to win in matches with fewer and fewer restrictions.

On August 5, 2018, the OpenAI Five managed to win a best of three vs a team of 99.95th percentile Dota players in front of a live audience (Figure A1-11).

Figure A1-11. *Screencap from the game OpenAI Five vs. Humans*

OpenAI managed this entirely by self-play training, using their general-purpose AI Training system named Rapid. Each bot received 180 years' worth of training each day, running on 256 GPUs and 128,000 CPU Cores.

In August 2018, OpenAI Five participated in the International 2018, the annual Dota 2 World Championship. Initially, the bots were defeated by pro player teams from Brazil and China. But with further improvements and training, in April 2019, the bots competed against OG, the world champions of the International 2018, and won 2–1. In the same month, OpenAI allowed the public to play against OpenAI Five in an online event. The bots managed to win 38,654 out of the 42,729 public games against teams from all over the world.

APPENDIX B

Optional Setup Steps

Following are a few optional steps in setting up your tools that may become useful in some scenarios.

Switching the Backend in Multibackend Keras

This is how to switch the backend of Keras is done in the keras.json file, which is located at *%USERPROFILE%\.keras\keras.json* on Windows. The default keras.json file looks like this:

```
{
    "floatx": "float32",
    "epsilon": 1e-07,
    "backend": "tensorflow",
    "image_data_format": "channels_last"
}
```

Switching which backend Keras uses—which by default is TensorFlow—can be done using the backend parameter. You can set the backend parameter to either tensorflow, Theano, or cntk in the keras.json file, and Keras will start using the specified backend when a Keras code runs next time.

However, when switching the backend, we need to make sure to switch the image_data_format parameter too. For tensorflow or cntk backends, it should be channels_last. For theano, it should be channels_first.

© Thimira Amaratunga 2021
T. Amaratunga, *Deep Learning on Windows*, https://doi.org/10.1007/978-1-4842-6431-7

So a keras.json for CNTK should look like:

```
{
    "floatx": "float32",
    "epsilon": 1e-07,
    "backend": "cntk",
    "image_data_format": "channels_last"
}
```

And a keras.json for Theano should look like:

```
{
    "floatx": "float32",
    "epsilon": 1e-07,
    "backend": "theano",
    "image_data_format": "channels_first"
}
```

Why is this `image_data_format` parameter so important?

The `image_data_format` parameter affects how each of the backends treat the data dimensions when working with multidimensional convolution layers (such as Conv2D, Conv3D, Conv2DTranspose, Copping2D, and any other 2D or 3D layer). Specifically, it defines where the channels dimension is in the input data.

Both TensorFlow and Theano expect a four-dimensional tensor as input. But where TensorFlow expects the channels dimension as the last dimension (index 3, where the first is index 0) of the tensor—that is, tensor with shape (samples, rows, cols, channels)—Theano will expect channels at the second dimension (index 1)—that is, tensor with shape (samples, channels, rows, cols). The outputs of the convolutional layers will also follow this pattern.

So the `image_data_format` parameter, once set in keras.json, will tell Keras which dimension ordering to use, in its convolutional layers.

Mixing up the channels order would result in your models being trained in unexpected ways.

Apart from setting the parameter in keras.json, you can manipulate it in the code as well. You can get and set the `image_data_format` through the keras.backend package.

To get the `image_data_format`, you can use the `image_data_format()` function:

```
from keras import backend as K
print(K.image_data_format())
```

To set the `image_data_format`, pass the string either channels_first or channels_last to `set_image_data_format()` function:

```
from keras import backend as K
K.set_image_data_format('channels_first')
```

You can also set it per layer, using the data_format parameter in the 2D and 3D convolutional layers:

```
model.add(Conv2D(20, (5, 5),
                 padding="same",
                 input_shape=(height, width, depth),
                 data_format="channels_first"))
```

When manipulating the `image_data_format` programmatically, just make sure to keep track of what you change it in to, and keep it consistent throughout your models code. Otherwise you might mess up training of your model.

Installing OpenBLAS for Theano

Installing OpenBLAS is only needed if you are running Theano on CPU. TensorFlow has its own internal CPU optimizers, and thus does not need (or use) OpenBLAS. But with Theano, it is recommended to have OpenBLAS setup, as it sometimes doubles the speed at which deep learning models train on it when using CPU.

This is for your reference only, as we have not used Theano or OpenBLAS in this book.

OpenBLAS has prebuilt binaries for Windows available only for some of its versions. Therefore, you will have to use an older version. The last version with all the required Windows binaries was OpenBLAS v0.2.15, which you can download from the OpenBLAS SourceForge Page.[1]

---

[1]"OpenBLAS - Browse /v0.2.15 at SourceForge.net," `https://sourceforge.net/projects/openblas/files/v0.2.15/`, [27 Oct, 2015].

You will need to download both the OpenBLAS-v0.2.15-Win64-int32.zip and the mingw64_dll.zip files (Figure A2-1).

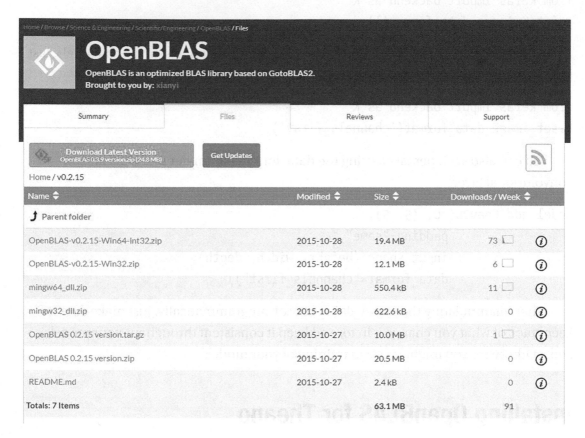

Figure A2-1. *OpenBLAS downloads page*

Once downloaded, first extract the OpenBLAS-v0.2.15-Win64-int32.zip file to a globally accessible location on your hard disk (something like `C:\Dev_Tools\ openblas\`).

Then extract the mingw64_dll.zip, and copy its contents (3 DLL files) to the bin directory of your extracted OpenBLAS directory (Figure A2-2).

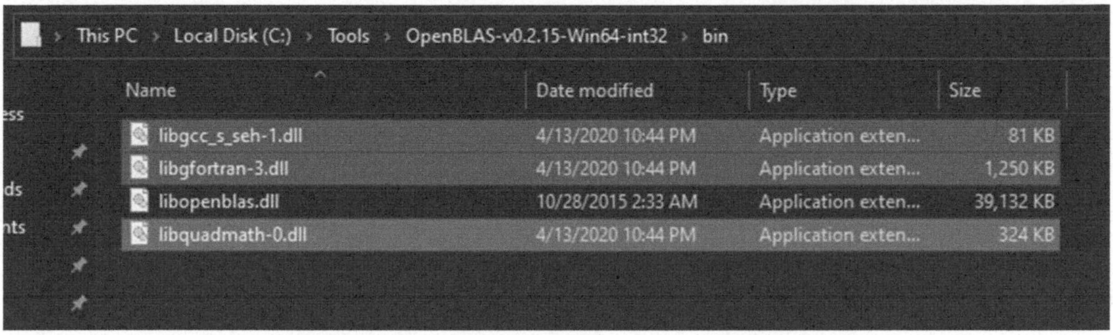

Figure A2-2. *Mingw DLL files added to OpenBLAS bin directory*

If you extracted OpenBLAS to `C:\Dev_Tools\openblas\`, then `C:\Dev_Tools\` `openblas\bin` will have the libopenblas.dll in it. When you extract mingw, it will have 3 more DLLs—libgcc_s_seh-1.dll, libgfortran-3.dll, and libquadmath-0.dll. Copy those to `C:\Dev_Tools\openblas\bin` also.

Finally, add the `C:\Dev_Tools\openblas\bin` directory to your system path.

Index

A

AlexNet, 312, 313
AlphaGo, 320, 321
Anaconda, 19, 20, 33
Artificial intelligence (AI), 1–3, 13, 14
Atari assault-v0 environment, 310

B

Bottleneck features
    definition, 147
    VGG16 model
        accuracy, 154
        bird_classify_bottleneck.py, 149
        compiling, 153
        data generator, 151, 152
        layers, 153
        load, 152
        packages, 149, 150
        save/evaluate/graph, 153, 154
        training history graph, 154, 155
        training parameters, 151, 152
        training steps, 149
        utility functions, 150, 151
    workflow, 147, 148
Box2D BipedalWalker-v3
    environment, 310
build_lenet() function, 73

C

CartPole problem
    build model, 297, 298
    definition, 293
    elements, 294
    histogram, 300
    methods, 301
    packages, 295, 296
    trained, 299
CelebFaces Attributes (CelebA), 272
Classifier, 101, 110
classify_image(), 224, 227
Computer vision, 10
    detecting faces, images, 244–246
    detecting faces, video, 246–248
    image processing tasks, 233
    images, 234–239
    libraries, 23–25
    OpenCV, 233
    real-time deep learning object, 248–251
    software libraries, 234
    video files, 242–244
    Webcams, 240–242
Convolutional filters, 69, 74, 75, 112, 124, 125, 130
Convolutional neural networks (CNNs), 7, 69, 260, 312, 313
cv2.resize() function., 80